SHAMBHALA DRAGON EDITIONS

The dragon is an age-old symbol of the highest spiritual essence,
embodying wisdom, strength, and the divine power of transformation.
In this spirit, Shambhala Dragon Editions offers a treasury
of readings in the sacred knowledge of Asia. In presenting
the works of authors both ancient and modern, we seek to make
these teachings accessible to lovers of wisdom everywhere.
Each Shambhala Dragon Edition features Smyth-sewn binding and is
printed on acid-free paper.

THE HUNDRED THOUSAND

SONGS OF *Milarepa*

Volume Two

The life-story and teaching of the greatest Poet-Saint ever to appear in the history of Buddhism.

SHAMBHALA   *Boston & Shaftesbury*   1989

THE HUNDRED THOUSAND

Songs of *Milarepa*

Volume Two

TRANSLATED AND ANNOTATED

BY *Garma C. C. Chang*

Shambhala Publications, Inc.
Horticultural Hall
300 Massachusetts Avenue
Boston, Massachusetts 02115

Shambhala Publications, Inc.
The Old School House
The Courtyard, Bell Street
Shaftesbury, Dorset SP7 8BP

9 8 7 6 5 4 3 2

Printed in the United States of America

Distributed in the United States by Random House
and in Canada by Random House of Canada Ltd.

Distributed in the United Kingdom by Element Books Ltd.

Library of Congress Cataloging-in-Publication Data
Mi-la-ras-pa, 1040–1123.
The hundred thousand songs of Milarepa.
(Shambhala dragon editions)
Translation of: Mgur'bum.
Reprint. Originally published: Boston, Mass.:
Shambhala Publications, 1977.
Includes index.
1. Mi-la-ras-pa, 1040–1123. 2. Lamas—China—
Tibet—Biography. 3. Spiritual life (Buddhism)
I. Chang, Chen-chi, 1920–   . II. Title.
BQ7950.M557A3 1989   294.3'923'0924 [B]   88-13782
ISBN 0-87773-095-4 (v. 1)   ISBN 0-87773-096-2 (v. 2)

PART TWO

MILAREPA
AND HIS HUMAN
DISCIPLES
(Continued)

TSERINMA AND THE MUDRĀ PRACTICE

Obeisance to all Gurus

L ATE on the night of the eighth day of the Month of the Fire Chicken, a great light shone upon Milarepa's quiet hermitage in Chu Bar.[1] Milarepa then sensed a fragrant odor he had never smelled before and heard the sound of approaching voices. While he was wondering about them, the Auspicious Lady of Long Life [Tserinma], well-dressed and wearing beautiful ornaments, appeared with her sisters — one bringing various kinds of incense; one, many delicious foods and drinks; one, musical instruments; another, fine and pretty clothes; and still another, beautiful flowers. They all bowed down before the Jetsun, circumambulated him many times, and offered him desirable oblations conjured by their miraculous powers. Then they sang in chorus:

> Oh perfect, precious, destined and well-endowed
>   Guru,
> Is "Laughing Vajra" the name that Buddhas and
>   Gurus call you?
> Did not your parents name you "Toubagha,"[2]
> While people call you "The Great Accomplished
>   Repa"?
> Are you not the one with three wondrous names?
>
> To the left of the mountain, Lhaman Jalmo,
> Stands your hut by the bank of Lodahan River.
> The King of the Nagas sounded
> His magic conch-shell trumpet,
> And into a wish-fulfilling Palace
> Was this hut transformed.

On this river-bank in Medicine Valley,
You, a wondrous yogi,
Industriously practice the Pinnacle Teachings.
Renouncing the Eight Worldly Desires,
From Saṃsāric temples you are freed.
Through our wondrous powers
We five girls have come
To praise and sing for you
With sweet words and tuneful voices.
We represent the four known types of womanhood
Called Lotus, Conch, Mark, and the Elephant.[3]
Pray practice Karma Mudrā with us.
Will you grant our prayer?
Do you know well
The four techniques of Karma Mudrā
Called falling, holding, turning back, and
        spreading —
If so, you may apply them now,
For your servants are prepared.

It is said in the Supreme Tantra,
[That the qualified yogi] should attract the
        maids of Heaven,
Of Nāgas, of Asuras, or of human kind.
It also says that of all services
The best is Karma Mudrā.
Thus we come here this evening.
Pray witness this, oh great Yogi,
Whose naked body is full of splendor
        and radiance.

The Jetsun answered:

At this late hour
I hear your tuneful voices raised,
And your thoughts expressed in song.
[From whence come you, fair ladies?]
Does not your abode
Stand on the shining summit,
The Snow Mountain's crystal peak?
Towers not a palace
Under the canopy of clouds
'Midst the flower-galaxy of stars?

Long are your lives and great your powers —
This of your mercy is the meed.
Your fortune rivals that of the God of Wealth —
This of your bounty is the meed.
Your servants are faithful and obedient —
This of your patience is the meed.

In practicing meritorious deeds
You are full of aspiration —
This is the sign of your diligence.
The fact that you have met me in this life
Proves your good wishes in past lives.
I sing this song for you
To reveal the deep relationship.

I am a follower of Nāropa's Lineage,
Who has mastered Prāṇa and Bindu.
'Tis true that of all offerings
A qualified Mudrā is the best.
Most wondrous indeed are the four perfected
        Mudrās.

The radiant Face and Lotus promote bliss;
The shell-shaped Nāḍī speeds the ecstasy;
The Mark in the deep recess prevents all waste;
While through the "Elephant" Reality is realized.

You are the auspicious, noble, and fault-free
        Lady of Long Life.
In your secret Wisdom Lotus
Lies the bīja,[4] "Bham" shaped like the sign "ĕ";
The male gem is likened to the blue bīja "Hum";
And, when combined with "Pad," fixes
        Tig Le well.
When Wisdom and Skill together join
The Bliss of Two-in-One is offered best.

The Four Blisses and Four Moments are
The essence of the Four Bodies of Buddha.
Like the crawling of a tortoise
[Slowly Tig Le] should drip down.
Then hold it in the Central Channel,
And like a coursing beast,

Reverse it [to the head].
Later when you spread it,
Use the Liberating Mudrā.
"Tig" is Nirvāna Path!
"Le" the Bliss of Equality;
"Las"[5] means the various actions and plays,
"Kyi" the intercourse 'twixt Bliss and Voidness;
"Phyag" is this and that to hold;
And "rGya," to embrace Nirvāna and Samsāra.

"Las" is to contact this and act on that,
"Kyi" to do this and that for the associate;
"Phyag" is the Union of the Bliss and Void;
While "rGya" is not to go beyond.
This is the speed-path of Union,
A path full of retained-bliss,
A path to consummate the accomplishment
Of the Illuminating-Void,
Leading toward undiscriminating Dharmakāya,
Directing one to the perfect Sambhogakāya,
And leading to the Manifesting-Void of the
        Nirmānakāyas.
This is a path of bliss — of voidness, of no
        thoughts, and of two-in-one,
A path of quick assistance by a goddess.
Following this inspiring way
You, fair ladies, will reach Liberation,
And, in the Realm of No-arising will remain.
Oh gifted fairies, you are indeed well qualified!

The Karma Mudrā was then performed, during which the five goddesses offered Milarepa their bodies, words, and minds — also many
foods and drinks to please him.

Among the five Ḍākinīs — the Auspicious Lady of Long Life, the
Drogmanzulema of Lashi Snow Mountain, the Mannmo of Linpa
Draug, the Tsomanma of Nepal, and the Yidagmo of Yolmo Snow
Mountain[6] — the Auspicious Lady of Long Life was the one who gained
the best Karma Mudrā inspiration from the Jetsun.

This is the story of how the Repa, "Laughing Vajra," the great Yogi
who was capable of attracting and using goddesses for his Mudrā practice, met with the Lady of Long Life; and in which the songs of in-

quiry and the answers, named "The Rosary of Bliss-Void Wisdom," are found.

.After sincere prayers and offerings to the Deities, the two brother yogis — the compilers of this story — received a delightful revelation of permission, upon which the story was written.

Samaya Ja Ja Ja! [Warning: Secret! Secret! Secret!]

The story of the Lady of Long Life and Milarepa, including several preachings of Mila and the requests of the five Ḍākinīs, was compiled and preserved by Ahtsarya Bodhi Radsa and Repa Shiwa Aui.

This is the end of this wondrous account, composed of three successive stories.

NOTES

1 Lit.: " . . . . in the quiet dwelling, the Palace of the Nirmāṇakāya of Chu Bar."

2 Toubagha (T.T.: Thos.Pa.dGah.): Milarepa's first name, given him by his father. See W. Y. Evans-Wentz' "Tibet's Great Yogi Milarepa."

3 The four different types of Shajhaṁa, or women qualified to serve as "Mudrās." "Shell," "Mark," "Lotus," and "Elephant," are all figurative terms designating the various patterns of physical make-up of the Shajhamas.

4 Bija means the seed, core, or Essence of a Mantra.

5 Karma Mudrā is translated in Tibetan as "Las.Kyi.Phyag.rGya." "Las" is equivalent to the Sanskrit word "Karma," meaning Action; "Kyi" is a preposition meaning "of," and "Phyag.rGya." is the equivalent of "Mudrā," meaning symbol or gesture. "Las.Kyi.Phyag.rGya." can thus be translated literally as "Action of Symbolic Teachings Practiced Through Concrete Actions." It is customary in Tibetan poetry, to break down a phrase and use its every component word to begin a line, thus making the poem more illustrative.

6 Compared with Story 29, the names do not correspond. However, the translator presumes these are different names for the same Ḍākinis — one series being their formal names and the other, designations given according to the places from which they came.

ADMONISHMENT TO
REPA DORJE WONSHU

Obeisance to all Gurus

A T ONE time when the Jetsun Milarepa was living in the Regba Dhujen Cave of Dinma Drin, he gave instructions to his disciples and patrons and set them to meditating; as a result they all gained good Experiences.

Among the disciples there was a very industrious young man, a descendant of the Tiger Tribe.¹ His deep faith in the Jetsun was confirmed when Realization had dawned upon him. In an assembly he said, "Dear Jetsun, when I think of the miseries of Saṃsāra and the happiness of Liberation, I cannot sit in idleness for a single moment. Please accept me as your servant and I will meditate day and night with you. Also, when I think of your merits and the noble deeds of the Gurus in our Linage, all worldly merits and virtues become trifling and worthless. Pray, therefore, grant me the quintessential teachings of the Dharma."

In reply Milarepa sang:

> My Lineage is the Lineage of Dorje-Chang,
> My great-grandfather was the noble Tilopa,
> My grandfather was the great Paṇḍita Nāropa,
> My father is Marpa the Translator,
> I am the Yogi Milarepa.
> These, with the fountainhead of profound Instructions,
> Make the six mainstays of my background.
>
> Now I shall tell you of the "Six Deceptions":
> Monasteries are like collecting-stations
> For hollow driftwood —

Though they claim
That the priestly life is divine and pure,
It is deceptive and illusory to me;
Of such companions I have no need!

I am a man who cherishes peace of mind
And abhors all gossip and accusations!

When the Dumo-heat is kindled within,
All woolen clothes are useless;
Of burdensome robes I have no need,
And for disheartening housework I have no desire.

When detestation arises within,
All things and possessions lose their worth;
For business I have no appetite;
For accumulating wealth I have no desire.

When perseverance and industry grow within,
Sons and disciples cease to be important;
I have no need for meetings and visitors
For they would merely interrupt devotion.

When the Pith-Instructions are practiced,
Dharma preachings lose significance;
Since they only incite one's pride,
I have no need for books and learning!

This is the Song of the Six Deceptions
In which the Pith-Instructions may be found.
Think on it, and bear it well in mind.

"This is indeed wonderful," said the young disciple. "Now, for the sake of ignorant sentient beings like us, I pray you to sing a song relating to your own Six Merits and Greatnesses." Milarepa then sang:

Seldom in my life have I boasted of "greatness,"
But for praising the greatness of the Lineage
I now sing the Song of the "Six Greatnesses": [2]

Great is the benevolence of Gurus and Buddhas!
Great is the grace of Yidhams and Deities!
Great is the power and might of the Protectors!

Great are the oral instructions of the Whispered
    Lineage
Great is Mila's perseverance,
And great the faith of his disciples!

Now I shall sing the Song of the "Six Joys":
Joy it is to stay in the land of no-man;
Joy it is to think of my Guru's instruction;
Joy it is to sit on the hard cushion beneath me;
Joy it is to remain in the solitary cave;
Joy it is to meet hunger and cold with
    indifference;
Joy it is to practice the Krunkol Exercises.[3]

Now I shall sing of the "Six Gatherings":
In the daytime people gather here
And at night the Ḍākinīs come.
Morning and evening, food and clothes are
    brought.
The Wheels-of-Bodhi gather in my living soul,
The outer world and my mind gather into one.

Now I shall sing of my "Six Keeps":
In Ragma I have a keep called "Bodhi-Practice,"
In the Red Rock Gem Valley I own the "Eagle
    Keep,"
On the summit of Red Rock is my "Sky Keep,"
In the Mon region there's the "Tiger Cave
    and Lion Keep."
Also I have the "Plantain Keep" of Kadaya Crystal
    Cave,
And at White Horse-Tooth Rock I have the
    "Central Keep."

Now I shall sing of the "Six Goodnesses of
    Mila":
Good is the view of Mahāmudrā,
Good is the practice of the Six Yogas of Nāropa,
Good is the profound practice of the Skillful
    Path,
Good is the inborn fruit of the Trikāya,
Good is the grace of the Ghagyuba Sages,
Good are the Pith-Instructions of Milarepa.

Oh faithful patrons and disciples,
Evildoers are many, but virtue-practicers are
    few.
All sufferings are of sins the retribution,
All joys of virtues are the meed,
Yet both are due to all that one has done.

Let us now make a vow to meet
Again and again in future times!

Hearing this song, all the disciples and patrons were very much impressed and pleased. They then left for their homes. The young man, however, was taken as a servant-disciple by the Jetsun. Later he became one of the close-sons of Milarepa, and was known as Daugom Repa Dorje Wonshu.

This is the story of Repa Dorje Wonshu.

NOTES

1 Tiger Tribe (T.T.: Rus.sTag.).

2 The Tibetan text, on folio 172, mentions only five Greatnesses. This could be a "copygraphical" error. The translation is based on the corrected version of the fifth Greatness.

3 Krunkol Exercises (T.T.: hKhrul.hKhol.): Various specially designed physical exercises to further a yogi's meditation progress, and to overcome the hindrances that he may encounter in his Yoga practice.

33

MILAREPA'S MEETING WITH DHARMA BODHI

Obeisance to all Gurus

A T THE time when Milarepa was setting in motion the Wheel of Dharma at the Belly Cave of Nya Non with Rechungpa and his other son-disciples, there were five contemporary, great accomplished yogis. They were the Gurus Tsem Chin of La Dud, Dhampa Sangje of Dinrin,[1] Shilabharo of Nepal, Dharma Bodhi of India, and Milarepa of Nya Non.

Once Dharma Bodhi was invited by Shilabharo to Bhalbo Dson to preach the Dharma. Many Tibetans as well as Nepalese went to pay homage to him. A number of Milarepa's disciples also wanted to go. Rechungpa gave many reasons to Milarepa, urging him to visit Dharma Bodhi. In answer to his request, Milarepa sang:

> By the Gurus' grace
> Many accomplished Sages come.
> The wondrous Dharma thus spreads far,
> And with joy are blessed all living beings.
> Many pilgrims paying homage to the Sages
> Show that a few destined persons will emerge.
>
> The Dhampa Sangje of Dinri,
> The Guru Tsem Chin of La Dud,
> The Shilabharo of Nepal,
> The Dharma Bodhi of India,
> And the Milarepa of Gung Tang —
> All have attained the Wisdom.
> Each has succeeded in meditation,
> Each knows the Illuminating Mind-Essence.

They all are capable of working miracles,
They all possess the overflowing Void-Compassion,
They all work wonders and produce amusing marvels.
As to the spontaneous making of songs,
I am the best of all the five;
My perseverence and austerity are also greater;
Nothing special or superb have they.
I see no need to go;
But you, my sons and disciples,
Should do so by all means!
It is not because I think ill of them
[That I remain behind]
But merely that I am too old to journey [there].
I now make a sincere wish that I may meet
Them in the Pure Land of Oujen.
Oh my son, do not be bewildered,
But have confidence [in me].

Rechungpa said, "If you do not go, people will think that you are proud and jealous, and they will so accuse you with much reviling. By all means, please go!" In reply, Milarepa sang:

I pray you, ye accomplished Beings
To cleanse all sins and evil-doing.

He who cares what people say
Will only make himself confused.
Journeying to many places
Merely hinders one's devotion.
Meddling in too many things
When visiting a holy Guru
Will confuse and irritate the consorting Deities.
Treading the Path of the deep Tantra,
Should one's mind divided be,
Never can he attain accomplishment.
Great is the blessing of the Accomplished Ones,
But too many visitors produce ill will.
However, Rechungpa, do go to see
Him with your brothers [if you so wish].

Rechungpa replied, "[Your unwillingness to go will directly cause] people to commit sinful deeds. And so please go! We will also be greatly benefited if you will grant our request." After such persistent entreaties, Milarepa finally gave in, saying, "All right. In that case let us go to greet Dharma Bodhi." Upon the Jetsun's consent, Rechungpa and the other disciples all cried for joy. They said, "Indians all like gold; therefore we should obtain some for him as a token of our welcome." In commenting on their suggestion, Milarepa then sang:

> I pray you, ye accomplished Beings,
> To remove the cravings of this poor mendicant;
> I pray that all my deeds may accord with the
>   Dharma!
> Why practice the Bodhi-Mind
> If one's acts are in conflict with the Dharma?
> He who has attained Samādhi
> Ne'er needs a companion!
> He who has experienced self-liberation
> Ne'er needs a consort!
> Else what would be the use and meaning
> Of his long work in meditation?
> If I, Milarepa, pursue gold,
> My renunciation will be pointless.
> Dharma Bodhi wants no gold,
> Else his accomplishment would be valueless.
> Dordrag Rechungpa wants no profit,
> Else his apprenticeship would be meaningless.

The Jetsun continued, "You go first — I shall follow you." Thus he dispatched them. On their way, in doubt, they all thought, "Will the Jetsun really come?" With this misgiving, as they approached Bhalbo Dson, lo and behold! Milarepa, who had transformed his body into a pagoda, [suddenly] descended in the midst of them like a shooting-star falling from the sky. Seeing this miracle, Dharma Bodhi was very much impressed, and all Milarepa's disciples were struck with great surprise and joy. The whole party then approached Dharma Bodhi, who was surrounded by crowds of people. Seeing Milarepa and his disciples coming, Dharma Bodhi of India at once descended from his seat and prostrated himself before Milarepa of Tibet. Thereupon, people all thought that Milarepa must be even greater than Dharma Bodhi; but they were also confirmed with a faith that both men were no different from the perfect Buddha. The two accomplished beings then sat together on one seat and conversed joyfully with each other. Dharma Bodhi said to Milarepa, "I am very pleased that you always remain in solitude. This is indeed remarkable." In reply to this praise, the Jetsun sang:

I pray you, ye Nirmāṇakāya Gurus,
For blessings from the Accomplished Ones
   of the Whispered Lineage!

To Dharma Bodhi of India and the gifted
Tibetans and Nepalese assembled here,
I, Milarepa, the Yogi of Tibet
Sing a song of Wisdom Experiences,
Lest people fail to recognize an accomplished
   being.

The Five Twisted Nāḍīs are straightened by
   Prāṇa-Practice,
The Five Winding Prāṇas are straightened by
   the Taming Practice,
The Five Sullied Elements are burned out,
And all Five trunks of the poisonous Passion-
   Mind are overthrown.
In the Central Channel the savage
Karmic wind of errant thoughts is pacified.
Now there is no need for me
To entangle myself with evil companions.

Dharma Bodhi then said, "The way you have conquered the 'adversaries' is indeed wonderful. Now please tell me of some good methods to this end." In response, Milarepa sang:

I pray to all accomplished Beings,
I pray that, through your blessing,
A companion may be found within me.

When the Mother of the Five Pure Nāḍīs
Meets the Father of the Five Pure Prāṇas,
The Five Sons of the Pure Elements are born,
And the face of Self-Mind, the Five Purities,
   is seen.
In the Beyond-Measure-Palace of the Central
   Channel,
The proclaimer of Buddha achievement
Shouts to the Four Rainbow Cakras.[2]
To the armies of the Web of Myriad Forms[3]
For discipline [I] give the order of non-
   clinging.

By realizing that all forms are self-awareness,
I have beheld my consort's face — the true
    Mind Within.
So none of the sentient beings in the Three
    Great Worlds
Eludes the embrace of this great Thatness.
This is my companion, the wonderful Bodhi-Mind.
Happy it is to consort with her always,
For never will she take leave of me!

Upon hearing this song, Dharma Bodhi was very much pleased. He said, "Truly the inner experiences of a yogi are beyond description. Nevertheless, please tell us briefly about [your understanding] of the View, Practice, and Action." In response Milarepa sang:

He who can watch his mind without distraction
Needs no talk or chat;
He who can absorb himself in self-awareness,
Need not sit stiffly like a corpse;
If one knows the nature of all forms,
The Eight Worldly Desires will vanish of
    themselves.
If no desire or hatred is within his heart,
He needs no pretense or show.
The great Wisdom and Trikāya
That transcend Saṃsāra and Nirvāṇa both,
Can never be achieved by search and aspiration;
Never can one attain them
Without first receiving blessing from the Lineage.

Dharma Bodhi then said, "Your View, Practice, and Action are truly marvelous." Milarepa replied, "Now please tell us your understanding on the profound Key-Instructions gained in your practice." Dharma Bodhi then sang:

For the gifted ones in this assembly
I pray to the wondrous Succession of the
    Practice —
Through this propitious Karma
Soon may we all behold [your holy faces].

If one cannot subdue habitual thinking and
    wandering thoughts,

What will be the use of observing the mind?
If one cannot conquer ego-clinging and
    pleasure-craving,
What will be the use of meditating for an age?
He who does not strive for altruistic deeds,
Will be o'ertaken by his pride
And gain no progress.
If one follows not the Guru's guidance,
What benefit can he gain
By being with pleasant friends?

Pretense and vanity directly cause disgrace,
Quarrels and discord bring misfortunes.
If one always tells the truth,
It often smites another's heart.
If one practices not altruism
How can he attain Buddahood?
*The instructions one has learned will
    become profounder*
If restfully he remains alone.
Oh you great Yogi of Tibet,
You are proficient in poetry and song —
I am not good at chanting or at singing,
But now, exhilarated, excited, and inspired
I can sing this song for you.
May we soon, in the Pure Land of Great Happiness
All sing the holy hymns [together].

Dharma Bodhi and Milarepa continued their delightful conversation for some time, then both took their leave.

When Milarepa and his disciples returned to Nya Non, people in the village brought wine to welcome them, and asked about the meeting with Dharma Bodhi. In answer, Milarepa sang:

When rises the sun or moon,
All Four Continents are bright;
When moisture and warmth abound,
Fruits will ripen on the trees;
When mother and son together meet,
The pain of longing ceases;
When an accomplished one appears
The world is gay and prosperous!

When Dharma Bodhi came to the wood of Bhalbo
      Dson,
I, Milarepa of Tibet, went there to see him.
He rose from his seat
And made obeisance to me.
Thus people were caught in surprise and doubt.
Folding his two hands and bending both his
      knees
He bowed down before me.
This symbolized the Truth of Two-in-One.
He asked about my health and welfare —
This symbolized the all-embracing Whole.
In answer to his kind inquiry
I showed him the [signless] Mahāmudrā.
In the Temple of Non-dual Purity
We had an illuminating talk of no-words,
      with joy.
A pure wish in our past lives
Had brought about this meeting.
I must have had a Karma-link with him before,
When Buddha descended to this world.

This meeting with my brother-friend
Was delightful and auspicious.
It will be heard and asked about
In far-distant lands.

Hearing this song, the patrons of Nya Non were all very much
pleased and excited. It is said that because of Dharma Bodhi's obeisance, the Jetsun's fame and fortune became even greater than before.

This is the story of Milarepa meeting with Dharma Bodhi.

NOTES

1 Dinrin: This name also appears as Dinri.

2 The Four Rainbow Cakras: The literal translation of this phrase should be
"The Rainbow Place or State of the Four Cakras." It actually denotes the state
of thorough liberation and ultimate Enlightenment. The mind of one who has
reached this state becomes the All-knowing Wisdom, and his body, the radiant and

magic-like Rainbow Body (T.T.: hJah.Lus.). The Tantric expression of "attaining the Rainbow Body," or "reaching the Rainbow State," thus signifies the achievement of Buddhahood.

3 Web of Myriad Forms (T.T.: sGyu.hPhrul.Dra.Wa.): This may also be translated as "The Magic Manifestation Web, or Net." This is an important term, reflecting the basic Tantric view on the Realm of Totality, which is strikingly similar to the philosophy of Hwa Yen. To explain it very briefly, all manifestations are unsubstantial, delusory, dream-like and magic-like, devoid of any self-nature. Because of this very unsubstantial or void nature, all manifestations can arise simultaneously in the same place without hindering one another — in fact each and every manifestation can arise in another's place simultaneously in an interpenetrating manner. Thus, using a graphic expression to describe this awesome, interpenetrating state, "Manifestation Web," or "Web of Myriad Forms" is used in the Buddhist Scriptures. See "The Essence of Buddhism," by D. T. Suzuki, The Buddhist Society, London. See also the translator's forthcoming book, "The Philosophy of Hwa Yen Buddhism."

34

THE CHALLENGE
FROM THE LOGICIANS

Obeisance to all Gurus

Having fully mastered the Mind-realms of himself and others, Jetsun Milarepa was able to cause Dharma Bodhi of India to make obeisance to him. His fame thus spread afar. The people of Nya Non, at that time, all made offerings to him for the benefit of both the living and the dead. With ever-increasing fortune he remained happily in the Belly Cave of Nya Non to help sentient beings.

Now there were some scholar-monks [logicians and theologians] in the Nya Non Monastery, who were very jealous of Milarepa. They vilified him by calling him a heretic, and heaped many abuses upon him.

At one time, a mild famine broke out at Nya Non, and many villagers went to the scholar-monks for loans [in order to buy seeds for] sowing. The monks said to them, "Since we do not practice or know anything about heretic teachings, we have never received any offerings from you people for performing the rites for the dead. Our largess is used for the single purpose of providing provisions for studying and practice of the immaculate Dharma, which of course is of no help to you. Now if you want a loan you should go to your heretic teacher to whom you gave all your belongings when you had them." Thus the peoples' request was rejected. One among the borrowers commented, "Well, to some extent what the monks have said is quite true. We may regard the Jetsun as our refuge in this life and the lives after. But we have needs in this life too. We should, therefore, also make offerings to the scholar-monks." Then the villagers made an agreement and compromised with the monastery.

Not long after this incident the scholar-monks held a conference under the leadership of Lodun Gedunbum and Radun Dharma Lhodre.

One conferee said, "Milarepa must be chased out of this place, other-wise we can never attract more people or spread our teachings. Be-sides, Milarepa's teaching is heretical and evil, he surely deserves to be ousted." But the elders replied, "It would not look well if we drove him out, people would criticize us. The best way is to send three of our most learned scholars who are well-versed in Sanskrit, logic, philosophy, and the Sūtras to challenge him in debate on Buddhist doctrines. Since he is so ignorant, possessing nothing but a tongue, he will not be able to answer our challenges and arguments. Out of one hundred questions, at best he may answer but one or two; then we can scorn and abuse him. Mortified by such a disgrace, he will run away of his own accord." Three most learned scholars were then sent to the Jetsun. When Rechungpa saw them coming he was not pleased. He went in and asked Milarepa, "There are three scholar-monks here who want to see you — should I let them in?" The Jetsun replied, "My Guru Marpa said to me, 'You should devote your body, mouth, and mind to benefit sentient beings in all possible ways; even in your daily conversation you should try to serve them.' By all means let them in. I will see them." Then they were led in and given water to re-fresh them. Milarepa said, "The power of one's faith can split rocks, crack the earth, and divide the water. Now, please preach for me the teaching of the Sūtras." The leader of the scholars then rose from his seat snapping his fingers, and said proudly, "Yes, we are teachers who have mastered the Three Learnings[1] and their disciplines and possess the three robes of the Dharma — the symbol and source of all merits. I may or may not preach for you the teaching of the Sūtras, but now let me ask you first: What merit do you possess that you, a layman, have been receiving and enjoying people's offerings and gifts without the slightest qualm and with so much confidence?" In answer to his question, the Jetsun sang "My Realizations from Meditation":

Embodied in my Guru's nectar-like instruction
Is the pinnacle Dharma of the Ultimate Truth —
The essence of all teachings from Scriptures
     and from Reason,
To which all scholars and priests aspire in
     veneration.
Pray may He not depart from me
But ever sit above me
As my glorious adornment.

[To you learned scholars]
I now relate my devotion-practices

By dividing them into three groups.
The first group that I practice,
Is the Arising Yoga of my Patron Buddha,
The second is the Nāḍīs, Prāṇas, and Bindus,
The third is the Mahāmudrā.

In the four periods of each day
I practise the Yoga of Bodhi-Mind.
In accumulating the true Bread of Faith
I contemplate the Voidness;
In accumulating the Karmic Bread of Faith
I offer the Dorma;[2]
In accumulating the Bread of Self-faith
I give oblations to the deities.
To the ghosts I give away the Dorma remnants.
I am a yogi who turns the Wheel of Nourishment.
Having realized the Voidness of all things
I am qualified to receive and enjoy offerings.

One of the scholars said, "As a person with maimed hands can never climb mountains, so one without knowledge of Buddhist studies can never attain Liberation. As a blind man sees nothing in the chapel, so one without experience of meditation will never see Reality. To practise the Arising Yoga one must first know *how* to practice it. Now you said that you have done so, but tell us how?"

The Jetsun then sang:

When I practise the Arising Yoga of the Patron
    Buddha
I see my body, vivid like a rainbow yet void,
Of which no substance whatsoever can be found.
So have I freed myself from all desires.

All talk is like an echo in a deserted valley.
For it I have neither fancy nor aversion.
So have I exhausted all likes and dislikes.

The Illuminating-Void of Mind
Is like the radiance of the sun and moon,
Without limitation or attribute.
Dissolved into it, my ego-clinging becomes
    nought.

The common human body, word, and mind
Are themselves the Body, Speech, and Wisdom of
    the Self-Buddha.
Being free from all that's vulgar,
I always feel great happiness and joy.

I am happy because my deeds are in accord
    with Dharma,
I am inspired because I follow
The right Dharma Path.

"What you have said may be correct," commented the scholar. "Now
tell me how you practise the Nāḍīs, Prāṇas, and Bindus?" In reply the
Jetsun sang:

In practising the Nāḍīs, Prāṇas, and Bindus
I meditate on the Three Channels and
    Four Centers.
As the attachment to body is exhausted
The ego into nought dissolves itself.
The Key-words of the [Five] Elements[3] are
    purified,
So they vanish not, but become illumined.
I behold the self-face of Reality,
So there is no chance for me to make mistakes.
The Prāṇas all are gathered in the Central
    Channel,
And thus they hit the vital point.
The White and Red Forces unite within me,
The experiences of bliss, illumination, and
    non-thought spontaneously arise,
And so the knots of doubt and ignorance are
    untied.
I practice the Dharma by heart and not by mouth,
I conjoin together the Mother-and-Son-Light
And exterminate the complex of desires.
As form and Void into one are merged,
My mind is at ease and full of joy.
I am every happy
For I never fall into the trap
Of mere conceptualization of the Void.
As all confusions have vanished into Dharmadhātu
I feel but joyful and gay!

The scholar then said, "The marmots who live underground can sleep [hibernate] for four months during one flow of the Prāṇa-current without even slightly shaking their bodies. Remaining under the water for any length of time, the fishes can still survive. They can do so merely because of their [inherited] Prāṇa powers, yet these animals cannot be conceived of as possessing any merit, as their minds are completely blind! You should know that all merits consist in one's understanding. Now tell me, how do you practice your so-called 'Mahāmudrā'?"

The Jetsun sang:

> When I practice Mahāmudrā,
> I rest myself in the intrinsic state,
> Relaxingly without distraction or effort.
> In the realm of Voidness,
> I rest myself with Illumination.
> In the realm of Blissfulness,
> I rest myself in Awareness.
> In the realm of Non-thought,
> I rest myself with a naked mind.
> In manifestations and activities,
> I rest myself in Samādhi.
> Meditating on the Mind-Essence in such a manner
> Numerous understandings and convictions arise.
> By Self-illumination all is accomplished without
>   effort.
> Looking no more for Enlightenment,
> I am extremely happy.
> Free from both hope and fear,
> I feel very joyful.
> Oh, what a pleasure it is to enjoy
> Confusion when as Wisdom it appears!

"It is true that from your mouth no [meaningful] thing can come out but your tongue," remarked the scholar. "What you have just said seems not so bad, but it is like an imitation of the original thing. Now tell us who is your Guru?" The Jetsun replied, "I attain all my knowledge through studying my mind within, thus all my thoughts become the teachings of Dharma. So long as I do not become separated from my own mind, I am always accompanied by sūtras. I have realized that all manifestations are Mind, and the mind itself is the illumination. These are my Gurus." Whereupon he sang:

I shall now tell you who my Gurus are.
My Gurus are the Jetsuns,
Whose immaculate Bodies manifest as the Buddha's
     Pure Land.
The purified Five Prāṇas are their thrones,
The purified Five Nāḍīs are their lotus seats,
The purified Five Elements are their Sun-and-
     Moon cushions.
The void Mind-Essence is my Guru's body;
My Guru is Dorje-Chang, with the Wisdom-Body;
My Guru is Tilopa, with the Six Miraculous
     Powers;
My Guru is Nāropa, with the Net of Myriad
     Spells;[4]
My Guru is Marpa, to whom I owe the
     greatest debt.
They sit e'er upon my head as my glory.
If you have a pair of clear and sincere eyes
You will see them as real Buddhas.
If with sincerely and faith you pray to them,
The rain of grace will ever fall upon you.
If you offer practice and devotion,
The treasury of Accomplishments will be opened
     to you.

Having heard this song, faith in the Jetsun was aroused in the three scholars. They all bowed down to him and said, " 'Ignorance, blindness, and confusion — these three evils have created all misfortune in the world!' How true this is! How true this is! With our blind minds we thought that you were an ignorant man who took people's offerings by [deceiving them] with your crazy Dharmas. But you have answered our challenging questions with ease and without the slightest hesitation. We now regret very much the quarrel we have imposed upon you. Please forgive us. Since we do not have the opportunity or merits to meet your Gurus, we shall look up to you and pray to you with sincerity and veneration, for you are even greater than the 'Treasury-of-Accomplishments.' Pray now vouchsafe us the Initiations and instructions." So they besought Milarepa in a very humble and respectful manner. The Jetsun was greatly pleased. He then gave them the Initiations and Pith-Instructions, and set them to meditating. Later, they all gained Experiences and Realizations, and became the three enlightened snow-lion-like yogi-scholars.

Now, at this time the people of Nya Non held a great festival in
the village and invited the Jetsun and all his disciples, including these
three scholar-priests, to attend. A throne was prepared for the scholar-priests Lodun[5] and Dhar Lho[6] — and also a row of seats for the
other scholar-monks. A throne and more seats were made ready for
the Jetsun and his Repa disciples.

The three scholar-priests who were sent to dispute with the Jetsun
came. Dressed like yogis, they appeared as Repas sitting on the lower
seats, and drank wine from the Kapāla [skull-cup], draught by draught.
When Lodun and Dhar Lho saw this they were convulsed with rage,
and said to themselves, "You scoundrels, dirty lice, betrayers! As long
as you stay here, our doctrine will be disparaged and confounded! We
will talk to these dirty traitors and get rid of them in an appropriate
manner." Lodun then got up from his seat and said to the Jetsun,
"You are an extraordinary yogi, so you must have a sound knowledge
of logic. Otherwise, acting like this, you will degrade the Dharma, ruin
yourself and others, and disqualify yourself as a Dharma-practicer.
Therefore, please give us a simple proposition in accordance with the
rules of logic." The Jetsun replied, "My dear scholar, you should try
to rest yourself in the inborn Dharma-Essence instead of in words and
talk. In daily life you should always attempt to subdue your desires.
Correct understanding and merit can only grow from within, otherwise you will be driven into the Miserable Realms by jealousy and the
Five Kleśas. So please do not ruin yourself! I do not understand the
logic of your School. My own 'logic' is that of the Guru, of the Pith-
Instructions, of diligence and perseverance, of remaining in solitude,
of meditating in the hermitage, of producing the Realizations and
true understanding within, of the sincere patrons with true faith, and
of being a genuine and worthwhile receiver of patronage. Being bound
by the 'logic' of jealousy and evil cravings, one is liable to experience
the 'logic' of Hell and suffer the 'logic' of pain. I do not know any
'logic' other than this. In order fully to describe my 'logic,' I shall
sing you a song, so listen to me":

I bow down to my Kleśa-free Gurus.

Alas, at this time of defilement,
Great is people's jealousy!
Please listen to me, Lodun and Dhar Lho.
If from my mother's womb I did not come,
How could I have drunk her milk?
If she fed me not on her sweet milk,
How could I have eaten the three kinds of grain?

If I did not eat the grain,
How could I have grown up?
If I did not grow up,
How could I have crossed the door?
If I did not cross the door,
How could I have wandered in all countries?
If I did not visit all countries,
How could I have found my gracious Guru?
If I did not meet my Guru,
How could I have received the Pith-Instructions?
Without instructions how could I meditate in
    solitude?
Without meditating in solitude,
How could the inner Experience and Realization
    arise?
Without the Realizations and the inner-heat,
How could I keep warm
In a garment of sheer cotton cloth?
If I cannot live in a cotton robe
How can the patrons have faith in me?
If my patrons have no faith in me
How can you, oh teacher-scholar, be jealous
    of me?
If jealousy and hatred had ne'er arisen in you,
How could you, oh teacher-scholar, go to Hell?

On the high plateau yonder
The wild beasts run and play,
Making the hounds keen and jealous;
Is not this the very reason
For the hounds becoming angry?

In the Belly Cave of Nya Non
I, the worthy Milarepa, stay.
This makes you, the teacher-of-words, painfully
    envious.
Is not this the very reason you are so distraught?
Seeing the alms offered by my patrons,
You, the learned priest, became jealous.
Is not this why you were angry and confused?
Oh great teachers and scholars,
Cling not to meaningless words and empty talk
Deeming them to be the Truth!

Even heretics can play with them.
One can waste two-and-thirty lives and gain
     nought,
If his mind but follows words.
It would be much better, therefore,
To conquer the devil of egotism.
I have no time to waste in words, words, and
     still more words!
Nor do I know logic or how to pose a proposition.
Therefore, you are the one
Who wins the argument to-day!

Dhar Lho then said, "I asked you in the language of Dharma, but you did not answer my question in Buddhist terms. Instead, you have sung a deceptive song to cheat gullible folk. Who cannot sing this kind of trash? Your song may deceive fools, but never me. If you cannot answer my questions today with scholastic language in Buddhist terms of academic tradition, but [shamelessly] still intend to receive alms from people with your deceiving songs, you well deserve to be trampled down." Saying this he seized a handful of earth and threw it in the Jetsun's face. The Jetsun brushed it off, smiled at him, and said, "How can you, the scholar who adheres to words and books merely for the sake of the pleasures of this life, act in accordance with the Dharma? Driven by your powerful Karmas and sins, all your learning and priestly disciplines will only bring you more unhappiness. As I understand them, all Dharmas are remedies for human passions and desires; but the way in which you practice them will only *increase* your passions and desires. Therefore, my Dharma and yours are completely different and contradictory. Since we do not speak the same language nor believe the same principle, how can we find a common base from which to discuss the Dharma?"

Now seeing all these things, Rechungpa thought to himself, "Although I am not worthy even to match a single hair of my Guru's head, if I do not beat this sinner who is now trying to hurt the Jetsun, I shall then violate the Samaya Commandment [Tantric Precept]; but if I punish him I will create great merits." He then picked up a stick and rushing towards the priest, was about to strike him. At once the Jetsun caught his arm, saying, "Rechungpa, my son! The wealth that cannot be used when one is in want, the kinsmen who do not assist when one is in need, and the Dharma that cannot help when one is under [adverse] conditions, will only make one more miserable. You should control yourself and try hard to think of the Admonishments. I shall now sing a song to awaken your good thoughts and Awareness."

I bow down to Marpa, my gracious Guru and
    my glory,
The great Jetsun, the shelter of all beings!
I pray you save us from doing evil deeds!

Oh Rechungpa, my son,
Calm yourself and listen to me!
Those hypocritical Buddhists who "talk big"
Become commoners at once
When they meet with adverse conditions.
Because their intentions are evil
From wrong-doings they will always suffer.
If you ever fight with people,
You violate the precepts through and through!
Calm yourself my son
And listen to your Guru!

In the vast firmament of the peerless Dharma,
My eagle-child of Awareness learns to fly;
But never should he pride himself on his flying
    power,
Lest he fall into the sectarian abyss.

Rechungpa, listen to your Guru's words!
In the great ocean of the Dharma Practice
My fish-child of Awareness learns to swim;
But never should he pride himself on his power
    of swimming,
Lest he fall into the net of confusion.

Rechungpa, listen to your Guru's words!
On the Snow Mountain of Dharma Actions,
My lion-child of Awareness learns to fight;
But he should never pride himself on his
    fighting power,
Lest he be lost in the snowstorm of desires.

Rechungpa, listen to your Guru's words!
In the Precious Land of Dharma-Accomplishment
My child of Awareness learns to trade;
But never should he trade with shrewdness,
Lest he lose the great pearl of Dharma-Essence.

Rechungpa, listen to your Guru's words
And try to keep your temper,
Lest you be scorched by anger!
Rechungpa, discipline yourself
And quench your passions!

Hearing the Jetsun's song, Rechungpa calmed down. The patrons in the assembly all blamed the scholar-priests. Rechungpa was also slightly criticized [for his outburst]. After this incident, the patrons were all confirmed with a deeper faith than ever in Milarepa. It was the scholar-priests who first had the intention of slandering the Jetsun, but in doing so they had only disgraced and discredited themselves.

Being frustrated and humiliated, Dhar Lho, Lodun, and some other monks again went to the Jetsun [on the following day] to seek revenge. They brought much meat and many books with them. When they arrived, they asked permission to see the Jetsun in order to apologize for their conduct of the day before. Rechungpa said, "There is no need for apology, nor for further debate, and there is no necessity for you to meet the Jetsun." While Rechungpa was trying to stop them, some other disciples [slipped into] the Jetsun's room and besought him to see the priests. He said very kindly, "The best thing is not to do any wrong, but if you have, and can repent of it with sincerity afterwards, this is also very good. Now, let the scholar-priests come in and talk to me." Thus he accepted the interview. The priests then offered the meat and said, "Yesterday, you were in the right. We regret what we did. In apology, we offer you this meat. Using these books as frames of reference for judgment, let us now discuss the Buddhist teachings in a friendly manner." The Jetsun replied, "Dear teachers, the proverb says, 'Judging from the complexion of his face, one knows whether the man has eaten or not.' In the same light, the fact that one knows or knows not the Dharma, can easily be detected by whether or not he can conquer his own ego-clinging desires. If he can, that proves he knows and also practices the Buddhist teachings. One may be very eloquent in talking about the Dharma, and win all the debates, but if he cannot subdue even a fraction of his own ego-clinging and desires, but merely indulges himself in words and talk, his victories in debates will never bring him any profit but will only increase his egotism and pride. This is the cause of wandering forever in Saṃsāra and falling to the bottom of Hell. Therefore, as I can see, all this argumentation is harmful and destructive. Your apology for [your misconduct yesterday] is very good indeed. Now we have finished our discussion and you may return to your home."

Dhar Lho then said, "Only Buddha can say whether one has conquered his ego-clinging and desires. One may not be able to subdue his ego-clinging, but that does not mean his knowledge about Buddhism and eloquence in debate condemns him to fall into Hell and wander in Saṃsāra forever; to say that is to say knowledge and learning are sinful. One may claim that scholarship itself is a great sin, but this will not absolve him from his [conceit] of being virtuous, nor protect him from doing the wrong thing even with a right intention. This perhaps will cause his direct fall to the bottom of Hell. Therefore, it is of great importance to learn well and to distinguish what is right and what is wrong. For these reasons we must discuss the Buddhist teachings. Since I am familiar with the rules and manners of conducting a debate, I suggest that you choose a topic in which you are well-versed, and propound a proposition in its light. We will then evaluate it and give you our opinion. On the other hand, if you think that we are not well-learned scholars, you may ask us any question you like and we will try to answer it." The Jetsun replied, "If you must insist, I have no other choice. Both of us are known to the people here. They have heard of us, see us, and know us well. I shall now take up a topic beyond both erudition and ignorance. I will ask you some questions; also I will propound my proposition [on Buddhist teachings]. Now, please answer me, Is space obstructing or non-obstructing?" The scholar replied, "No one would ever ask this kind of question. But since I have given my word just now, I must give you my answer: Of course space is non-obstructing — what else could it be?"

"But I think space is obstructing," said the Jetsun.

"What is your reason for daring to make such a presumptuous assertion?"

In the meantime, Milarepa had entered the "Samādhi-of-Solidifying-Space" and replied, "Let us see whether space is obstructing or non-obstructing! Now, will you please stand up and move around, or stretch your limbs?"

The scholar then tried to move but found he could not do so. He had to remain in his original posture, unable even to open his mouth, and sat stiffly there [like a dead image]. Whereupon the Jetsun [levitated] and walked, stood, lay down, and sat in the lotus posture, right out in space. Then he emerged from Samādhi and said to the scholar, "You have maintained that space is non-obstructing, but why cannot you move your body?"

"This is because you have learned evil spells and black magic from your Gurus. What happened to me was simply due to your evil mantras and sorceries; it is a well-known fact, recognized by all sentient beings, that space is non-obstructing."

Milarepa then asked, "Is it true that without conceptualization and rationalization, space is regarded by all as non-obstructing? Do the animals also consider space to be so? You and your teachers, who deem that it is, are now refuted by your own experiment. All of this may be due to my 'black magic,' but the fact that the obstructing nature of space has been proved to you is quite sufficient. Now, I shall give you my proposition: I declare that the rock in front of us is non-obstructing. What is your reaction to *this* statement?"

The scholar replied, "Unless you apply your evil mantras and sorceries [again], the rock cannot be otherwise than obstructing."

To this the Jetsun said, "In accordance with what you suggested in the beginning [((that each party may test the other in any subject), I now want to test your magic powers], for I do not think that you are well-versed in this subject. Now, please perform some magic to make the rock in front of us become non-obstructing."

"To be able to make magic, and to be willing to do so, are two quite different things," replied the scholar. " 'Capable of making' does not mean being allowed to make. Only you evildoers play these black-magic tricks to cheat others."

"Just now you gave me the impression that you seem to know and can do everything," said the Jetsun. "What you called 'forbidden magic,' is now being performed like rainfall by infinite Buddhas throughout the universe."

Lodun then said, "Just as space became obstructing a while ago, now please demonstrate a spell for making the rock non-obstructing."

Whereupon, the Jetsun entered the Samādhi-of-Space-Exhaustion, making the rock permeable, and then passed through it from the top to the bottom and from one side to the other; also, he kept half of his body in the rock and half outside of it. Then, he threw the rock up and let it fall. Finally he lifted up the rock with his hand, and cried to Rechungpa, "Bring a pillar!" Rechungpa brought a pillar-shaped stone and set it up. [Milarepa then placed the huge rock upon it] leaving his hand-prints indented on the rock. These marks can be seen to this very day.

The scholar Lodun then said, "It seems that you have made the rock non-obstructing. If this is not delusive magic, *we too* should be able to pass through the rock. Now tell us, can we also do it?"

The Jetsun replied, "Of course! If the rock were *obstructing*, should I not then have been killed when it fell?"

The scholar, Dhar Lho, then said, "The rock never touched *me*. If there was no rock in the first place, what is the use of talking about its non-obstructiveness?"

"The fact [that you did not feel the rock come down and crush you] is the very proof that it is non-obstructing," replied the Jetsun. "That you fail to feel a thing does not imply the non-existence of that thing."

Now Dhar Lho became even more angry than before, but Lodun began to be uncertain, and to waver. He thought, "All this seems to be genuine. We skeptical and incredulous scholars are always very difficult to convince. If these performances are not created by magic but are proofs of his accomplishment in the Path, I should acquire from him the teaching of the Six Pāramitās." He then asked, "Will you please tell us how to practise the Six Pāramitās?" In answer Milarepa sang:

Oh Three Great, Precious Refuges,
Sitting on my head as my joy and glory,
I pray with sincerest heart
That you may never leave me.
I pray you to fold me in your compassion,
I pray that you attend me with kind thoughts,
I pray you to grant Ultimate Truth to all
          sentient beings.

The Mahāyāna Yogi hears not the Dharma of
          mere words;
In the truth of Voidness, [he knows] there is
          no practice.
So he renounces of himself the Ten Vices.

If from parsimony one cannot free oneself,
What is the use of discussing charity?
If one does not forswear hypocrisy and pretence,
What is the use of keeping discipline?
If one abjures not malicious revilings,
What is the use of exercising pretentious
          "patience"?
If one abandons not indifference and inertness,
What is the use of swearing to be moral?
If one conquers not the errant thoughts within,
What is the use of toiling in meditation?
If one does not see all forms as helpful,
What is the use of practicing the Wisdom?
If one knows not the profound teaching
Of forbidding and allowing,
What is the use of learning?
If one knows not the art of taking and rejecting,
What is the use of speaking on Karma-causation?
If one's mind does not accord with Dharma,

What is the use of joining the Order?
If the poisonous snake of Kleśa is not killed,
The yearning for wisdom only leads to fallacy.
If venomous jealousy is not overcome,
One's yearning for Bodhi-Mind will be an illusion.
If one refrains not from hurting people,
His longing for respect and honor
Is merely wishful thinking.
If one cannot conquer ego-clinging and prejudice,
His craving for the Equality-of-Dharma
Only brings wrong views.
If one cannot subdue the demon, clinging-ego,
His Kleśas will be great and his Yoga bound
          to fail.
If one's actions conform not with the Dharma,
He will always hinder the good deeds of others.
If one has not yet absorbed his mind in Dharma,
His babbling and prattling will only disturb
          others' minds.
Therefore, do not waste your life in words and
          chatter
But try to gain the assurance of no-regret
And the confidence of facing death!

"Well, I admit that you have heard of the Six Pāramitās," commented Dhar Lho. "Now tell me how should one practise the Ten Pāramitās?" In answer to his challenge, Milarepa sang:

Oh gracious Jetsun, Marpa the Translator!
I pray you to quench the "dharmas of jealousy,"
I pray you to protect us in these evil times.

Now, listen to me Dhar Lho, you evil-minded scholar!
Without remembering or thinking of death
You have indulged in words and arguments.
For the past two-and-thirty years
You have failed to realize this fact.
But you can gain far more
If you devote yourself to actual practice.
Alas, in this time of defilement,
Great are people's passions and desires,
And unbearably glib are sinful people's tongues.

On the Other Shore[7] of Non-ego which I have reached,
There is no distinct Pāramitā of Charity.
On the Straightforward Other Shore on which I live
There is no distinct Pāramitā of Discipline.
On the Other Shore of No-Separation-from-Devotion,
There is no distinct Pāramitā of Diligence.
On the Other Shore of the Immediate-Presence
    where I dwell,
There is no distinct Pāramitā of Concentration.
On the Other Shore of Realizing-the-Absolute,
There is no distinct Pāramitā of Wisdom.
On the Other Shore of All-Perfections where I live,
There is no distinct Pāramitā of Means.
On the Other Shore of Conquering-Four-Demons,
There is no distinct practice called
    "Pāramitā of Power."
On the Other Shore of Two-Benefits[8] where I dwell,
There is no distinct practice called "Pāramitā
    of Vow."
Since the faulty Kleśas are themselves Illumination,
There is no thing outstanding
To be known as "Wisdom."
This is the right way of practicing the Dharma;[9]
Empty words are useless and help little!

"Your practices and understanding are indeed right!" exclaimed Lo-dun. On the other hand, Dhar Lho remarked, "Your words are like third-hand imitations; they cannot stand close examination. As to the magic and sorcery, even pagans can perform them perfectly. The Ten Pāramitās you have just talked about are merely nominal, they are not at all in accordance with these books. Now, we should discuss the subjects indicated in *them*." [He pointed to the books in front of him, and continued]: "All human knowledge should be examined and evaluated through logic.[10] Logic is the most important science of all learning. If one knows logic, all other studies become secondary. Therefore, I shall first discuss logic with you. If you can answer my questions I shall then acknowledge you. Generally speaking, logic is the study of judgment and definitions, of which the most important subjects are the studies of direct experience, of inference and deduction, of 'sufficient reasoning' and 'false-reasoning,' of 'non-decisive proofs,' and of the patterns for constructing propositions. Now, tell me about all these things!"

The Jetsun replied, "Teacher, your body and mind are both possessed by devils. Since you have neither faith in yourself and in your Yidham, nor any veneration toward Buddha Himself, how can I expect you to agree with me? When I drink the soup of your favorite Dharma-of-no-Compassion, my tongue and palate are burned. When I eat the food of your beloved Dharma-of-no-Renunciation — which tastes like [a dish of] vegetable greens cooked with dust and ashes but without any salt or seasoning — my stomach is filled with arrogance and egotism! Then from the upper part of my body I belch with self-conceit and vomit the waste of jealousy; from the lower part I break the wind of slandering and discharge the feces and urine of vanity. I am then caught by the deadly sickness of injuring-all. Therefore, I know nothing about your teachings, which, if used as an antidote, would only worsen the sickness, and as a Dharma would only lead people to sin. What I understand is that all manifestations [consist in] Mind, and Mind is the Illuminating-Voidness without any shadow or impediment. Of this truth I have a decisive understanding; therefore not a single trace of inference or deduction can be found in my mind. If you want me to give some examples of 'false-reasoning,' your own knowledge is a 'good' one, because it is against the Dharma; and since this 'false reasoning' only enhances your cravings and makes them 'sufficient,' it is a good example of 'sufficient reasoning.' Your hypocritical and pretentious priestly manner contains the elements of both 'false' and 'sufficient' reasoning, which in turn stand as a good example of 'non-decisive proof.' "

Hearing the Jetsun's remarks, Lodun covered his head with his shawl and laughed; Dhar Lho shook his head, burst out laughing, and cried, "Thank you for correcting my 'spelling'! You are the one who can hardly imagine the difference between the head and the tail of my feces, but yet takes himself as the Holy Buddha. How amusing! How ridiculous! You said that both my body and mind are possessed by devils, but who is the witness of that? If it is because of scholarship and knowledge of logic that I praise myself and denounce others, you are just like me: for you even talk as if you were Buddha Himself, and humiliate me even to *this* extent! By the same token, you also have your own 'logic.' In brief, you have no merits or fortune to [learn the right doctrine]. Besides, instead of answering my question correctly, you have puffed out a lot of nonsense and big words — bigger than the penis of an ass! I think you had better hide it, sit quietly, and shut your mouth."

The Jetsun replied, "I wanted to sit quietly, but you would not let me! Naturally you have no need for my 'logic,' but my 'logic' has brought me happiness and peace. Therefore it is very helpful and important. Since I was talking to you from the viewpoint of the innate

Truth which just hit you on the spot, it appeared as if I were prais-ing myself. The minds of all sentient beings are void yet illuminating. They can neither be affected by the defilements of Saṃsāra nor by the glories of Nirvāna. This very mind is called the Buddha of Uni-versal Origin, or the Treasury of Buddhahood.[11] It is only because we do not understand ourselves that our minds are veiled by temporal blindness; we, as a result, begin to wander in Saṃsāra and become miserable sentient beings-of-desire. He who [fully] realizes his own mind, is called the Enlightened One, the Pure One, or the Buddha, and he attains Nirvāna. Lord Buddha said:

'The Matrix of Buddhahood permeats all sentient
  beings.
All beings are therefore Buddhas in themselves.'

"Also He said:

'Sentient beings are Buddhas in themselves,
Yet are they veiled by temporal defilements;[12]
Once the defilements are cleansed,
Then will they be Buddhas.'

"[Buddha also said]: 'He who realizes his own mind, knows that the mind itself is the Wisdom, and no longer searches for Buddha from other sources. This is the highest teaching one can practice.'

"[As I understand] it, whoever realizes the inborn Illuminating-Void Mind becomes Buddha. I consider that the Ultimate Truth is no other than the realization of one's own mind, but you scholars have no faith in this. As to your body and mind being in the hands of devils, evidence can be shown, and all people here may witness it. However, this would hurt and damage you too much, therefore it is better that I do not talk about it."

The scholar replied, "How wonderful is this! You say that my mind and body are in the hands of devils; if you have any convincing proof why don't you bring it out now? I think I am much better than those fakers who cheat people through deceptive sorcery and gloomy songs."

The Jetsun smiled at him and said, "Well, if you insist, I have no choice but to convince you. Now, pay attention and try to understand what I am going to say! A thing that you cherished with great affec-tion is now in someone else's hands. Is not this very action [of giv-ing a cherished thing to another] itself a sufficient proof that your body and mind are possessed by devils?"

Hearing this, Dhar Lho was nonplused. His face first turned green and then black. Although the Jetsun now tried to stop Rechungpa from [further] exposing Dhar Lho's scandals, Rechungpa would not listen and went forward to a girl (among the visitors), who had little faith towards the Jetsun but great faith in Rechungpa, and took a bracelet off her wrist. Dhar Lho was so ashamed that he became utterly speechless. Then, [recovering himself], he turned on the Jetsun and Rechungpa, attacked them outrageously in abusive language, and walked out. Rechungpa was so delighted that he showed the bracelet to everybody. Afterwards Rechungpa went again to the girl's home and obtained a rosary [that the scholar had given her], brought it back, and showed it to all. People were thus convinced of Dhar Lho's infamy.

Meanwhile, the scholar Lodun thought, "If the information was not given to Milarepa by others, he must be a genuine and great [accomplished being]. I must think of a way to test him." Then remarking, "We have had enough discussions and debates today," he returned home. On that same evening he poured blood into his begging-bowl but filled his skull-cup with milk,[13] and inverted the images of Gautama Buddha and his attendants. He said to himself, "If he knows what I have done, then he is really an accomplished being and has genuine miraculous powers."

The next day Lodun went to the Jetsun again. Upon his arrival, he first met Rechungpa, who said to him, "Well, my dear scholar, have you come to disgrace yourself and the Dharma again?" Lodun replied, "No, this time I have come to pay homage to the Jetsun, for I now have great faith in him." Saying this he slipped into Milarepa's room. The Jetsun smiled at him and commented, "My dear teacher, you don't have to test me like this. I see all the secrets hidden in your heart as vividly [as if they were in my own hand]. You have poured the Essence of the Five Poisons[14] into the monks' utensil [the bowl] and poured the juice supposed to fill the begging bowl, into the skull-cup. Also you purposely inverted the Buddha's and Bodhisattva's images. Now please do not do such reactionary things, things that no Dharma-follower would dream of doing. Please pour the right drinks into the right vessels, and put the images back in their correct positions." When Lodun heard this remark he was nonplused and frightened half to death. His faith in the Jetsun then rose high. "Pray preach me the Dharma that you practice yourself," he implored, "for I am now fully convinced!" Milarepa replied, "It is very good that you now consider yourself convinced. But my teachings cannot be given to the wrong person, one who is not capable of receiving them. Listen to my reasons":

I bow down to Marpa, the Translator;
I pray you to enable me, the mendicant,
To observe the Secret Precepts.

The divine teachings of the Secret Doctrine
Are precious yet formidable!
Should I give them to you, the bigoted scholar
Who knows nothing but words and argument,
It would be a sheer waste!

If one absorbed in meditation talks nonsense,
His meditation will be ruined and interrupted.
The teachings of Tantra should be practised secretly;
They will be lost if demonstrated in the marketplace.
Accomplishment is attained by practicing
       the Bodhi-Mind;
A great Yogi will go astray
If he follows priestly rules.
The Pith-Instructions are meant for good Vessels;
They will but wasted be,
If given to the incapable.
If one adheres first to seclusion
But later abandons it,
His efforts will all be wasted.
The songs of yogic experience are profound,
But if one sings them to all people,
It will only lead to waste and pride.
There are too many ways in which
To lose oneself and squander life!
In answer to your question
I have said enough today.

The scholar said again, "You may not like to tell me your inner
Experiences, but apparently you seem to have brought forth the Wisdom through your meditations. Now please tell me briefly about your understanding of the Initiations, Path, Stages, View, Practice, and Action." The Jetsun replied, "I know nothing of your teaching concerning these topics, but mine is as follows":

I bow down at the feet of Marpa.

I sing in answer to your question.
Please listen and think carefully,

And for a time forget your criticism!

The best scenery is nought-to-see —
That is the Mind-Essence of Illumination.
The best gain is nought-to-get —
That is the priceless treasure of Mind-Essence.
The best food for satiation is nought-to-eat —
That is the food of beyond-form Samādhi.
The best drink is nought-to-quaff —
That is the nectar of the Bodhi-Mind.
Wisdom is but Self-awareness,
Beyond all words and talk!
This is not the Hīnayānist's world,
This is no realm for fools.
The highest Initiation is that of "This."
He who realizes the truth of "nor-high nor-low,"
Has reached the highest Stage.
He who realizes the truth of no-action,
Is following the Supreme Path.
He who realizes the truth of no-birth, no-death,
Obtains the best that he can hope for.
He who realizes the truth of no-inference,
Has mastered the best logic.
He who realizes the truth of no-great, no-small,
Understands the teaching of the Supreme Vehicle.
He who realizes the truth of no-virtue and no-evil,
Has acquired the Supreme Means.
He who realizes the truth of not-two,
Has attained the Supreme View.
He who realizes the truth of no-observations,
Knows the supreme way to meditate.
He who realizes the truth of no-accepting and
        no-abandoning,
Knows the supreme way to practice.
He who realizes the truth of non-effort,
Approaches the highest Accomplishment.

This truth cannot be understood by
Arrogant and self-conceited teachers —
The prideful scholars of mere words,
And the "great yogis" who prejudge.
For they are those who aspire to Liberation
But only find enslavement.

They are caught by the "two-clingings."
They want emancipation but only find confinement;
They want release, but are bound instead.
They sink down, down to the bottom of Saṃsāra;
They wander, wander in the Three Gloomy Realms.

After this, the scholar Lodun's pride and arrogance were completely broken down. He prostrated himself before the Jetsun and asked him for the Dharma, but he was not able to get the Instructions from the Jetsun at that time. Confirmed with great faith, he said to Milarepa, "The debates we have had are indeed 'true debates,' I admit that you have won."

He then returned home and said to Dhar Lho, "I am convinced that what Milarepa has said is true, and that we logicians have little sincerity, faith, or devotion; nor do we have the pure thoughts and spirit of renunciation. I am now really skeptical about the usefulness of our knowledge. Truly, I do not know whether this knowledge is helpful or obstructive to the course of Liberation. I also regret very much that I thought his genuine superpowers were morbid sorceries." Dhar Lho replied, "The change in your attitude merely shows that you have no confidence in the Dharma; what you have said is like childish babbling. I think he is possessed by a great devil, and his magic powers and telepathy are merely devil-inspired. He does not know one iota of Buddhist teaching. Nor did I have an affair with that woman; his slanderous accusation was absolutely untrue!" Saying this he died, full of hatred and vicious thoughts. Because of his hate and cravings, he became a fearful demon after death. Later, the Jetsun told his disciples, "Because of Dhar Lho's ill-omened attack on me, he has now fallen to the far edge of Saṃsāra!" Thus, those scholars who slandered the Jetsun all incurred loss for themselves.

Later the scholar Lodun put himself in the Jetsun's care. After meditating for some time he eventually became the foremost of the five scholar-yogis in the ranks of the close-sons of Milarepa. His story will be related in the pages to follow.

This is the story of Milarepa overcoming the ill-intentioned challenge [of the scholars] through his miraculous powers and wonder-performances.

NOTES

1 The Three Learnings (T.T.: Slob.gSum.): the learnings of Precept, of Meditation, and of Wisdom.

2 Dorma: See Story 30, Note 7.

3 Key-words of the Five Elements: Each of the Five Elements that constitute the physical body is symbolized by a specific key-word (bīja), i.e., the Fire Element bīja, "Rūm," the Space Element bīja, "Ā" and so forth.

4 See Story 33, Note 3.

5 Lodun: His full name was Lodun Gedunbum (T.T.: Lo.sTon.dGe.hDun. hBum.).

6 Dhar Lho: His full name was Radun Dharma Lhodre (T.T.: Ra.sTon. Dar.Ma.bLo.Gros.).

7 Other Shore: "Pāramitā" is translated by both Chinese and Tibetan scholars as "Reaching-the-Other-Shore," meaning reaching the Nirvāṇa beyond Saṃsāra. Some Western scholars also translate this term as "Perfection."

8 The Two Benefits: deeds that lead to the benefit of oneself and that of others.

9 In addition to the Six Pāramitās practiced by Bodhisattvas, four more are given for the advanced stages. They are: the Pāramitās of Means, of Power, of Vow, and of Dharma Clouds, subsequently assigned for the practice of Enlightened Bodhisattvas of the 7th, 8th, 9th, and 10th stages.

10 Logic (T.T.: Tshad.Ma.), meaning measurement, standard, correct thinking, and so forth. "Tshad.Ma." is derived from the Sanskrit word "Pramāna," signifying [that which is] prior to opinion or thinking; the means of acquiring right knowledge.

11 The Treasury of Buddhahood (T.T.: bDe.gÇeg.sÑiṅ.Po.; Skt.: Tathāgatagarbha). This term may also be translated as "the seed or cause of Buddhahood," without which the attainment of Buddhahood is not possible no matter what spiritual efforts may be made.

12 Temporal defilements: All "defilements" (T.T.:. Dri.Ma.), such as passions, desires, ignorance, etc., are in their deepest sense, rootless, delusory, and temporal. To regard them as something concrete or permanent is erroneous and misleading.

13 Skull-cup, or Kapāla (T.T.: Thod.Pa.): the human skull used as an essential utensil in Tantric practice. It is employed by Tantric yogis as a cup to fill with wine as an offering to the deities. In rare cases, in the performance of certain rituals of the Fierce Deities (T.T.: Khro.Wo.), blood, semen, urine, feces, and saliva — the so-called "impurities" and "filthy things," as men regard them — are offered to the deities. The main purpose of this curious rite is to eliminate discriminative thoughts and to transcend both the realms of purity and impurity. This is strictly Tantric. No Hīnayāna or other Mahāyāna School practices it.

Here the scholar Lodun reversed the customary way of offering in Hīnayāna, and in the Tantra, to test Milarepa.

14 The Essence of the Five Poisons: The Five Nectars (T.T.: bDud.rTsi.lÑa.) of Tantrism are the five major "filthy" discharges, i.e., urine, feces, semen, blood, and spittle. Milarepa refers to blood here as the Essence of the Five Poisons. See Note 13.

35

RECHUNGPA'S THIRD
JOURNEY TO INDIA

Obeisance to all Gurus

THROUGH his miraculous powers the Jetsun Milarepa had conquered the scholar-priests in their ill-intentioned debate and had won the argument. However, his heart-son, Rechungpa, was not satisfied with this victory, for he thought that the Jetsun had not answered the monk's questions in a scholarly manner. "The only way," Rechungpa thought to himself, "to conquer these scholars, who cannot even be convinced by the evidence of miracles, is through logic and argument, or by black magic and curses. I might ask the Jetsun to teach me black magic, but it is not likely that he would. Oh, confound it! These damned scholars who belittle genuine miracles as sorceries! They certainly deserve to be dealt with! But the Jetsun will never do it. Well, it is true that my Guru is well-versed in the Pith-Instructions for attaining Buddhahood in one life, but in order to beat these scholars, I shall go to India to learn logic and science." He then went to Milarepa and told him of his intention. The Jetsun said, "Rechungpa, if we had been defeated in the debate, how could the scholars have credited us with pure [thoughts]? If you go to India merely for the purpose of learning the art of debate, you are then doing something wrong and worthless. [That also means that you will] forsake meditation practice. In learning 'semantics,' you may acquire some knowledge about words, but still you will not be able to win all the debates, nor can you master the whole study of letters. Only Buddha can answer all questions and challenges, but to achieve Buddhahood one must practice. Therefore, the best way is to abjure the world, renounce all thoughts and wishes of this life, and devote oneself to meditation. One may slay people by black magic, but if he cannot deliver the victims [from Samsāra], both he and the victims will be damned. Formerly

I used black magic to curse my enemies, but because of this sinful deed I had to go through many painful trials under Marpa. Life is very short, no one can tell when death will fall upon him. Therefore please forget everything else, and concentrate on your meditation."

[In spite of his Guru's advice], Rechungpa pressed the Jetsun to grant him permission to go to India. Milarepa then said, "If you insist upon ignoring my advice, you may go to India; but I am not sending you there to study logic and science. When I was with Marpa, I received from him only four of the nine complete teachings of the Formless Ḍākinī Dharma Series. He said that the other five were still available in India, and also prophesied that a disciple in our Lineage would later secure them from [a teacher of] Nāropa's Transmission. Thereby many sentient beings will be benefited. Since I have been devoting myself to meditation, I have not yet attended to this matter. These teachings, therefore, are still to be obtained. I am now old and sick, also I have fully realized my own mind — there is no need for me to go. I think it fitting that you go to India to procure them. You will, however, need some gold for your journey."

Thereupon, the Jetsun and Rechungpa collected all the gold that people had offered them, which totaled quite a large sum. Then Shindormo and Lesebum, together with many patrons, prepared a sacred banquet as a farewell party for Rechungpa. In the assembly, the Jetsun presented his disciple with all the gold, and said, "Rechungpa, my son! Listen to my song and think about it. You should try to secure the teachings in India in this manner:

> I bow down to Marpa, the Translator.
> Pray bless us that we keep to your Tradition.
>
> This uninformed son of mine, the loser of debate
> And full of doubts, has stopped his meditation
> And is about to wander far away to study.
> This is the very thing a yogi should avoid!
>
> Rechungpa, when you arrive in India,
> Try to secure the Formless Ḍākinī Dharmas
> Of the great Paṇḍita Nāropa's Succession;
> But, never give yourself to studying words!
>
> In the beginning I met the right person,
> I put myself in the hands of Marpa.
> In the middle, I practiced the right teaching,
> Meditating on the White Rock Mountain.[1]

At the end, I asked for alms in the right places
    for alms;
I beg here and there without friends or kinsmen.
Since I have disposed of Saṃsāra and Nirvāṇa
And have nor hope nor fear in my mind,
I shall ne'er regress in my meditation.

When with my Guru Marpa on that steep hill
He once said to me:

    "The King of the Mighty Wheel holds
        [It as] the Jewel,
    And the Bird with Five Families
    Flies in [It's] expanse of Dharma-Essence.[2]
    Five special teachings in India still survive:
    First, the Lamp of Illuminating Wisdom,
    Second, the Wheel Net of Nāḍī and Prāṇa,
    Third, the Great Bliss of Precious Words,
    Fourth, the Universal Mirror of Equality,
    And Fifth, the Self-liberation Mahāmudrā.
    These five teachings are still taught
        in India."

I am now too old to go,
But you, child of Marpa's Lineage,
Should go to India to learn them!

Rechungpa was delighted. He picked up the best piece of gold, tossed it to the Jetsun as [his farewell offering], and sang:

    Bless me, my teacher,
    Let me risk my life
    To fulfill the Gurus' will.
    Pray help me get the Ḍākinīs' Teachings as prophesied.
    With your great Wisdom-Compassion
    Pray e'er protect, and ne'er part from me.
    Pray, at all times look after this, your son,
    Who has no kinsmen and no friend.
    Pray conquer all his hindrances
    And save him from going astray!
    Pray safeguard him where'er he goes in India —
    A land of danger, and full of bandits!
    Pray lead him to the right teacher,

As he wanders on alone in that foreign land!

In response, the Jetsun sang:

My son Rechungpa, on your way to India
Remember these seven Trinities of counsel:

The Skillful-Path of Tantra,
The Guru's Pith-Instruction,
And one's own judgment,
Are three important things for your remembrance!

Respect and serve the learned,
Have faith in your Guru,
Be determined and perservering.
These are three things you should remember.

Rightly to direct the Life-stream [Prāṇa],
To enter the Dharma-Essence,
And to master all the teachings,
Are three techniques you should remember.

The views of the Bliss-Void,
Of the myriad forms,
Of reasoning and following the scriptures,
Are three essentials you should remember.

A partner qualified in Mudrā,
Experience of the bliss therein,
And the "Elephantine Work,"[3]
These are the three delights you should
    remember.

To instruct an idler brings misfortune,
To speak of one's experience leads to loss,
In towns to wander damages one's Yoga.
These are three dangers to remember.

To join the assembly of the Brethren,
To attend the meeting of Ḍākinīs,
And be present at the [secret] feasts,
Are the three occasions not to miss.

Think of the meanings of this song,
And put them into practice!

Rechungpa made many obeisances to the Jetsun and then set out for India. Accompanying him were fifteen monks, their leader being a Ningmaba Lama[4] called Jidun. In Nepal, both Rechungpa and Jidun had some success [in spreading the Dharma]. They also met Dipupa's disciple, Bharima.

[When they asked the King of Ko Kom in Nepal] for a "Travel-Permit," the King said, "It is wonderful that you, the heart-disciple of the great Yogi who refused my invitation before, have now come to me." He was delighted and granted all Rechungpa's requests. Arriving in India, Rechungpa met Dipupa and obtained all the teachings he wanted. Dipupa also had great faith in Milarepa. He entrusted Rechungpa with his gift — an aloewood staff — to present to the Jetsun upon his return to Tibet.

On this journey Rechungpa also met the accomplished Yoginī, Magi,[5] and he received from her the teaching of the Buddha of Long Life. He also learned much black magic and many deadly spells from pagan Indians.

On his way home, Rechungpa again met Bharima in Nepal. As to the story of Bharima correcting the jealous translator-scholars, and Rechungpa's other adventures in Nepal and India, the reader may refer to Rechungpa's Biography, in which all is told in full.

In his illuminating [Samādhi] Milarepa foresaw Rechungpa's return. He then went to Balkhu plain to welcome him. Thus, the father and the son met again.

This is the story of Rechungpa and Dipupa.

NOTES

1 White Rock Mountain (T.T.: Brag.dKar.rTa.So.): Literally "White Rock Horse Tooth [Mountain]."

2 The meaning of these two statements is very enigmatic. The translator presumes that the first statement, "The King of the Mighty Wheel [Cakravarti] holds [It as] the jewel," is an expression of praise for the Teaching of the Ḍākinī. "It," in the brackets, in both the first and second statments implies the total teaching of the Ḍākinī.

3 The "Elephantine Work" (T.T.: sPyod.Pa.Glañ.Chen.): The advanced yogi acts fearlessly, with great inspiration, for his own need in various unusual acts, that common people may judge him as "crazy" or "immoral."

4 Ningmaba Lama (a free translation): literally, "a Lama who follows the teaching of the Great Perfection (T.T.: rDsogs.Chen.Pa.)." rDsogs.Chen. is the Ningmaba version of Mahāmudrā.

5 Magi: an outstanding woman philosopher and yogini of Tibet. She was the founder of the gGod. School.

36

THE REALIZATION
OF MEGOM REPA

Obeisance to all Gurus

WHEN the Jetsun Milarepa was living in the Belly Cave of Nya Non, a merchant of the Mes tribe[1] came to see him and became filled with an unshakeable faith toward him. He offered Milarepa and his sons all that he had. [He was then given the name of Megom, and became a disciple.] Having received the instructions, he set out to meditate and gained outstanding Experiences and Realizations. Thereupon Milarepa initiated him with the Two-in-One-Pointing-out-Demonstration of the View, Practice, and Action. Immediately, with infinite joy and delight, he beheld the self-face of the Immanent Realty.

After the ceremony, while Megom was preparing a sacred feast in honor of the occasion, he was asked by Drigom Repa, "Do you really understand the Dharma and the instructions? How have your inner Experiences developed?"

Megom replied, "By the mercy of my chief Guru[2] and the Gurus in the Lineage, I am now fully convinced by these teachings. Nothing either good or bad can alter my conviction. For the rest of my life all I need is my Guru's instructions. I have made up my mind, and sworn, to remain in hermitages all my life."

Hearing this, the Jetsun was very pleased and said, "Quite right, Megom. For him who has faith in his Guru and in the instructions, the Experiences and Realizations are bound to develop. They may not arise quickly, but one must have the determination to mediate alone [until they do]. Now listen to my song:"

I bow down at the feet of Marpa.

Oh Megom, and all my disciples here,

403

Please listen, think, and practice what I sing —
The song of an old man
Who is an expert in these things.

Because confusion is uprooted in me,
I realize that Self-awareness is my Guru.
He who has not realized this truth,
Ne'er should leave an accomplished teacher.

All thoughts and forms are but the Holy Truth.
If one has not realized this truth,
He should ne'er neglect the Holy Scriptures.

Try to renounce all desires and craving!
If aversion toward worldly things
Has not arisen in one's mind,
He should watch and discipline himself!

Try to realize the sole truth of Non-being.
If one has not yet experienced this truth,
He should closely watch his Karma.

Try to understand that Nirvāṇa and Saṃsāra
          are not two.
If one has not reached this understanding,
He should practice the equality of the Two Truths.[3]

Try to realize the oneness of self and others.
He who has not yet done this,
E'er should hold to Bodhi-Mind.

Try to let Realization of itself arise.
If of itself it has not done so,
Never forsake the rules and rites.

Try to transcend the Chief and Ensuing Samādhis.[4]
He who has not passed through both realms
Should follow the Skillful Path in solitude.

Try to let the Experience perpetually arise.
He who cannot yet do this
Should continue with the Three-Points practice.[5]

Try to realize the self-nature of Trikāya.
Until this has been realized,
Practice the Arising and Perfecting Yoga.

Try to make yourself
Always relaxed and free.
If you cannot do so,
Keep your vows and precepts!

In great joy, Megom cried, "Jetsun, you are most kind to instruct me in the two-in-one nature of the View, Practice, and Action by combining them into one teaching!" Whereupon he sang:

I pay homage to the gracious Jetsun.

Joyful it is to see the Two-in-One,
Cheerful it is to meditate thereon,
Delightful it is on it to act,
Oh, marvelous are these three "Two-in-Ones"!

If one knows not the View of Two-in-One,
How can he understand that all things
Are but the Dharmakāya?
If one knows not how to practice the Two-in-One,
How can he realize that all pains are glories?
If one knows not the Action of Two-in-One,
How can he spontaneously relinquish worldly wants?

All sentient beings in the Six Realms
Are but the Wisdom of Nirvāna.
This is the View of Two-in-One.
All positives and negatives
And the Wisdom of the Whole
Are but the Dharmakāya.
This is the Practice of Two-in-One!

Like the moon reflected everywhere in water,
Like a rainbow that by no one can be held,
Like lamplight shining brightly [in the dark],
Such is the Action of Two-in-One.

The core of the View
Lies in non-duality,

The Essence of the Practice
Lies in non-distraction,
The "pivot" of the Action is
To embrace and absorb.
That is Enlightenment!

This is the understanding
Your son gained in his devotion!

All the disciples profited greatly from this song. Then on the eve
of his departure to meditate in solitude, Megom asked the Jetsun to
give him a teaching, effective yet easy to practice. The Jetsun replied,
"Great merits have grown in me since I practiced these instructions.
You should also follow them. Now listen to my song":

I, the Yogi Milarepa, see the Essence
By gazing nakedly upon It!
I see Beyond-playwords, clear as the sky!
By letting go, I see Reality;
By resting at my ease, I realize
The voidness of all and everything.
I relax, relax, and come to the Self-Realm;
I let go, let go, and in the flow of Awareness
The pure and impure become one!

Because I search for nothing,
Thoughts and ideas are all cut off;
The perils of Saṃsāra are thus forever crushed!
Since I realize that Buddha and my mind are one,
I no longer wish for accomplishment!
As the sun disperses darkness,
When Realization dawns upon one
Kleśas and Nhamdogs vanish by themselves!

Hearing this song, Megom was filled with joy. As instructed by his
Guru, he then went to a hermitage and meditated there alone. Later
he gained many merits on the Path, attained superb Experiences and
Realizations, and became one of the close sons of the Jetsun, known
as Megom Repa, who [in his lifetime] helped many well-endowed
men.

NOTES

1 The text reads, "Rus.Mes.Yin.Pahi.Tshon.Pa.Shig.". "Rus.Mes." literally means "ancestral lineage," but here the translator presumes "Mes" is the name of a tribe, and not to be understood as "ancestral" in the original meaning of the word.

2 Chief Guru: A Buddhist yogi may have many Gurus. However, the most important Guru is he who brings the yogi to the initial Enlightenment; this Guru is considered as one's *Chief Guru*. Not only is he more important than the others insofar as he has actually opened one's mind to the Prajñā Truth, but also he is the main reliance of the yogi in his progress on the Path. The first priority should be given to him in service, worship, and prayer, as shown by the relationship between Milarepa and Marpa.

3 Two Truths (T.T.: bDen.Pa.gÑis.): These are the Mundane and the Transcendental Truths. The former deals with the basic principles of the phenomenal world, and the latter with the Ultimate. See also Story 29, Note 11.

4 Chief and Ensuing Samādhis (T.T.: mÑam.bShag. [and] rJes.Thob.): The Chief, or Main Samādhi is the real Samādhi stage; the Ensuing Samādhi is the after-Samādhi stage, i.e., the daily activities in which the Samādhi experience still prevails to some degree.

5 The Three-Points practice: The translator presumes that this refers to the practice of observing the nature of the three successive stages of any passing event, i.e., the beginning, the middle, and the final phases. By observing them, one's inner Experience can be widened.

37

SAHLE AUI AND HER UNDERSTANDING

Obeisance to all Gurus

THE Jetsun Milarepa went for alms to Ngogang from the Belly Cave of Nya Non. He stayed at La Shin for half a day, and then proceeded to Nagchar. On his way there he met a pretty young girl about sixteen years of age, with dark eyebrows and gleaming hair, well-dressed and well adorned. She was on her way home from fetching water. The Jetsun said, "Dear lady, will you offer me a meal this evening?" The girl replied, "If we who live by the road gave food to every alms-beggar we would be preparing meals for them all the time." Saying this she entered the house and left Milarepa outside.

That night the girl had an auspicious dream. The next morning, recalling her dream, she thought, "Generally, sentient beings are veiled by blindness. They cannot recognize the Buddha nor the Jetsun Milarepa, who is the Buddha too. Without his grace and blessing, I would not have had that dream last night. Can that yogi be Milarepa himself? I will go and find out."

She then prepared some food and took it to the Jetsun. "My dear Yogi, who are you?", she asked.

"I am an alms-beggar who lives in your neighborhood."

"Are you not the Jetsun Milarepa from the Belly Cave of Nya Non?"

"Yes, you may say so."

Hearing this, a faith that was strong enough to dissolve her entire body at once arose within her, and her hair stood on end. She bowed down before Milarepa and cried, "Yes, yes — now I understand! This is why I had such a wonderful dream last night!" The Jetsun then asked her, "What was the dream?"

"I dreamed that a sun and a moon were in my house, but they did not shine. Then another sun and moon appeared in the East, bright and radiant. They lit up the dark sun and moon in my house, and made them shining bright. Then they (the dark ones) rose up and united with the sun and the moon in the East. The whole universe was thus illuminated. Will you please accept me as your servant, so that I can develop myself in the Dharma?"

The Jetsun replied, "I believe you can." Then he blessed her with his Samādhi power and returned to the Belly Cave.

Soon after, the girl visited the Jetsun, bringing a friend with her. She gave Milarepa a nugget of gold, and sang:

> Please listen to me,
> Great Repa Yogi, the accomplished One.
> When I look at human lives
> They remind me of dew on grass.
> Thinking thus, my heart is full of grief.
>
> When I see my friends and relatives,
> They are as merchants passing in the street.
> Thinking thus, my heart is grieved and sad.
>
> When I see goods hard to earn
> They remind me of the honey
> Of hard-working bees.
> Thinking thus, my heart is filled with grief.
>
> When I see my native land,
> It suggests a den of vice.
> Thinking thus, my heart is sad.
>
> By day, I contemplate this truth,
> At night, I think about it without sleep.
>
> Because of my good deeds in former lives,
> I was born this time a human being.
> My past life drives me from behind,
> Cooking and household duties pull me on.
> I draw closer to death every minute.
> This decaying body
> At any time may fall.
> My breath, like morning-fog,
> At any time may disappear.
> Thinking thus, I cannot sleep.
> Thinking thus, my heart is sad.

Oh, my Father Jetsun,
For the sake of Dharma I visit you.
Pray bless, protect, and pity me,
And grant me the holy Teachings!

To test whether the girl could really devote herself to the Dharma, or whether she might still be interested in worldly things, the Jetsun said, "I do not want your gold. It is very seldom that the rich can practice the Dharma, though they may have great ability in other things. Since you are still very young, I think it is better for you not to renounce the world completely. Now, hearken to my song":

I bow down to the gracious Marpa,
The incarnation of the wheel-turning King!

In the luxuriant garden of the Joyous Heaven[1]
The flowers are sweet-smelling and exquisite,
But common bees can never find them,
Though a hundred flowers they may touch!

On the Tsanglin Continent,[2] south of Mount Sumeru,
There is a bathing pool with Water-of-Eight-Merits
Which common birds can never find,
Though they may locate all other places.

To the north of Bodhgaya
Grow Tsandan, trees of healing,
Which cure all congestions.
But not all sick men can find them,
Though they gather other herbs.

On the border between Nepal and Tibet
Is found the Refuge of the grieved,
He is the immanent Buddha, the good Wadi.[3]
Men without merit cannot see Him.
They may see other images of Buddha,
Yet no faith will grow in them.

In the endless ocean of Samsāra
Wander lonely crowds,
Oft falling to the Lesser Realms.
If once born as human beings,
Few can make provision

For their "souls."
Vain and deluded, they will lose
Once more what they have gained!

To be born a human being
Is rarer than a star that shines by day.
If blessed enough to win a human body,
Many will waste it by running after pleasures,
But few can tread the Path of Dharma.
Though hundreds the gate may enter,
Few can keep the disciplines.

By the grace of my Father Guru
I have realized that all forms are golden;
I have no need for your precious gold.
This is my reply, my faithful patroness,
A song with five parables and six meanings.
The enthusiasm that you now have
Is transient and can be changed;
A will that is not shaken is ever hard to come by;
And so, dear lady, I suggest that you go home.
Trust in the Dharma, is the advice I give.
Take care of your dear husband
As though you served a god.
Maintain your house and fields
And give your children love.

Worship Gurus and Buddhas above;
Protect and help the poor below;
In between look after your in-laws
And keep on good terms with your neighbors.
Now you have been blessed by this old man
Who wishes you prosperity, long life, and success.
May you always have the boon of finding holy
    Dharma.

She bowed down before the Jetsun and said, "I am not interested
in worldly pleasures, but utterly disgusted with everything in Saṃsāra.
Please allow me to give my reasons." Whereupon she sang:

I bow down to the gracious Jetsun.
Pray fulfill my wishes with your blessing,
Pray judge my words and my sincerity.

Pray, great Repa, listen to this girl's request.

With ignorant and bewildered mind
I have thought and searched.
In the depths of my heart
I have reflected on the transiency of life.
I have seen death strike down both young and old
Since first I saw the light of day.

Life is precarious and fleeting
Like dew upon the grass.
Time flies unnoticed, and then life is o'er.
I have never seen or heard of an immortal man.
I am certain beyond doubt
That I shall die one day.
I have no freedom or choice
Of where to go when I am dead.
I am sad and fearful
When I think of the pains that I
In Lower Realms might bear.

This world is but a play —
The endless toil of housework,
The struggle for a living,
Leaving one's gracious parents,
Giving up one's life to one's betrothed —
If into the Lower Realms one falls,
Progress and Liberation will be lost.

Sometimes to myself I thought,
How does it make sense —
Freely to give yourself with your parents' goods
To someone who for life enslaves you as a servant?

At first a lover is an angel,
Next a demon, frightening and outrageous,
In the end a fierce elephant,
Who threatens to destroy you.
Thinking thus, I feel sad and weary.
Now, this maid shall devote herself to the Dharma,
Now, she will join her Vajra-brothers![4]

Most men are but credit-collectors;

Seldom does a gifted one appear.
First they steal your youthful beauty,
Next they snatch your food away,
Then they pull jewels from your hands.
Thinking thus, I feel sick at heart.
Now, I shall devote myself to practicing the Dharma.
Hereafter I shall foster the children of Wisdom.

Houses and temples are like prisons;
At first, they break your heart,
Then they give you an aching back,
In the end, they leave you in despair.
Thinking thus, I feel sick at heart.
This maid will now devote herself
To building a chapel for the immortal Dhyāna.

'Tis meaningless to worship symbols and the Sūtras
Except for those who have real faith and sincerity.

I see people fighting over land,
Then they quarrel over water,
In the end, blows are exchanged.
Thinking thus, I feel sick at heart.
Now I shall farm the land of self-discipline,
Now I shall devote myself to practicing the Dharma.

If one adheres to the Bodhi-Mind
His merits will surely grow.
Yet should he crave for wealth
He will commit much sin in his endeavors.

In the beginning, burning desire consumes one,
Then is he possessed by pride and jealousy,
In the end he fights his foes in desperation.
Thinking thus, my heart is filled with grief.
Now I shall devote myself to the Dharma,
Now I shall cultivate goodwill to all men.

Clearly we see others' faults
But seldom see our own.
How, then, can harmony exist among us?
Even the immaculate Buddha,
All-knowing and all-perfect,

Was found with faults by sinners.
How, then, can peace exist among us?
Thinking thus, I feel sad and weary.
Now I shall devote myself to the Dharma,
Now I shall look at the self-face of my mind.

All things appear like gold to you,
The Nirmāṇakāya of the Buddha!
One may not have experienced this,
Yet [in reality] there is neither existence
        nor non-existence.
To conquer my greed and clinging
I now offer you my most cherished thing.

As the Lord Buddha said,
"One should renounce belongings
That increase one's craving.
All possessions, like magic, are delusive —
One should give them away
For good purposes and charity."
Following this injunction of the Enlightened Ones
I now offer you this gold.
Accept, please, this small token of my faith
And grant me your instructions.

Whereupon the Jetsun Milarepa accepted the gold from the girl
and then returned it to her, saying, "If you have determined to practice the Dharma, disregarding life and death, you have already entered
the gate of Dharma. Now you should prepare offerings for the Gurus
and the Patron Buddha."

A sacramental offering was then made on a grand scale. The Jetsun ordained her as a Geninma[5] in accordance with the general Buddhist Rules,[6] initiated her into the esoteric Tantric Order, and gave her
many verbal instructions. He then named her "Sahle Aui," and ordered her to meditate. In a very short time she gained good Experiences and merits, and learned to meditate alone. The Jetsun then
said to her, "I am very pleased with your faith and perseverance; the
Experiences and Realizations that you have now gained will enable
you to meditate independently in solitude. You should go now into
the mountains and meditate by yourself. Until we meet again, remember these words from my heart." Whereupon he sang:

Great is the blessing of qualified Gurus!

Safe is the shelter of the Three Jewels!
Mighty is the merciful power of the Guards
        and Ḍākinīs!
To you all I pay sincerest homage!

My voice and melody may not be good,
But this song will surely carry
The blessing of the Lineage,
And illustrate the gist of Buddha's teaching.

Listen, faithful Sahle Aui, the woman devotee!
If you want to cleanse the rust from the mirror
        of your mind,
Look into the depth of the pure sky!
And meditate in quiet mountains
Blessed by accomplished beings!

To stay alone in a hermitage
One should know how to observe
The deep Essence of the wavering mind.
Listen carefully, Sahle Aui,
As I tell you how to meditate.

To have faith unshaken
While a Novitiate of Dharma is wonderful;
Like a mountain standing firm,
Meditate with steadfastness.
To win the merits of the Buddha,
Disregard both pain and pleasure!

Like a river flowing on and on,
Meditate without interruption.
To receive the blessing from your Guru,
You should have incessant faith.

Like the firmament, devoid of edge or center,
Meditate on vastness and Infinity.
To understand the innate Truth,
Unite Skill and Wisdom.

Like sun and moon in all their glory,
Meditate clearly without darkness.
Knowing that all beings are your parents,

Love and show compassion to them.

Use the ocean as a parable.
Meditate without drowsiness or distraction.
To see directly the Self-mind,
You should follow straight the Guru's words.
Like this great earth,
Meditate with unshaken firmness.
To make yourself a vessel of the Dharma
Meditate beyond all words.
To realize that all things are holy Dharmas,
Watch your mind.

At all times and in all you do
Provide for yourself with care.
Deck yourself with the ornament of discipline,
Wear the clothes of patience, made of sheepskin,
Ride on the wonder horse of diligence,
And enter the holy City of Dhyāna.
With the Jem of Wisdom you will be enriched.
Forget not to repay the bounty of your Guru,
But give him the best offering —
All you have experienced and realized.
Do you, my faithful daughter, understand what
        I have said?

With an even greater faith in the Jetsun than before, Sahle Aui gave a great feast in his honor. Then, obediently, she renounced all worldly affairs and went to meditate on the mountain of Nonyul in the Nya Non area, while Milarepa left for the Red Rock of Drin.

Some time later the Jetsun saw in his so compassionate mind a beam of glittering light shoot from a crystal stūpa, [a sign that Rechungpa was having trouble in his devotions]. The fact was that Rechungpa was having difficulty with his breath-control as a result of the black-magic practices that he had learned from the heretics. Seeing this, the Jetsun thought, "What hindrance is my son Rechungpa having now?" He then flew from the summit of the Red Rock Mountain toward Lashi. Half way there he landed at Rechin Meditation Cave leaving his footprints on the rock. Again absorbing himself in the illuminating Samādhi, he observed the fortunes of Rechungpa and saw that neither Rechungpa's body nor life would be affected, but that some unorthodox thought was hindering his mind.

Milarepa then set out for Nya Non to learn the whereabouts of his female disciple, Sahle Aui. On the way he met some monks who told him that Sahle Aui was still meditating in the cave to which she had first gone. They said that she never spoke or moved her body, but sat still like a dead corpse all the time. They believed that she must have gone astray in her meditation. Milarepa thought, "To absorb oneself in Samādhi like that is a good thing and not a hindrance." He then went toward the girl's abode. Meanwhile, in an illumination, Sahle Aui also saw the Jetsun coming, so she went to the edge of the valley to welcome him.

After making obeisances and inquiring after his health, Sahle Aui sat down to one side quietly, without uttering a word. In order to examine her meditation experience, Milarepa sang:

> Oh, Sahle Aui, the hermit
> Who took the Dharma to her heart,
> With faith and veneration
> You first relied on your Guru;
> And through his blessings
> Your mind has ripened.
> Sipping the heavenly nectar of the Skillful Path
> A real knowledge of Dharma has grown in you.
> Without sloth and laziness in your devotion
> The Warm-Experience that all saints have had
> Has now grown within you.
>
> Since no hindrance has arisen,
> You may as well keep silent now.
> As hunger is not killed by poisonous food,
> Nor Liberation reached by a wrong path,
> Efforts so made will be wasted.
>
> Deer stay in the mountains,
> What is the use of that?
> The black-bird Dorge can sing,
> What is the sense of that?
> The white-bellied Gyuar Mo[7] can hold Life-Prāṇa
>   well,
> What is the benefit of that?
> The Dombu Tukar[8] is skilled in mixing elixirs,
> All pagan yogis practice the Samādhi of No-thought,
> The Brāhmans are ascetic all their lives,
> What is the good of that?
> Parrots can talk with eloquence,

But he who follows not
The Path of Liberation,
For all his passionate striving
Hardly can emancipate himself.

The human mind is like a whirling vortex.
Through the power of Samādhi
One may suppress desires and wandering thoughts,
But this alone will never ferry one
Across the ocean of Saṃsāra!

To practice the Tsandali Yoga of Forms,[9]
One needs Wisdom beyond form.
To practice the Tsandali at the Heart-Center,
One must recognize the Bardo Illumination.
To practice the Ultimate Tsandali of Immanence,
One must realize the State beyond birth and death.
To practice the Tsandali Yoga of Bindu and Nāḍī
One must cease clinging to all forms.
The Central Channel, Dhuti,[10] is beyond
    all efforts and acts;
It is non-acting, self-existent, originally pure.
[Seeing it], the knots of the two clingings
Will spontaneously unravel.
This is the foremost truth of Mahāmudrā.
Dear Sahle Aui, have you realized it yet?

Presenting her inner Experience to the Jetsun, Sahle Aui sang:

The holder of the Lineage of Dorje-Chang,
The one who was prophesied by all Ḍākinīs,
By the grace of Tilopa and Nāropa
Mastered the Four Tantras, the knowledge profound.
He was Marpa, of the Whispered Succession!
By his grace in the Ten Directions,
You have raised many crops;
By his grace, you have borne immaculate fruits
One after the other!
With your blessings, I have gained the great
    Freedom.
To you, the glory upon my head,
I ever pay my homage.

You are the compassionate one,

The great Repa from Gung Tang
Whose fame has spread afar to all lands.
To you, the crowning gem upon my head,
I pray with great sincerity and faith.
Oh, my Father Guru, it is through your grace,
That we, confused wrong-doers, were converted
     to the Dharma.
It is you who led us to the right path.

You ripened the unripened,
You emancipated those who were not free.
You made me realize that all
Manifestations in the outer world
Are unreal and magic-like.
I have thus seen the Mother of the Illuminating
    Dharmata,[11]
I have thus realized that flowing thoughts
Are phantom-like projections;
As waves rise from the sea
They will vanish into it again.
All doubts, errors, and
Temptations in the world
Are thus wiped out!
Following the clear Path
I have gained true knowledge,
Understanding what the Tantras mean.
Truth of the lesser path should not
Be taken for the higher.
By craving it one cannot reach Buddhahood.
I now sincerely ask you, my Guru,
To instruct me in the Tantra.

Comparing my experience with my Dharma-brother
    Ngan Tson's,
I cannot help but feel a deep respect for him.
Like food, my conceit and wrong ideas
    are swallowed;
Thus my long, leaden slumber has been shortened.
I have now renounced all men,
And given myself to meditation.
For many years I have avoided soft cushions,
And contemplated on Mahāmudrā without distraction.
I am a woman aspiring to Nirvāṇa,
Who, from Voidness and Compassion would n'er depart.

Free from conceit and arrogance,
I shall e'er be glad to learn the Doctrine.
Ever in you I trust as in the Buddha.
With all Ḍākinīs caroling with me,
This is my song to you, my gracious Guru.

The Jetsun, very much pleased, said, "You have gained good understanding and Experiences from your meditation. It is indeed difficult to win Realization like this. Although you have now entered the Path of the Omniscient Ones, you should still remain and meditate in solitude."

Obeying this injunction Sahle Aui again meditated in the hermitage. Later on she became one of the four foremost yoginī disciples of the Jetsun. During her lifetime she performed a great service to the Dharma and benefited many sentient beings. The story of her life may be found in a book written by Ngan Tson Dunba Shun Chub Jhalbo.

This is the story of Sahle Aui.

NOTES

1 Joyous Heaven (T.T.: dGah.lDan.).

2 Tsanglin Continent (T.T.: hDsam.Glin): the Southern Continent. (See Story 2, Note 16.)

3 Wadi (T.T.: Rañ.Byañ.Wa.Ti.; lit.: the self-born Wadi): a famous Buddha image legendarily believed to have descended from Heaven.

4 Vajra Brothers, or Brothers-of-Vajra (T.T.: rDo.rJe.sPun.): Those who are initiated by the same Guru are Vajra brothers.

5 Geninma (T.T.: dGe.bsÑen.Ma.): the laywoman Buddhist who has taken a vow to observe the five basic virtuous rules.

6 General Buddhist Rules (T.T.: mDo.Lugs.; lit.: Sūtra Traditions): This implies the Rules and traditions that one finds in the general Mahāyāna Schools whose doctrines are based on Sūtras but not on Tantras.

7 White-bellied Gyuar-Mo (T.T.: Gyur.Mo.lTo.dKar.): According to the text, Gyuar-Mo seems to be a hibernating animal, presumably a porcupine.

8 Dombu Tukar (T.T.: Dom.Bu.Thugs.dKar.).

9 Tsandali Yoga (Skt.: Caṇḍālī Yoga) is called in Tibetan the "gTum.Mo." (Heat) Yoga. See W. Y. Evans-Wentz' "Tibetan Yoga and Secret Doctrines," 2nd ed., 1958, pp. 171-210. See also the translator's volume, "Teachings of Tibetan Yoga."

10 Dhuti: This is the abbreviation of Avadhūtī, the Central Channel.

11 Mother of the Illuminating Dharmatā: The illuminating Dharma-Essence is here referred to as "Mother," a symbol of "origin" or foundation, upon which all dharmas depend.

38

THE STORY OF
THE YAK-HORN

Obeisance to all Gurus

Having helped Sahle Aui, the outstanding Yoginī, to further her devotion, Jetsun Milarepa went toward Balkhu to welcome his heart-son Rechungpa [upon his return from India. On the way there] he stayed at Betze Duyundzon [the Land of Pleasure] for some time. As Rechungpa was approaching from Gung Tang, the Jetsun saw in a vision that he was suffering from pride. [With this knowledge in mind] he went to welcome Rechungpa.

When the father and son met in the center of the Balkhu plain, Rechungpa thought, "I have now gone twice to study in India. Heretofore, I have been following my Guru's instructions to serve the Dharma and sentient beings. My Jetsun Guru's compassion and grace are indeed great, but I am much more learned in Buddhist philosophy and logic than he. Now he has come to welcome me, I wonder if he will return the obeisance to me when I bow down to him." With this thought in mind Rechungpa prostrated himself before Milarepa and presented him with the Ahkaru staff that Dipupa had given him to offer to the Jetsun. But Milarepa gave not the slightest sign that he would even consider returning the courtesy. Rechungpa was very displeased. However, he said, "Dear Guru, where did you stay while I was in India? How is your health? How are my Repa brothers? Where shall we go now?"

The Jetsun thought, "How is it that Rechungpa has become so proud? He must either have been possessed by demons or affected by the evil influence of pagans. No matter what the cause, I must rescue him from this hindrance of pride!" So he smiled and answered Rechungpa's questions in this song:

421

I am a yogi who lives on a snow-mountain peak.
With a healthy body I glorify the Maṇḍala of
        the Whole.
Cleansed of vanity from the Five Poisons,
I am not unhappy;
I feel nought but joy!
Renouncing all turmoil
And fondness for diversion,
I reside alone in perfect ease.
Forswearing the bustle of this world,
Joyfully I stay in no-man's land.
Since I have left embittered family life,
I no longer have to earn and save;
Since I want no books,
I do not intend to be a learned man;
I practice virtuous deeds,
I feel no shame of heart.
Since I have no pride or vanity,
I renounce with joy the saliva-splashing debate!
Hyprocisy I have not, nor pretension.
Happy and natural I live
Without forethought or adjustment.
Since I want nor fame nor glory,
Rumors and accusations disappear.
Where'er I go, I feel happy,
Whate'er I wear, I feel joyful,
Whatever food I eat, I am satisfied.
I am always happy.
Through Marpa's grace,
I, your old father Milarepa,
Have realized Saṃsāra and Nirvāṇa.
The Yoga of Joy ever fills my hermitage.

Your Repa brothers are well;
On hills remote they make progress in their
        meditations.
Oh, my son Rechung Dorje Draugpa,
Have you returned from India?
Did you feel tired and weary on the journey?
Has your mind been sharpened and refreshed?
Has your voice been good for singing?
Did you practice and follow your Guru's
        instructions?

Did you secure the teachings that you wanted?
Did you obtain all the various instructions?
Have you gained much knowledge and much learning?
Have you noticed your pride and egotism?
Are you altruistic in your thoughts and actions?
This is my song of welcoming for you,
On your return.

In reply, Rechungpa sang:

Obeying my Guru, I went to India.
My journey was hazardous and full of fear,
I underwent great pain and toil —
But the trip was well worthwhile.
I saw Dipupa, the great Tantric Master,
And met Magi, the great Yoginī.
Also I saw the wondrous Patron Buddha
And witnessed fulfillment of the Ḍākinīs'
        prophecy.
I have unmistakably attained
The longed-for Pith-Instructions —
Those of the Illuminating Wisdom Lamp,
The Wheel Net of Prāṇa and the Nāḍīs,
The Universal Mirror of Equality,
The Lantern of the Great Bliss Injunctions,
The True Words on the Mirror of Self-Mind,
The Supreme Form of the Sun-like Realization,
And the Self-liberation Mahāmudrā.

I drank Nectar — the Essence of Immortality,
I received teaching on the Bardo,
The Pith-Instructions on Dhyāna practice,
On the Five Gems and Symbols Three.
I was told how to practice the Six Yogas,
And how to win what I wanted in the world.
The Mothers and Ḍākinīs gathered for me
All these wonderful instructions.
The Deities and Gurus were all well pleased,
And my mind united well with theirs.
Like a rain of flowers,
Accomplishments fell upon me.
Heavenly food was fed into my mouth,
The Pith-Instructions were put into my hand.

In farewell, the Deities wished me good luck.
My desires were met and success was won.
Like the rising sun
My heart is bright with joy.
Now I am back, my Jetsun Guru!
Now I give you the Ḍākinīs' teachings!
Please observe them,
Praise and serve them —
The holy Dharmas that have brought me my achievement.

Then Rechungpa gave the books [that he had acquired in India] to the Jetsun. In order to clear up Rechungpa's pride and arrogance, Milarepa sang:

Do not be proud and pompous,
My little child, Rechungpa,
Whom I have nurtured from your teens.

In a tuneful voice I sing for you
A golden-rosary of song with meanings deep.
Keep it in your mind, if you agree with it.

Goddesses cherish the Formless Ḍākinī Dharmas,
[But] he who strives to become too big
Is liable to be slain by villains.
The hoarded goods of wealthy men
Provide enjoyment for their enemies;
To indulge in luxury and pleasure
Is the cause of poverty and death.
He who does not know his limit
And acts above his station,
Is stupid as a fool.
If an officer ill-treats his servants,
He harms his country.
If a servant respects not his master,
He will lose his mind
And bring misfortune on himself.
If a Doctrine-holder cannot behave,
He will destroy the Dharma.
He who does not keep the Ḍākinīs' teaching secret,
Disturbs and offends them.

Oh, my son, your pride in what you learned

Will lead you well astray!

To preach a lot, with empty words,
Ruins your good Experience and meditation.
To be swollen with pride and arrogance
Proves you have betrayed the Guru's precepts.
Nothing gives cause for more regret
Than disobedience of the Guru.
No one is more distracted and confused
Than he who ceases to meditate in solitude!
Nothing is more fruitless
Than a Buddhist who renounces not his kin!
Nothing is more shameful
Than a learned Buddhist who neglects his meditation.
Nothing is more disgraceful
Than for a monk to violate the rules.

My son Rechungpa, if you agree with what I say
You should hold it in your heart;
If you disagree, do whate'er you please.
I am an old man fearing death,
And with no time for chat and gossip.
You are young and self-conceited,
Whoever remonstrates with you, you will condemn
      him in return.

Oh, my gracious Guru, Marpa the Translator,
Pray help me, the poor beggar
Who forever abjures all wordly desires!

Picking up the books and the Ahkaru staff, Milarepa ran ahead with great speed by means of his miraculous power. Rechungpa could not catch up with him. He ran, gasping and panting, after his Guru as he sang this song:

Oh, please listen to me, my Father Jetsun!
How could a son ever disrespect his father?
I only pray you to accept the teachings I have
      attained.
I was given, beyond any doubt or possible error,
The instructions on the Formless Ḍākinī Dharmas.
From the profound, and the profoundest, doctrines
I have gained conviction!

I pray you to understand this, my dear Guru!

In addition, I also attained the Yoga of Longevity,
The Ḍākinīs' Symbolic Secret Words,
The principles of the Vajra Body,
And the instructions of the Mother Buddha.[1]
I now offer them all to you, my Jetsun Guru!
Also I have attained
The profound Tiger Protection, the Cures of Diseases,
And the Teaching of Dispersing Demons.
All these golden instructions I now offer to you.

Upon my shoulder I have brought back
The Medicine of Six Merits,
And the elixirs of gods and goddesses;
Now I offer them to you, my gracious Guru.
This marvellous staff made of the supreme Ahkaru
    plant
Was used by Ḍākinīs to rest upon.
It is a priceless and wondrous thing,
Symbolizing the Tantric teachings of Dipupa;
I now offer it to you, my Jetsun Guru.
Please appreciate these wonderful teachings
And have pity on me, the weary Rechungpa!
Please commiserate me, and give me
A chance to stop running and panting!
If you would please, please do so,
It would be the best charity.
If one can satisfy the hunger and thirst of others,
It is of the greatest merit.
To console people in distress is the best giving;
To serve people with kindness and show them the
    right path
Is the obligation of all Dharma-followers,
As taught by Buddha, our Lord.

The Jetsun heard Rechungpa singing this song while he was running after him. When the song was finished, the Jetsun stopped. He
then sat down on the ground and replied to Rechungpa, singing:

It is fine that father and son are in harmony —
Maintaining harmony with people is a great merit;

But the best merit is to keep harmony with one's
    father.
If one is discordant with all the people he knows
He must be a person ominious and obnoxious.
Yet even more ominious is discord between father
    and son.

Good it is to maintain harmony with one's father
    by right deeds,
Good it is to repay one's mother's kindness and
    bounties,
Good it is to act in concord with all.

One's wish can be fulfilled
If he is on good terms with his brothers;
To please one's Guru
Is to gain his blessings;
To be humble is to succeed.
A good Buddhist is one who conquers all bad
    dispositions.

Kindness is toleration of slanders;
To be modest is to gain fame and popularity;
To maintain pure discipline
Is to do away with pretense and concealment;
To live with a sage is to gain improvement;
To be indifferent is to stop all gossip;
To be good and compassionate is to advance one's
    Bodhi-Mind.
These are the things a wise man should do,
But a fool can never distinguish friend from foe.

Where the [actual practice of the] Path is
    concerned,
The Formless Ḍākinī Dharmas do not mean too
    much.
My relationship with you
Is much deeper and more important
Than the Tantric staff of Dipupa.
Of the accomplished Mother Magi
There is no better disciple than I.
If Ḍākinīs keep their secret teachings from me,
To whom will they impart them?

In the golden Maṇḍala
I have enjoyed many sacramental festivals.
With the Patron Buddha, Dorje Paumo,
I have had much longer acquaintance than you.
There is not a land of Ḍākinīs and Bha Wos[2]
That is unfamiliar to me.
Much more than yourself,
I am concerned about the things you are doing.
Oh, Rechungpa, do not be proud and go astray!
Let us go into the mountains and meditate in
    solitude!

Thereupon, the Jetsun and Rechungpa set out together on their journey. This is the first chapter of Rechungpa's meeting with the Jetsun at Yaug Ru.

As the Jetsun and Rechungpa proceeded along the road, Rechungpa again thought, "Had this been another Guru, I would have had a good reception and been most hospitably treated upon my return from India. But my Guru lives under such poor conditions himself, naturally it would be impossible for me to expect any comforts or pleasures from him! I have been in India and have learned so many of the Tantric teachings! A man like me should not practice his devotion as an ascetic, but should practice it with pleasure and enjoyment." With these arrogant and evil ideas in his mind, strong thoughts, full of infidelity toward the Jetsun, arose within him.

At once, Milarepa read Rechungpa's mind. He then pointed to a yak's horn lying along the side of the road, saying, "Pick up this yakhorn and bring it with you." Rechungpa thought, "Sometimes my Guru wants nothing as he always claimed, but at others 'his hatred is much stronger than that of an old dog, and his greediness is greater than that of an old miser,' as the proverb says. After all, what is the use of this torn-out yak-horn?" He then said to the Jetsun, "What good can this piece of waste do us — leave it alone!" The Jetsun replied, "To take a small thing like this will not increase one's greediness, and sometimes these discarded things are very useful." Saying this he picked up the yak-horn and carried it himself.

When they reached the central part of Balmo Baltang Plain where no hiding-place could be found for even a small mouse, the heretofore clear sky suddenly became darkened by gathering clouds. Then a great storm, accompanied by violent hail, arose. In the midst of this onslaught Rechungpa covered his head in such haste and confusion that he completely forgot even to look at his Guru. After awhile, when the hail began to abate, Rechungpa started to search for Milarepa, but could not find him. For a time he sat upon the ground and waited. Then he seemed to hear the Jetsun's voice coming from the yak-horn which had been left beside the road. He walked toward the place and saw it was undoubtdly the same yak-horn which the Jetsun had taken a few moments before. Rechungpa then tried to pick it up, but it was so heavy that he could not move it, even an inch. Then he bent down and looked into it, and saw Milarepa seated comfortably within with ample room to spare; his body was no smaller, and the horn no larger than before, just as the reflection of a large image may be seen in a small mirror. He heard the Jetsun sing:

The grace of my Guru enters into my body.
If one's body remains like a commoner's
He is not a great yogi.
Rechungpa you should pay homage to my miraculous
    body.

The grace of my Guru enters into my mouth.
If one makes nonsensical remarks
He is not a great yogi.
All Pith-Instructions are found in my song.
Rechungpa, you should bear them in your heart.

The grace of my Guru enters into my mind.
If any unfaithful thought ever arises in one's mind
He is not a great yogi.
Rechungpa, you should pay homage to my power of
    telepathy.

Oh, son Rechungpa, your mind is like a nimble bird;
Now it flies high, and now it swoops low.
You should observe this unstable change,
Stop thinking so much,
And devote yourself to the Repa's practice!

If you think you can match your Guru,
Now you may come into this horn.
Come in right now —
Here is a spacious and comfortable house!

Rechungpa, your Enlightenment is like the sun and
    moon;

Sometimes they shine bright, but sometimes they are
      darkened by clouds.
You should observe this unstable change,
Stop thinking so much,
And devote yourself to the Repa's practice!

If you think you can match your Guru,
You may come into this horn.
Come in right now —
Here is a spacious and comfortable house!

Son Rechungpa! Your behavior is like the mountain
      wind;
Now it blows fast and violent,
And now it blows gentle and slow.
You should observe this unstable change,
Stop thinking so much,
And devote yourself to the Repa's practice!

If you think you can match your Guru,
You may come into this horn.
Come in right now —
Here is a spacious and comfortable house!

Son Rechungpa, your accomplishments
Are like the crops in the field.
Sometimes they grow badly, and sometimes well.
You should observe this unstable change,
Stop thinking so much,
And devote yourself to the Repa's practice!

If you think you can match your Guru,
You may come into this horn.
Come in right now —
Here is a spacious and comfotable house!

If one's mind can master the domain of space
He can enter this horn and enjoy it.
Come in right now, my son, your father is calling!

It wouldn't be nice
If a son refuses to enter his father's house.
I am a sick and worn-out old man

Who has never been in India in all his life;
His insignificant body is frightened
By the dangerous road outside,
Therefore inside this horn he stays!
Son Rechungpa, you are young, and have been in
    India.
Also, you have studied under many learned and ac-
    complished Gurus.
You should now step into this horn
With your splendid and prominent body.
Of little value is this rotten yak-horn;
Surely it will not inflate one's egotism and desire.
Come in, Rechungpa, come and join your father in-
    side!

Rechungpa thought, "There seems to be plenty of room there; can I also get in?" Thinking this, he tried to enter the horn, but he could not even get his hand and head in, [let alone his whole body]. Then he thought, "The Jetsun's miraculous power may, or may not be genuine, but he can surely produce hail." Putting his mouth close to the horn, Rechungpa sang in a quavering voice:

Oh, my father Jetsun Guru, please listen to me!
Whether the View, Practice, Action, and Accomplish-
    ment
Of your servant and son, Rechung Dor Draug,
Be high or low, bright or dim, great or small,
Better or worse, it makes no difference;
He shall continue to pray to you.
Whether his cotton robe be dry or wet,
He shall continue to pray to you.
He may or may not match his father,
But he shall continue to pray to him!

Milarepa came out of the horn. He gestured toward the sky, and at once the storm began to abate, the clouds to disperse, and the sun to break through. Immediately the air became very warm, and before long, Rechungpa's clothes were dried.

After resting a while, the Jetsun said, "Rechungpa, I knew from the beginning that your trip to India was unnecessary. Being quite satisfied with the teaching of Mahāmudrā and the Six Yogas, I did not go to India. I am very glad that you have now returned with the teaching you wanted."

"Dear Lama, I am very hungry and cold," said Rechungpa, "let us go to the tents over there and beg some food."

"But this is not the time to beg alms," replied Milarepa.

"I do not know whether it is the time to beg alms or not, but I know that I am starving to death right now. By all means let us go."

"Very well, we shall go. I think perhaps it would be better to go to the first tent."

"But in begging alms one must not look only for rich people, and neglect the poor," said Rechungpa. "Therefore let us go to that small brownish tent near the lower end [of the terrace]."

So they went toward the small tent. When they reached its entrance to ask the host for alms, a fearful old woman came out and said, "A yogi should stick to poverty all the time. Good yogis always refuse our offerings, even when brought to them. But greedy people like you, never content with what they already have, always come after others' belongings. All the things that I had to spare for charity, I already gave to some beggars this morning. Nothing is left now. You had better go somewhere else to beg." Upon hearing these malicious remarks, the Jetsun said, "The sun is about to set; it makes no difference whether we get food or not this evening, so let us find a place to sleep."

That night the Jetsun and Rechungpa slept nearby. About midnight, they heard a noise in the tent. Then it subsided and all became quiet again. The next morning when the sun arose, the Jetsun said to Rechungpa, "Go over to the tent and take a look inside." Rechungpa did so, but he found nothing left in the tent except the corpse of the old woman who had refused to give them alms the evening before. Rechungpa then informed Milarepa of what he had seen. The Jetsun said, "The food and other things must be hidden somewhere underground," and they went over to the tent together.

The fact was, that regardless of her malicious talk, the hour had come for the old woman — the land was full of epidemics at the time. [They found that] her jewelry had all been stolen by the nomads. Left behind on the ground was nothing but a small bag of butter, some cheese and barley flour, and a pail of yogurt. The Jetsun said to Rechungpa, "Son, all things are like this. Last evening this old woman was full of stinginess and worry, but now she is dead. Oh, in sooth one should give alms to those in need." Thereupon, Milarepa and Rechungpa prepared a sacramental offering for the dead woman with the things that were left. Rechungpa then packed up the remnants of the edible food and was about to carry it away with him, when the Jetsun said, "It is not good for one to eat the food of a corpse without benefiting it. The proverb says, 'The old men should eat the food and the young men should produce it.' Now, carry the corpse upon your shoulder and I'll go ahead to lead the way!"

With misgivings that he might be contaminated by the filth of the corpse, Rechungpa unhappily carried it upon his shoulder while the Jetsun went ahead to guide them on the road. When they reached a marsh, the Jetsun said, "Now put the corpse down." He then placed the point of his staff at the heart of the corpse, and said, "Rechungpa, like this woman, every sentient being is destined to die, but seldom do people think of this fact. So they lose many opportunities to practice the Dharma. Both you and I should remember this incident and learn a lesson from it." Whereupon, he sang the "Song of Transiency and Delusion," having six parables:

> Oh, the grace of the Gurus is beyond our compre-
> hension!
>
> When the transiency of life strikes deeply into
> one's heart
> His thoughts and deeds will naturally accord
> with Dharma.
> If repeatedly and continuously one thinks about
> death,
> He can easily conquer the demon of laziness.
> No one knows when death will descend upon him —
> Just as this woman last night!
>
> Rechungpa, do not be harsh, and listen to your Guru!
> Behold, all manifestations in the outer world
> Are ephemeral like the dream last night!
> One feels utterly lost in sadness
> When he thinks of this passing dream.
> Rechungpa, have you completely wakened
> From this great puzzlement?
> Oh, the more I think of this,
> The more I aspire to Buddha and the Dharma.
>
> The pleasure-yearning human body is an ungrateful
> creditor.
> Whatever good you do to it,
> It always plants the seeds of pain.
> This human body is a bag of filth and dirt;
> Never be proud of it, Rechungpa,
> But listen to my song!

When I look back at my body,
I see it as a mirage-city;
Though I may sustain it for a while,
It is doomed to extinction.
When I think of this,
My heart is filled with grief!
Rechungpa, would you not cut off Saṃsāra?
Oh, the more I think of this,
The more I think of Buddha and the Dharma!

A vicious person can never attain happiness.
Errant thoughts are the cause of all regrets,
Bad dispositions are the cause of all miseries.
Never be voracious, oh Rechungpa,
But listen to my song!

When I look back at my clinging mind,
It appears like a short-lived sparrow in the woods —
Homeless, and with nowhere to sleep;
When I think of this, my heart is filled with grief.
Rechungpa will you let yourself
Indulge in ill-will?
Oh, the more I think of this
The more I aspire to Buddha and the Dharma!

Human life is as precarious
As a single slim hair of a horse's tail
Hanging on the verge of breaking;
It may be snuffed out at any time
Like this old woman was last night!
Do not cling to this life, Rechungpa,
But listen to my song!

When I observe inwardly my breathings
I see they are transient, like the fog;
They may vanish any moment into nought.
When I think of this, my heart is filled with grief.
Rechungpa, do you not want to conquer
That insecurity now?
Oh, the more I think of this
The more I aspire to Buddha and the Dharma.

To be close to wicked kinsmen only causes hatred.

The case of this old woman is a very good lesson.
Rechungpa, stop your wishful-thinking
And listen to my song!

When I look at friends and consorts
They appear as passers-by in the bazaar;
Meeting with them is only temporary,
But separation is forever!
When I think of this, my heart is filled with grief.
Rechungpa, do you not want to cast aside
All worldly associations?
Oh, the more I think of this,
The more I think of Buddha and the Dharma.

A rich man seldom enjoys
The wealth that he has earned;
This is the mockery of Karma and Saṃsāra.
Money and jewels gained through stinginess and toil
Are like this old woman's bag of food.
Do not be covetous, Rechungpa,
But listen to my song!

When I look at the fortunes of the rich,
They appear to me like honey to the bees —
Hard work, serving only for others' enjoyment,
Is the fruit of their labor.
When I think of this, my heart is filled with grief.
Rechungpa, do you not want to open
The treasury within your mind?
Oh, the more I think of this
The more I aspire to Buddha and His teachings.

The corpse of the old woman was buried [in the swamp], and her soul was delivered to the Dharmadhātu. Thereupon the Jetsun and Rechungpa took the edible food with them and set out for Betze Duyundzon.

This is the second chapter, the story of the yak-horn.

Later, while the father Jetsun and the son Rechungpa were residing at Betze, Rechungpa gained great improvement in his meditation. In an Experience of great joy, numerous thoughts appeared in his mind. Being aware of this, the Jetsun said, "Rechungpa, what have you experienced in your meditation lately?" In relating his Experiences, Rechungpa sang:

> Living with my Guru, I had
> An Experience powerful like a sharp knife;
> With it I have cut inner and outer deceptions.
> Because of this I am happy and gay!
>
> In the midst of many manifestations,
> I felt as if I were a radiant lamp;
> All instructions thus became clearer than ever
>   before.
> Because of this, I am happy and gay!
>
> When I sat on the peak of a snow mountain,
> I felt like a white lioness,
> Predominating and surpassing all others in the world.
> Because of this, I feel happy and gay!
>
> When I dwelt on the hillside of Red Rock,
> I felt as if I were a majestic eagle;
> Forever have I conquered
> The fearful expanse of the sea.
> Because of this, I am happy and gay!
>
> When I roamed from country to country
> I felt as if I were a tiger cub, or a bee —
> Non-attached to all and utterly free.
> Because of this, I am happy and gay!
>
> When I mingled with people in the street,
> I felt as if I were an immaculate lotus
> Standing above all filth and mud.
> Because of this, I am happy and gay!
>
> When I sat among crowds in the town,
> I felt as if I were like rolling mercury —
> It touches all but adheres to nought.
> Because of this, I feel happy and gay!
>
> When I sat among faithful disciples,
> I felt as if I were the Jetsun Mila;

With cheer and ease I gave instructions through
    songs!
It is the blessing of my Guru
That brings me this joy.
It is through resting one's mind at ease
That Buddhahood is realized.

The Jetsun commented, "If not brought out by pride, these Experiences are fine; and you have truly received your Guru's blessings. Toward such Experiences, however, one needs certain understandings, in which you still seem to be lacking. Now listen to my song":

From the depths of my heart, when the great
    Compassion arose,
I felt that all beings in the Three Realms
Were enslaved in a prison of fire.

When the Instructions of the Lineage
Were imbibed in my heart,
As the dissolving of salt into water,
I experienced thorough absorption.

When the Wisdom shone bright from within,
I felt as if awakened from a great dream —
I was awakened from both the main and ensuing
    Samādhis;
I was awakened from both "yes" and "no" ideas.

When one secures the great bliss through *Viewing*,
He feels all Dharmas spontaneously freed
As mists of rain vanish into air.

When one comes to the Essence of Being,
The shining Wisdom of Reality
Illumines all like the cloudless sky.

When both pure and impure thoughts are cleared,
As in a silver mirror,
The immanent bright Wisdom shines forth.

When the Ālaya consciousness dissolves into the
    Dharmakāya,
I feel my body and soul break forth

Like the crushing of an egg when stamped upon.

When the rope-of-clinging is cut loose,
I feel the existence of Bardo disappear
Like the uncoiling of a snake.

When I act without taking or leaving,
My mind is always at ease and non-doing.
I feel as if I were a lion,
With the power of the Three Perfections.

The Illuminating Voidness, the Illuminating Wisdom,
And the Illuminating Manifestations
Are my three inseparable friends;
Like the sun shining from a cloudless sky,
I am always in the Great Illumination.
Like dividing the horses from the yaks,
The [outer] world and the senses are clearly
        distinct [from the inner].
The string of mind and Skandhas is forever cut!
Having fully utilized this human form,
I have now completed all Yoga matters.
Rechungpa, do you also have these Experiences?
Oh, my son, do not be proud and presumptuous!

Hearing this song, Rechungpa's mind was straightened out. Then
Milarepa said, "Now let us, father and son, go to Di Se or Lashi,
those remote mountains, to meditate." Rechungpa replied, "I am very
tired — my physical strength has reached the point of exhaustion. I
think it best that I go to a near-by monastery to recover [my strength],
otherwise I will not be able to meditate or travel at all."

"If a determination is made from the bottom of one's heart, one
can practice his devotion under any circumstances, at any time," countered the Jetsun. Thereupon, he sang a song called "The Six Sufficien-
cies":

Oh Son, one's own body suffices as a good temple,
For the vital points within are Heavenly Paradise.
One's own mind suffices as the Guru,
For all true understanding comes from it.
The outer phenomena suffice as one's Sūtras,
For they are all symbols of the Liberation Path.
The Food-of-Samādhi is sufficient to sustain one,

For the Father Buddhas will come and bless him.
The Dumo-heat suffices for one's clothing —
The warm and blissful dress of the Ḍākinīs.
To cut off all ties is the best companion;
To live alone is to become a friend of deities;
To regard all enemies as passers-by on the road
Is to avoid hatred.
The best remedy for all obstacles
Is to meditate on Voidness,
For they are all magic-like plays of the mind.
This is the right way for you to follow —
Against it, you will go astray!

I am an old man close to death,
Who has no time for chatting.
You are young, vigorous, and healthy
And would not listen my helpful advice.
To talk with honesty and straightforwardness
To prideful and greedy persons would be a sheer waste.
If you want to meditate, you may come along with me;
If you do not, you may do whatever you please.

The Jetsun was about to set out on his way, when Rechungpa
grasped his clothing in time [to stop him], and sang this song called
"The Eight Needs":

Though the best temple is one's own body,
We need a place for cover and sleep;
Without mercy, the rain and wind attack all.
Because of this, we always need a temple.

Though the best Guru is one's own mind,
We need a teacher to illustrate our Mind-Essence —
We cannot neglect for a moment to pray to him.
Because of this, we always need a Guru!

Though outer phenomena may substitute for the
      Sūtras,
Hindrances and doubts in any case will arise.
To clear them up,
A lucid reference to the Sūtras is necessary.
Because of this, we always need the Sūtras!

Though the food of Samādhi may be sufficient,
Provisions for nourishment are necessary;
On food this delusory body must live.
Because of this, we always need food!

Though the best clothing is the Dumo-heat,
Something to cover the body is necessary,
For who is not afraid of shame and disgrace?
Because of this, we always need clothing.

Though the best thing is to cut off relationships
    with all,
To get support and aid is ever necessary;
Good or bad, who has not some friends?
Because of this, we always need friends.

Though to avoid one's enemies is sufficient,
Sometimes one meets them on the road —
For who can be immune from hostility?
Because of this, we always need protection.

Though the best remedy is to view all hindrances
    as void,
The demons and ghosts are malignant and powerful;
To conquer the demon of ego
Is even more difficult.
Because of this, we always need safeguards.

To stay with my Guru, brings happiness;
To return to you brings joy.
Wherever you go, I will go.
But I beseech you, by all means,
To stay in the valley for a short time.

Milarepa replied, "If you have confidence, to follow my way will
be quite sufficient; otherwise, there will always be a need for something. Well, if by all means you are unwilling to go to no-man's mountain now, let us go to Bouto to preach the Dharma." Thereupon, the
Jetsun and Rechungpa went to Bouto of Red Rock.

This is the last chapter of the yak-horn story.

NOTES

1 Mother Buddha (T.T.: Grub.Pahi.rGyal.Mo.), a free translation.

2 Bha Wo (T.T.: dPah.Wo.; Skt.: Vira): the Brave One. This term refers to the male deities of Tantra. All male Tantric deities, except the chief Buddha in the Maṇḍala, can be considered as Bha Wos — the Brave Ones who can destroy evils and hindrances. Bha Wo is the counterpart of Dākinī, or a "male Dākinī." Dākinī, the female deity, is also called Bha Mo — the Brave Woman.

39

RECHUNGPA'S REPENTANCE

Obeisance to all Gurus

W HEN the Jetsun Milarepa and his son Rechungpa were approaching Drin on their way to Bouto, Rechungpa said, "I would like to stay in Drin tonight and meet the patrons." But Milarepa replied, "My son, let us first go to Bouto without the knowledge of our patrons, disciples, or the monks." In a displeased mood Rechungpa obeyed, and continued with Milarepa to Jipu Nimadson at Bouto of Red Rock. Upon their arrival, the Jetsun said, "Rechungpa, fetch some water and I will make a fire."

On his way back to the hermitage with the water, Rechungpa reached [a slope, from where he could see below him] the great, delightful plateau between Bouto and Jipu. He saw in the center, a mountain she-goat giving birth to a kid. Then the mother and daughter each gave birth to another kid; they, in turn, bore more kids, until eventually there were two hundred of them. These wild mountain goats frisked about so happily, with such innocence and spontaneity, that Rechungpa was amazed. He thought, "These mountain goats are even livelier and in many ways better than those of Baltang." With great interest, he watched them play for some time.

Meanwhile Milarepa, who had lit the fire, opened the books that Rechungpa had brought back from India, and said with great compassion: "I sincerely pray to all Ḍākinīs. I pray you to save and keep the Formless Ḍākinī's Dharma for which I sent from India — the teachings that will benefit the Doctrine and all sentient beings! I sincerely pray to all Guards of Dharma to destroy all heretical books of vicious Mantras that will certainly bring great harm to the Doctrine and to sentient beings!" After this prayer, Milarepa meditated for a short time; and then he burned most of the books until only a few incomplete folios were left.

Now while Rechungpa was watching the mountain goats at play, he saw a masterful goat take the part of a wolf and drive the flock across the ridge to the other side of the mountain. At this point Rechungpa thought, "Goodness! I have been dallying too long. I must go back at once, or the Jetsun will reprimand me."

He immediately started to return. When he reached a bridge leading to the cave, he saw smoke rising from it and smelled burning paper. He thought, "Are my books being burned?" When he entered the cave, he saw there was almost nothing left except the empty wooden covers! He felt as if his heart had been torn asunder. "Where are my books?" he cried to the Jetsun in great resentment. Milarepa replied, "You have been away for so long fetching water, that I thought you were dead and so I have burned all the unimportant books. As far as I am concerned, they were useless, and are merely temptations to distract one's mind and hinder one's devotion. By the way, what made you linger so long?"

In his pride, Rechungpa thought, "My Guru has now become very bitter and egoistic. He has affronted me sorely. Should I return to Dipupa and stay with him again or should I go elsewhere?" Thinking thus, Rechungpa lost all faith in the Jetsun. He sat there deadly quiet for some time. Then he said, "I was watching the wild goats at play, that's why I was late. Now the gold you gave me and the hardship I underwent in India have all become meaningless and wasted. I am leaving for another country now." Saying this, Rechungpa became hostile and disdainful to the Jetsun out of his bad faith toward him. Milarepa then said, "My son Rechungpa, you do not have to lose all your faith in me. All this should be blamed on your dalliance. If you want to be amused, I can entertain you. Now watch!"

Instantaneously, this wondrous vision took form: Upon Milarepa's head the Translator Marpa appeared clearly as Dorje-Chang, sitting upon the sun and moon Lotus Seat of Gems. Encircling him were the Gurus of the Transmission. To the right and left of Milarepa's eyes and ears, shone two suns and moons. From his nostrils streamed rays of light of five different colors like silk threads, from his eyebrows shone a radiant light. His tongue became a small eight-petaled lotus-seat with a sun and moon orb above it, from which sparkled brilliant and extremely fine letters — vowels and consonants — as if written by a single, split hair. From his heart rayed forth other beams of light, which then turned into numerous small birds. Whereupon, Milarepa sang:

Hearken to me, my son Rechungpa!

Above my head,
Upon the sun-moon orb of the Lion Seat
Sits my Gracious Guru Marpa —
The divine embodiment of Buddha Dorje-Chang!

Round him like a string of jewels
Are the Gurus of the Lineage.
If you behold them with faithful eyes
You will be blessed by the rain of grace,
And fulfilled will be your wishes.
Interesting it may be to watch the play of goats,
But how can it compare to *this* wondrous game?

Rechungpa, listen to me for a moment!
On the tips of my ears
A sun and moon shine, glowing as a radiant rainbow.
This reveals the Union of Wisdom and Skill,
This proves my steadfast Illumination.
Amazing it may be to watch the play of goats,
But how can it compare to *this* wondrous game?

Rechungpa, listen to me for a moment!
The five-colored rays from my nostrils,
Streaming like jewelled threads,
Are the essence of sound, a marvel.
This shows my mastery of Prāṇa
Through the Vajra-reciting Yoga.[1]
This proves that I have entered
The Central Channel of my Life-Force.
Amazing it may be to watch the play of goats,
But how can it compare to *this* wondrous game?

Rechungpa, listen to me for a moment!
At the mid-point between my eyes,
Appears the auspicious sign of the radiant
    Dsudbhu;[2]
This shows the essence of pure form,
This proves the blessed radiance of Buddha's
    compassion!
Amazing it may be to watch the play of goats,
But how can it compare to *this* wondrous game?

Rechungpa, listen to me for a moment!

A red lotus with eight petals opens in my mouth,
Adorned with a garland of consonants and vowels.
They are the symbols of all Vajra teachings —
That which is without end or limitation.
Beholding them with reverent eyes,
You will realize all Dharmas are your speech.
Amazing it may be to watch the play of goats,
But how can it compare to *this* wondrous game?

Rechungpa, listen to me for a moment.
From the center of my heart stream
Glowing beams of light.
This shows the Trikāya's immutability,
This shows the unity of mercy and the Void.
Amazing it may be to watch the play of goats,
But how can it compare to *this* wondrous game?

Rechungpa, however, paid no attention to the Jetsun's advice, but sat there silently and in deep resentment. He looked askance at the miraculous scene, but showed not the slightest sign of interest in it. Then he said, "There is nothing surprising in all this; it is more amusing to watch the play of goats!" Although the Jetsun had worked such a great miracle, Rechungpa showed neither interest nor admiration, but continued to demand that the Jetsun give back his books. For a while he merely sat there in persistent indignation and silence. Then he [got up], stamped heavily, and sat down again. Putting his elbows on his knees, and resting his chin on his hands, he began to hum [meaninglessly].

In the meantime, the Jetsun's body had become radiantly transparent; on his Secret Center appeared Buddha Dorje Danyi, on his Navel Center appeared Buddha Dem Chog, on his Heart Center, Buddha Jeba Dorje, on his Throat Center, Buddha Mahāmāya, between his eyebrows, Buddha Śākyamuni, and upon his head, Buddha Sungwong Duba, all encircled by many deities and their retinues. These divine bodies, vivid, yet devoid of any self-nature, were all distinctly visible under a great five-colored canopy of light. Whereupon, Milarepa sang:

My body is the Infinite Palace of Goddesses,
Wherein dwell all Buddhas [in the Universe].
In my Secret Center, where Bliss is preserved,
Dwells the Buddha Dorje Danyi and his retinue,
Glorifying my sealed Cakra of Bliss.
He embodies Buddha's Innate Wisdom.

In the Conjuration Cakra at my navel
Dwells the Buddha Dem Chog and his retinue;
This is the Cakra and two-and-sixty gods,
Where in essence dwells the Vajra Body.

In the Dharma Cakra in my heart
Dwells Buddha Jedor and nine deities;
They are the Essence of the Three Sattvas [?].
This is the Cakra of the Vajra Mind.

In the Enjoyment Cakra in my throat
Dwells the Buddha Mahāmāya and his retinue,
Symbolizing the enjoyment of all forms.
This is the Cakra where the Vajra is expressed.

In the White Conch Cakra between my eyebrows
Dwells Buddha Sākyamuni and many deities;
He is the symbol of Wisdom and Merits.
This is the Cakra of Unity!

In the Great Bliss Cakra in my head
Dwells Buddha Sungwong Duba and many gods;
This is the Cakra of Great Bliss,
Where the Nāḍīs and Bindus both unite.
Son, if you can identify your self with the Buddha,
The Divine Body will vividly appear;
Your flesh and blood will be transformed into
    the Rainbow Body.
Of all marvels, this is most marvellous.
Son, do not lose your faith
But increase your veneration!

Rechungpa said, "Your miracles are indeed wonderful, but my mind
will not be at ease if I cannot have my books back, so please return
them to me." The Jetsun then passed through rocks and other obstacles, flew by on a rock, walked and sat on water, poured fire and
water from his body, flew through and sat in the sky, and transformed
his body from one to many and from many to one. While doing so
he sang:

Rechungpa, listen to me for a moment.
Look, nothing can impede me!
This proves my mind with all forms has merged.

That I can ride upon a rock, flying through the air,
Proves I have mastered outer objects.
Walking on water as on earth
Proves I have unified the Four Elements.
The flow of fire and water from my body
Proves I have mastered all the Elements.
Transforming one body into many
And many into one,
Proves I can benefit all beings
By miracles.
Sitting, walking, and lying in the sky
Proves my Prāṇa rests in the Central Channel.
Amazing it may be to watch the play of goats,
But how can it compare to *this* wondrous game?
Son, if you lose not your faith,
Your prayers will be fulfilled.

Rechungpa said, "Your miracles are like child's play, you have demonstrated them so much that instead of being interesting, they are dull and tiring. If you are really compassionate, please return me my books."

Milarepa replied, "My son, do not lose faith in your Father! If you pray sincerely, you will realize that all manifestations are holy books. Now try to pray to me for this realization!"

Then Milarepa went to a narrow path used by merchants on their way to Drin. There he picked up a huge rock [that blocked the path], cut [a part of it] into pieces [with his hands] as if slicing a cake, threw the bits into the sky as if spraying water, and stamped on the [remaining] rock as though trampling on soft clay. Finally, with one hand, he threw this huge rock into the river in the valley below, and sang:

Rechungpa, listen to me for a moment!
On this narrow [mountain] path
Stood an iron rock with eight edges.
Its right edge was brushed when travellers mounted,
Its left when they the path descended.
One hundred blacksmiths with their hammers
Could not have split this gigantic stone;
A fire heated by one hundred bellows
Could not have melted it.
But behold,
I sliced it as I would cut a cake,
I threw the bits as I would sprinkle water,

I stamped upon it as I would trample mud,
And flung it like an arrow from a bow.
If with faith you look upon your father,
Wish-fulfilling rain will fall upon you;
The treasury of wish-fulfillment will be realized.
Interesting it may be to watch the play of goats,
But how can it compare to *this* wondrous game?
Try, my son, to change your mind at once!

Still without faith in the Jetsun, Rechungpa said, "If you can perform the miracle of restoring my books I shall then have faith in
you, otherwise I shall not be happy or satisfied." Whereupon, as though
spreading wings, Milarepa held out his robe and flew straight into the
sky above the precipice of the Red Rock. He fluttered and hovered
there like a hawk, and then darted to the ground like a flash of
lightning. While performing these miracles he sang:

Rechungpa, listen to me for a moment!
Here, on the peak of Red Rock stands
Sky Castle. Flying over it,
A huge hawk flaps its wings,
While small birds shake in fright.
No human being has flown here before,
None will fly here again.
Now look at this old man in flight,
Look at him soaring
Like a vulture in the sky.
See, he hovers like a hawk,
Darts to the ground like lightning,
And floats cloud-like in the air!
If you have faith in miracles
Through mastering the body,
Practice that mastery;
Then you can conquer and unite Saṃsāra and Nirvāṇa.
Amazing it may be to watch the play of goats,
But how can it compare with *this* wondrous game?
Try, my son Rechungpa, to straighten out your
        mind!

Milarepa's miracles, however, did not overly impress Rechungpa. He
only glanced at them indifferently and still had no faith in the Jetsun.
Then, once more, Milarepa held out his robe like a bird spreading
its wings, and flew into the sky. There he sang:

Rechungpa, listen to me for a moment!
On the peak of Red Rock in the Mon Mountains
Suddenly appeared a flock of goats
Without any reason,
A spontaneous play
Of non-arising Reality.

One goat played the wolf,
Chasing the flock o'er the ridge.
This symbolized the awareness
And the conquest of one's foibles;
This indicated the crossing
O'er the mount of dualism;
This was Milarepa's conjuration
To show Rechungpa the essential teachings!

To the miracles of your Father
You showed indifference,
But in the play of goats
You showed great interest;
This is indeed the sign
That you have lost your mind.
I have showed you such great miracles
Yet you have no faith in me.
When I think of men like you,
Faithless disciples all,
At this time of defilement
I feel sad, and sick at heart.

Rechungpa, listen to me for a moment!
Hard horn, and solid wood,
Can be bent if one tries;
But a harsh mind is hard to "bend."
Rechungpa, try to subdue your mind within!

Fierce tigers in the South,
And wild yaks in the North
Can be tamed if one tries;
But pride and egotism are hard to tame.
Rechungpa, try to subdue conceit within!

Mice under the ground,
And birds in the sky

Can be caught if one tries;
But a lost mind is hard to catch.
Rechungpa, try your own faults to see!

The Dharma of words
And speculation
Can be learned if one tries;
But the void Self-mind is hard to learn.
Rechungpa, try to meditate on the uncreated mind!

A son may leave his father
And his loving mother too,
But a bad temperament is hard to leave behind.
Rechungpa, try to change your temper and conceit!

Jewels, house, and land
One renounces if one tries;
But to renounce pleasure-craving is hard.
Rechungpa, try to give up your desire for pleasure!

Good jewels and a lovely sweetheart
If need be can be left,
But to leave a soft, warm bed is hard indeed.
Rechungpa, try to give up the "blind" sleep
     of a corpse!

Here and there hills and rocks
May meet face to face,
But to see the Self-face of your mind is hard.

The queen's and king's decrees
Can be evaded if one tries;
But no one can evade
Yama, the Lord of Death.
Rechungpa, make use of death for your devotion!

My son, try to correct your wrong ideas,
Abandon your bad actions,
Discipline your unruly mind,
Your impious thoughts restrain,
Avoid the demon of egotism.
When I come to die this shall I will for you;
No profounder teaching can I give you in my life.

Rechungpa, my son, bear my words in mind!

As Milarepa sang, he flew higher and higher into the sky until he disappeared. [Then, of a sudden,] Rechungpa was filled with remorse, and an unusual faith toward the Jetsun burst forth within him. He thought, "Because I could not control my temper and give away those worthless books, I have lost my Jetsun Guru. I have paid too great a price for those worthless books. The Jetsun has performed such great miracles for me, yet I still had no faith in him. Now he has forsaken me as though shedding a heavy burden, and has gone to the Ḍākinī's Pure Land. An unbeliever such as I can never be born there. What is the use of books without a Guru? I shall throw myself over this cliff and meet my death. I now make my last wish: In all my future incarnations may I always meet the Jetsun, and may my mind ever be at-one with his!" Having made this wish, Rechungpa plunged into the abyss below with every determination [to die]. He crashed on a great rock, from where he saw the shadow of the Jetsun. Crying with all his strength, he called to Milarepa in a most pitiful voice, and tried to fly after him, but could not do so. Nevertheless, he managed to walk [in the air] after Milarepa's shadow until he reached the waist of Red Rock cliff. He could not go a step farther but could see the Jetsun and hear his voice.

He saw Milarepa sitting in a cavity hollowed out from the side of the cliff with his other two transformed bodies sitting beside him, all singing together in response to Rechungpa's call of repentance:

> Rechungpa, listen to me for a moment.
> Look, from one Father Jetsun emanate two others!
> To them you should confess your sins,
> Of them you should ask of their well-being,
> From them you should receive the Tantric Precepts,
> And ask for Initiations and Instructions.
> Of them you should beg the profound Demonstration,
> In them should you take refuge,
> And place your confidence.
>
> If you have faith in my miracles,
> Your pride will be curtailed.
> Ill deeds indicate the victory of Yama;
> If of him you are afraid
> You should abstain from vices.
> Bad thoughts hinder one's devotion,
> So of them repent.

As the tears poured down his face, Rechungpa sang:

> Listen to me, Father Guru,
> Embodiment of wisdom and of blessings.
> Listen to Rechungpa, your blind and impious son,
> Who had no faith in your miracles.
> Listen, Jetsun Guru in the center,
> To you I make obeisance, and offerings.
> Of you I ask of your well-being and confess my sins.
> Oh, my Father Guru, it was you
> Who gave me the Precepts, Initiations, and
>   Instructions,
> It was you who enlightened me
> And gave me a lasting refuge.
> Save me, I pray, from stumbling,
> Protect me with your mercy,
> Safeguard this poor and impious mendicant.

Rechungpa managed to reach the place where Milarepa sat, and then hugged him with such great and overpowering emotion that he fainted. When he came to, Milarepa brought him back to the hermitage.

The Jetsun then said to Rechungpa, "If you wish to attain Buddhahood, you must practice the Pith-Instructions. Those books of polemics and the evil Mantras of the heretics had no value for us. The Formless Teachings of the Ḍākinīs are good and sound — these I did not burn, but I burned all the rest because they would only have caused one to fall into the Lower Realms, in spite of one's original intention to attain Buddhahood. Now hearken to my song:

> Rechungpa, my son,
> Whom from childhood I have cherished,
> You went to India for the Pith-Instructions
> But have brought back books full of arguments.
> You were thus exposed to the danger
> Of becoming a debater.
> You wanted to be a yogi,
> But books like those and their ideas
> Could make you a pompous preacher!
> To know both one and all, that was your wish;
> But if you are caught up in endless words,
> You will wreck the most important *one*.
> Your intention was to understand the Dharma,
> But if you are caught up in endless acts,

Greedy and arrogant will you become.
The immaculate Dharma for which I sent you
Has flown into the crevice of a rock
And is preserved by the Ḍākinīs;
You may recover it if you pray sincerely.
I have burned the magic books and evil Mantras
As an offering to the God of Fire;
Many will be helped by this.
Do not lose your temper,
Lest you be scorched by anger;
Do not distress yourself or grieve,
For that will hurt your mind and body.
Do not bestir yourself with many things,
But relax, and sit at ease,
Remembering your Guru
And his grace and bounties!

Rechungpa thought, "My Guru's words are absolutely true and do not differ from the Buddha's. I will now pray the Ḍākinīs to give me back my books." He sat and prayed, and in a short while the Formless Ḍākinī Teachings, together with other books that were beneficial to the Dharma and to sentient beings, all miraculously returned to Rechungpa's hand. He was delighted beyond all measure. He confirmed and imprinted on his mind a faith that Milarepa was Buddha Himself. He thought, "So far, I have served the Jetsun in many ways. Hereafter, I will serve him even better than before." This vow he kept, and lived up to it all his life.

Now, the disciples and patrons gathered to welcome Rechungpa. From the assembly Sevan Repa arose and said, "You must have learned and brought back from India both the Pith-Instructions, as prophesied by the Jetsun, and the science of logic. Now please tell us, how can we win a dispute should we ever become involved in one?" Milarepa said, "Rechungpa, you may tell them how to 'win' a dispute in the light of the Ḍākinīs' [teachings]." In response, Rechungpa sang:

The great Transmission Buddha, Dorje-Chang,
Will quench all disputes in the Lineage.
Our Guru, Buddha-Repa, will end
The disputes of craving teachers.
The Pith-Instructions and the Transmission's
    Skillful Path
Will quench all evil argument

Derived from constant thinking.
The omnipresent Mirror of Equality
Will reveal all concealed vices.
The precious teachings of the Great Bliss
Will burn all wandering thoughts in its Wisdom
    flame.
The Nāḍīs and Prāṇas in the Cakras
Will dispel at once all drowsiness and distractions.
The Teaching of the self-liberating Mahāmudrā
Will conquer the demon of ego-clinging to the
    Five Consciousnesses.
The Teaching of the radiant Wisdom Lamp
Will dispel darkness and ignorance.
The Act of Chu La[3] Swordsmanship
Will cut, with ease, the ties of worldly desire.

Milarepa commented, "What you have said is very good. But in addition, we need the Instructions on the View and Practice. Now listen to my song:

The View is the wisdom of the Void,
The Practice is the illumination of non-clinging,
The Action is the everlasting play without desire,
The Fruit is great immaculate Nakedness.

Concerning the view of Void-Wisdom,
The danger is to miss it
Through words and thoughts.
If absolute knowledge
Has not been gained within,
Words alone can never free one from ego-clinging.
Thus, you should strive for true understanding.

Concerning the practice of Illumination free
    from clinging,
The danger is to miss it
By adhering to mere concentration.
If Wisdom has not shone within,
Steady and deep concentration by itself
Will never lead to Liberation.
Wisdom never comes
With distractions and drowsiness;
You should thus work hard on mindfulness.

Concerning perpetual Action without desires,
The danger is to miss it
By indulging in idle talk.
Before all appearances have become
Aids in one's meditation practice,
"Tantric Acts" will be
Worldly desires disguised.
You should thus strive for purity and non-clinging!

Concerning the immaculate Fruit of Nakedness,
The danger is to miss it through your thought.
If ignorances are not purged within,
Hard effort will bring but small results.
You should thus strive to wipe out ignorance.

All present at the meeting were convinced by the truth of this song, and all were inspired with joy.

This is the story of the wild goats.

NOTES

1 Vajra-reciting Yoga (T.T.: rDo.rJe.bZlas.Pa.): A very important breathing exercise almost indispensible to all Tantric Yoga practices, it is also called the "Three Vajra Words Recitation." Describing this exercise briefly, the yogi recites the "Om" upon inhaling, "Ah" at the pause, and "Hum" upon exhaling, thus coordinating a complete breathing process with the recitation of three essential Vajra words.

2 Dsudbhu (T.T.: mDsod.sPu.): a circle of hair between the eyebrows in the middle of the forehead, one of the thirty-two superb marks of a Buddha, from which he sends forth divine rays of light.

3 The text reads: "sPyod.Pa.Chu.La.Ral.Gri.Yis.". The meaning of "Chu.La." is very obscure. "Chu" originally means water; it could therefore be interpreted as Act-of-fluidity — denoting the non-clinging and all-free attitude of an enlightened mind.

THE SONG OF "HOW TO GAIN HAPPINESS AND AVOID SUFFERING"

Obeisance to all Gurus

A T THE feast held for Rechungpa on his return from India by the patrons and disciples of Red Rock and Bouto, Jetsun Milarepa prophesied the coming of the peerless Gambopa. Then he was invited by the patrons to remain in Chu Bar. [While Milarepa was there], a great yogi [mediator] of the Lan tribe, having heard of his reputation and filled with enthusiasm and aspiration, arrived from Dagbo. As soon as he saw the Jetsun a Samādhi of bliss, illumination and non-thought arose within him. His faith confirmed, he said to Milarepa, "I am a yogi from Dagbo. I have learned many teachings, including the Great Perfection, from several Gurus; I have also practiced the Meditation-of-Distinctive-Observations,[1] and the [Tantric] Action-of-Equality.[2] I am not satisfied with the shallow experiences of mere understanding and have been greatly inspired by your reputation, therefore I now come to you for the Dharma. Please be kind enough to grant me the Instructions." The Jetsun asked, "Have you yet had these Experiences during your devotion? Now listen to my song":

> Have you missed the holy Guru's Pith-Instructions,
> Because of mere verbal knowledge?
> Have you missed the profound Distinct Wisdom
> Because of your Two Clingings?
> Have you lost the view of profound insight
> Because of the hindrance of dualism?
> In practicing the Meditation-of-No-Perception

Have you fallen into the pitfall of forms?
In practicing the Action-of-Equality
Have you gone astray through indulgence and
    skepticism?
Have you failed to understand that Nirvāṇa's fruit
Is found within yourself?
Have you thought the false experiences,
Contrary to the sayings of the Tantras,
To be genuine and sound?
Have you missed the intrinsically void Mind-Essence
By obstructing it with artificial thought?
When you practiced Yoga in solitude
Were you misled by demons in disguise?
As a potter turns his wheel,
The forces of ignorance
Turn one ever in Saṃsāra.

The yogi replied, "It is true that I have been like that. Now please initiate and instruct me in order to correct these faults." Milarepa granted his request and set him to meditate. After some time, the yogi, now called Lan Gom Repa, was still unable to get rid of his attachment to virtues, still thinking them to be concrete and with definite form. Many wandering thoughts rose in his mind, so that he could not free it; he had an urge to visit the town, and so forth. Milarepa was fully aware of this, so when Lan Gom Repa came to report his Experience and progress he said, "Lan Gom, you should not cling to the formality of virtuous deeds, but try to subdue your wandering thoughts about going to the town, and concentrate on your meditation; otherwise you can never free yourself from the Three Realms of Saṃsāra. Take heed of these things." Then Milarepa sang:

For him who keeps the tradition of the Lineage
All errors vanish in the Ultimate,
All things come with ease at the right time.
He who acts like this is a true yogi.

In the practice of Mahāmudrā
There is no room for thinking with a clinging mind.
When Realization of the State-Beyond-Playwords
    arises
There is no need to chant or keep the rules.

Yogis wandering in towns

Always yield themselves
To the will and favor
Of relatives and friends.
Their actions become pretentious,
Their talk nonsensical.
The light of the Void by hypocrisy is dimmed.
If in town one pays no attention to what people
    feel,
Troubles and worries will rain upon him.

To avoid fear and regret at the time of dying,
To escape the fatal chasm of Saṃsāra,
One should conquer the enemy — desire.
Remember always transiency and death,
And ever meditate in solitude.

He who observes not his mind *nakedly*,
Becomes apathetic and indifferent.
He who prays not with earnestness,
Is prone to be misled by false experiences.
If with great diligence and perseverance
He does not practice the profound teaching of
    the Skillful-Path,
He is prone to be vanquished by desires.
If he remains in a hermitage,
Merits will surely grow within him.

Lan Gom Repa thought, "The Jetsun's words have hit the crux of the matter: he is right about my faults." So he meditated in a hermitage without distraction until he gained superb Realizations. Then he came to report this progress to the Jetsun. Greatly pleased, Milarepa said, "That is very good; but you should still continue to practice like this until you attain Buddhahood. These are the important things you should always remember:

A son, a wife, and fame
Are three fetters for a yogi;
A Dharma-practicer should abandon them!

Goods, enjoyments, and prestige
Are three hindrances to a yogi;
A Dharma-practicer should abjure them!

Relatives, patrons, and disciples
Are three obstacles to a yogi;
A Dharma-practicer should forsake them!

Wine, fatigue, and sleep
Are three robbers of a yogi;
A Dharma-practicer should avoid them!

Chatting, joking, and entertainment
Are three distractions to a yogi;
A Dharma-practicer should abjure them!

The Guru, the Instruction, and diligence
Are three refuges for a yogi;
A Dharma-practicer should e'er rely on them!

Solitude, merits, and good companions
Are three staffs for a yogi;
A Dharma-practicer should ever use them.

Non-distraction, non-thought, and bliss
Are three good friends to a yogi;
A Dharma-practicer should e'er consort with them!

Relaxation, spontaneity, and naturalness
Are the three attributes of a yogi;
A Dharma-practicer should ever keep them!

Non-desire, non-hate, and supernormal powers
Are three signs of a yogi's success;
A Dharma-practicer should e'er achieve them!

Lan Gom Repa said, "Because of your blessing I have now relinquished all that should be relinquished, and can practice the right
Dharma spontaneously and with ease. I feel happy and cheerful all
the time." The Jetsun replied, "Yes, my son, this is correct. A yogi
who has completely abandoned all the faults and acquired all the
merits is always happy. If he does the opposite he will suffer all the
time. Therefore, he should always discriminate between right and
wrong for his own happiness and safety. Whereupon, he sang a song,
"How to Gain Happiness and Avoid Suffering":

He who knows his own nature

And the immanent Truth,
Is ever joyful.
He who wrongly acts
Is ever sad.

He who rests in the state of nature
And is ever spontaneously pure,
Is ever joyful.
He who surrenders to impulses and environments,
Being subject to hatred and to cravings,
Is ever sad.

He who realizes that all things are the Dharmakāya,
Freed from all fears, hopes, and doubts,
Is ever joyful.
He who is impatient, talkative, and rash,
Being overpowered by worldly desires,
Is ever sad.

He who knows that all things are his mind,
That all with which he meets are friendly,
Is ever joyful.
He who squanders his life away,
Carrying remorse to his grave,
Is ever sad.

He who has a thorough Realization,
At ease in the self-sustaining Reality,
Is ever joyful.
He who is enslaved by his desires,
Insatiable and always longing,
Is ever sad.

He who is freed from all forms without effort,
Always immersed in the Experience,
Is ever joyful.
He who merely follows words,
Unseeing of the mind,
Is ever sad.

He who renounces all worldly things,
Free from worry and consideration,
Is ever joyful.

A Buddhist who measures and stores up grain,
Cherishing the women and relatives he loves,
Is ever sad.

A yogi who discards all worldly ties,
Realizing all is magic and illusion,
Is ever joyful.
He who diverts himself, taxing
His body and mind with sensuality,
Is ever sad.

A yogi who rides the horse of diligence
Towards the Land of Liberation,
Is ever joyful.
He who is weighted with a stone
That pulls him to the bottom of Saṃsāra
Is ever sad.

He who avoids misunderstandings,
Amused at the play of his own mind,
Is ever joyful.
He who has sworn to practice Dharma
But indulges in sinful deeds,
Is ever sad.

He who has done away with fears, and hopes, and
     doubts,
Perpetually absorbed in the State of Origin,
Is ever joyful.
He who submits to the will of others —
Obsequious, artificial, and ingratiating,
Is ever sad.

He who leaves all "this and that" behind,
Always practicing pure Dharma,
Is ever joyful.

Lan Gom Repa and the other disciples were all greatly inspired [and filled with] joy. With the power of absorbing themselves in the unwavering Samādhi of Mahāmudrā, they were able to further their spiritual progress in this magic-like world of forms. The Jetsun was very pleased with Lan Gom Repa, who later became the patron, the disciple, and the Dharma brother of the Dagpo Rinpoche [Gambopa].

This is the story of Milarepa's intimate son, Lan Gom Repa.

NOTES

1 Meditation-of-Distinctive-Observations, or Meditation and Observation of the Distinctive Wisdom (T.T.: So.So.rTog.Pahi.Shes.Rab.Kyi.rTog.dPyod.).

2 Action-of-Equality (T.T.: Ro.sÑoms.): To set one free from fear and hope, likes and dislikes, Tantrism provides a practice for advanced yogis, known as the "Action of Equality." In the execution of this practice, the yogi is urged to do things against the standard of conventional values.

THE HOLY
GAMBOPA—MILAREPA'S
FOREMOST DISCIPLE

Obeisance to all Gurus

MARPA, in his interpretation of Milarepa's significant Dream of the Four Pillars,[1] foretold that the supremely exalted Gambopa, the heart-son of the great Yogi, Mila the Laughing Vajra, would appear as the Peerless Sage. The Patron Buddha, Vajra Ḍākinī, also told Milarepa that he would have one disciple like the sun, another like the moon, and twenty-five accomplished disciples like stars, and that Gambopa would be the foremost of all, like the sun.

The all-perfect Buddha, Sāykamuni Himself, also prophesied the coming of Gambopa in the Royal Samādhi Sūtra and elsewhere. For instance, in the Great Compassion Lotus Sūtra,[2] Buddha says: "Ananda! In the future, after my Nirvāṇa, a monk called the Physician [T.T.: hTso.Byad.] will appear in the North. He rendered outstanding services to the previous Buddha after having served hundreds of thousands of Buddhas in his former lives. He is well grounded in virtues and supreme thoughts and has entered the immaculate Path of Mahāyāna for the benefit and happiness of many sentient beings. He will appear as a well-informed man, highly versed in the Scriptures of the Bodhisattva's Doctrine, who speaks the words of the Great Vehicle and demonstrates faultlessly and perfectly the Mahāyāna teaching." And so at this time of five defilements, appeared in Tibet, the Snow Country of the North, Dagbo Lhaje [the Physician from Dagbo] whose fame was heard in all lands. He was a great Bodhisattva who had reached the Tenth (Final) Stage of the Path, and realized its direct insight. The Jetsun Milarepa foresaw him in his illuminating Samādhi. He blessed Gambopa with the grace of Samādhi, and attracted him with his mind power. It was he, the great Gambopa, who dawned upon the Buddhist religion and brought many sentient beings to the great Bodhi-Path. His life story is vast like the mighty ocean, of which this epitome of his biography is [but] a single drop.

The Lord Gambopa was born in the Seba Valley of Nyal in Tibet. His family was the Nyi Wa. His father, a physician called Wutso Gabar Jalbo, had two wives, Yunlaza and Sangdan Dranma, each of whom gave birth to a son. Gambopa was the eldest, and was called Dunba Dharmadraug. His father, being an excellent consultant in worldly affairs, trained him well so that he became proficient in speech and in consultation. When Gambopa was fifteen he had already learned many Tantric teachings of the Ningmaba, such as the Basic Tantra of Sungwa Nyinbo, Heruka Galbo, the Tantras of the Wrathful and Peaceful Buddhas and of the Great Merciful Net-Holder, and many other teachings of the Old School. He had also mastered the eight branches of medical science taught by his father.

At twenty-two he married the sister of the powerful [local] chieftain, Dharma Aui. She had all the admirable qualities of a lady. They had a son and daughter, but [a pestilence broke out in that area, and] the son died. Gambopa accompanied the corpse to the cemetery, and when he returned home, found that his daughter had also died. A few days later his wife caught the same disease. Every kind of medical treatment was tried, and prayers were repeated and sacraments held, but in vain.

After suffering great pain for a long time, she was still trying desperately to hold on to life. [Sitting beside her pillow] Gambopa recited the holy Sūtras to her. He thought, "She has been trying so hard to cling to life under such an ordeal, and will not let herself die peacefully. This must be due to her extreme attachment to something."

He then said to her, "Those who do not understand the true nature of Saṃsāra are toilworn and overburdened; those who are compelled to linger in Saṃsāra are miserable and pitiful. I am indeed sorry for those unenlightened people who are subject to intense attachment to their dream-like consorts and relatives. You will not let yourself die peacefully after enduring such a prolonged, unbearable ordeal. This must be due to your clinging to something or someone. If it is the house and land that you cannot abandon, I will offer them to the monks. If it is the jewels that you cannot give up, I will give them to the priests and the poor. What else is there that you cannot bear to leave? We met in this life because of our mutual vows in previous lives. But because of your bad Karma you have now caught this disease. I have tried everything to help, but have only made you suffer more. [This painful lesson has taught me] to decide that no matter whether you live or die, I shall devote my whole life to the Dharma."

His wife said, "I am now about to die. I am not attached to the land, the house, my jewels, or anything else. It is you that I cannot give up. I shall send for my brother [Dharma Aui] to prevent your being seduced by women. Besides, [as you have said], family life in Saṃsāra is without true happiness. I hope, my dear husband and physician, that you will now devote your body and soul to the Dharma."

Gambopa replied, "Even if you recover from this disease, we cannot stay together forever. If you die, I will devote my life to practicing the Dharma and will not marry again. Do you want me to swear to it before you?"

His wife said, "I know you are a man who will never go back on your word, but in order to set my mind at rest I would like you to take an oath before me. Please fetch a witness."

Gambopa then called in his uncle, Balsud, to be the witness, put the holy Sūtra, written with golden words, upon his head and took the oath. His wife said, "My dear physician, I shall see from a crack in my grave whether or not you dedicate your life to the Dharma!" Saying this, she took her husband's hand, gazed into his face with her eyes full of tears, and died.

Gambopa then divided his property into three parts, using one to pay for his wife's funeral and offerings, another for meritorious charities, and the third to provide for learning and practicing the Dharma. He then cremated his wife's corpse, built a stūpa, and made a number of Tsa Tsa[3] Buddha images with her ashes and bones. Later this stūpa became very famous, and people called it Jomo Chod Dan (the Stūpa of the Hostess). It can still be seen in the region of Nyal.

After the funeral and winding up his affairs, Gambopa felt very much at ease. He thought, "It is now time for me to practice the Dharma." He then went alone to Nyi Tong and meditated there.

Gambopa's uncle, Balsud, thought, "My poor nephew must be heartbroken after the loss of his dear wife. I must go to console him." So he went to see Gambopa, taking with him much wine and meat.

During their talk Gambopa said to his uncle, "Since my wife passed away I have been feeling very much at ease and happy." This remark made Balsud exceedingly angry. "Where could you find as good a woman as your [late] wife?", he cried indignantly. "Had Dharma Aui heard of this, he would have said that you were breaking the oath!" With this, he threw a handful of dust in Gambopa's face. Gambopa merely replied, "My dear Uncle, have you forgotten the oath I made before my wife with you as a witness? Am I not practicing the Dharma as I promised?"

"Nephew, you are quite right," said Balsud. "Though I have grown old like this, I seldom think of the Dharma. I really feel very much ashamed of myself! Prosper, my nephew, in your Dharma practice; I will take good care of your land and property."

After some time, without his relatives' knowledge, Gambopa went to the Bodor Monastery in the Pan region. There he saw Lama Bodorwa Rinchinsal, to whom he said, "Precious Lama, I am a native of Nyal, and I have come here for the Dharma. Please guide me through its gate and keep me for a time."

Bodorwa replied, "I have no charity to give you. You must provide your own food and clothing if you want to learn the Dharma." Gambopa thought, "If I had the means, I would not ask. According to the Tantra of Sungwa Nyinpo, to benefit sentient beings a Guru should have four kinds of compassion — the constant compassion, the spontaneous compassion, the compassion of granting benediction and prayers, and the compassion of guiding the disciples according to their needs. Only thus can a Guru help sentient beings. This Guru seems to be lacking in compassion. I doubt whether my Karma is linked with his, and I cannot venerate him."

He soon returned to his native land and prepared sixteen ounces of gold as a means for studying the Dharma. Then he went to the Jhajogri Monastery at Pan, received ordination from Lama Jhachil as a Bhiksu [a fully ordained monk] and was given the name of Sudnam Rinchin, the Precious Meritorious One.

Then under Professors Shapa Linpa and Shadulwa Tsinpa, Gambopa studied the Sāstras of Dodejan (Mahāyāna Sūtrālaṅkāra), Ngundojan (Abhismayālaṅkāra), Ngunbatso (Abhidharma Kośa), and others. In Mon, he studied the Tantras of Jedor, Sungdu, and others under Guru Lodan Sherab, and received the Initiations and Pith-Instructions from him. From Professors Nyurumpa and Jhajogripa, Gambopa learned numerous teachings of the Ghadamba School. Thinking, "Now I must practice these teachings," he meditated in Jhajogri.

The Jetsun Gambopa was a man whose intelligence and compassion were great, whose clingings and desires were small, whose industriousness and faith toward the Dharma were prodigious, and whose apathy and indolence were negligible. By day he studied Buddhism diligently, and at night he meditated strictly; or he circumambulated, and performed other meritorious acts. [Because of his compassion and purity], no insect ever grew on his body.[4] He could live comfortably without food for five or six days, and his body always felt blissful. He could absorb himself in Samādhi for many days, and all crude forms of lust, anger, and blindness dwindled away within him. As prophesied in the Golden Light Sūtra[5] all the signs preceding achievement of the Tenth Bhumi [the final and ultimate stage of Enlightenment of a Bodhisattva] had appeared unmistakably in his dreams.

Some time afterwards, Gambopa had a vision in which he saw a green yogi dressed in rags, who put a hand upon his head, and, wetting a finger with spittle, flicked it in his face. He [at once] felt his Dhyāna growing better and deeper. In addition, he gained a decisive [and immediate] understanding of Reality. In an Experience fraught with joy, his mind became clearer, lighter, and more alert than ever before. He told some monks in the town about this Experience, and they commented, "You were ordained a Bhiksu, and have been observing the immaculate precepts flawlessly. A monk like you, who dreams of yogis and the like, will come up against difficulties, for these premonitory dreams are conjured up by the [demon] Beghar. You should therefore go to your teacher, ask him to give you a holy recitation,[6] and invite a large group of monks to bless you with the rite of One Hundred Dorma Offerings." This Gambopa did, yet the vision of the yogi appeared more often than before.

At that time, in the Sunlight Happy Cave of Draugmar Bouto, the Jetsun Milarepa was setting in motion the wheel of Dharma, both of the Expedient and of the Ultimate Truth, for his heart-sons Rechung Dorje Dragpa, Shiwa Aui, Sevan Repa, and Ngan Tson Dunba; for his patrons Tsese of Drin, and Ku Ju, and for others. One day, the elders among the Repas said to Milarepa, "Jetsun, you are now very old. If one day you go to the Pure Land, we Repas will need someone who can act for you to help us in our difficulties and to further our progress on the Path. Our patrons also need a spiritual leader to increase their merits. Whom do you think can assume this responsibility? Whoever you have in mind should be given all the Pith-Instructions without reservation, and should be invested with power and status. Without such a man, neither our teachings nor our Lineage can spread widely, nor can our disciples be properly guided." Hearing their request, the Jetsun at first appeared slightly displeased. Then he replied, "Yes, indeed I shall have a good disciple, who will develop my teachings immensely. I shall, this evening, observe where he is and [will tell you] if you return early tomorrow morning."

The next morning, Milarepa arose earlier than usual, summoned all his disciples and patrons, and said:

"Like a Dharma-replenished vessel, the man who will receive my Pith-Instructions in full will soon come. He is a fully ordained monk, who bears the title of 'Physician,' and will hold my doctrine and spread it in all the Ten Directions. Last night I dreamed of his coming with a empty crystal vase, which I filled with nectar from my silver vase. This old father now has a son who will benefit numerous sentient beings and will illumine the doctrine of Buddha as the rising sun lights [the earth]. Oh, I am overflowing with joy and happiness!" In great delight Milarepa sang:

> I bow down to all Gurus,
> I pray to the Gracious Ones!
>
> In the East is found the White Lion's milk,
> The source of supreme strength;
> One will, unless one taste it,
> Never understand its power.
> Only after drinking can
> Its strength be felt most deeply,
> Yet only the Deva Indra can imbibe it.
>
> In the South, the great tiger
> Leaps with all his might;
> Great and majestic as this is,
> One can never understand it
> Without an actual contest.
> Only by vying with a tiger
> Can one fully appreciate its leap,
> But only the great Dombhi Heruka rides it.
>
> In the West, the Jurmo Fish has a bitter gall;
> Nothing in this world can taste more bitter,
> Yet, without directly sampling it,
> None can imagine how it feels.
> Only after tasting it
> Can one fully understand its bitterness;
> But only the Dragon Gawojobo has experienced it.
>
> In the North, great is the power of the Blue
>   Gem Dragon,
> Yet, without a formal contest,
> Its strength is never felt.
> Only after wrestling with this monster
> Can one fully understand its might,
> But only the athlete Deva Galugha matches it.
>
> The milk of the White Lioness in the East

Must be poured into a golden bowl,
Not into any common vessel
Lest the vessel break and the milk be lost.

The holy teaching of Nāropa and Medripa
Is deep and most profound,
Yet if one does not practice it,
One sees nothing deep therein.
Only after one has practiced can
One fully understand its depth.
This is the teaching my Father Marpa had!
This is the teaching Milarepa practiced.

Milarepa's Experience, insight, and instructions
Are always most effective and precise,
Yet those of little weight cannot receive them.
They are only given to the able student,
Yet they all will be imparted
To the monk, my coming heir.

One day Gambopa went out for a walk of circumambulation. At the gate [of the monastery] he overheard three paupers talking about their urgent need, as a great famine had broken out that year. One of them remarked, "At a time like this, our kind monks of Jhajogri give timely preaching to all Buddhists; they also invite everyone, without discrimination, to share their food. After we have eaten there, we can also beg a measure of the porridge left over and go to some pleasant place nearby to eat it together." Another suggested, "I have a better idea. Let us gather one full measure of half-ripened grain, make dough, and season it with pepper; then we can enjoy it together quietly in some abandoned house." The eldest said, "A cunning man always laughs and smiles, even if he is desperately hungry, while a good bird always flies like a vulture, even if it is starving. Let us, therefore, not say anything that might betray our yearning for food. Look! A Lama is coming this way! We had better not let him hear our conversation. It would shame us to be overheard. Besides, if you want to make a vow, you had better make a big one! Vow, therefore, to become the immaculate Son of Heaven —the great Emperor — protecting and spreading the holy Dharma and governing all Tibet here and now; or vow to become a yogi like Milarepa, the king of all yogis, who lives an ascetic life in the snow mountains to the West, sustained mainly by the food of Samādhi, dressed only in a thin cotton garment, and keeping his body warm by means of the blissful

Dumo. He is a yogi who practices the illuminating Mahāmudrā day and night. When he goes from one place to another, he flies. If you can renounce the world and practice the Dharma as *he* does, that would be the best of all; but if you cannot do this, you should vow to see his face at least once in this life." Saying this, the old man shed many tears.

When the Jetsun Gambopa heard the name of Milarepa, he could not stop the spontaneous arising of great faith toward him. The emotion that struck him was so great that he fell into a faint for half a day. When he came to, he shed many tears and made many prostrations in the direction of Milarepa's abode. Then he prayed with great sincerity, calling repeatedly, "Oh, Jetsun, Jetsun, please have pity on me! Please take care of me!" He then performed the ritual of the Seven Main Oblations as an offering to Milarepa. In a great and incessant inspiration, Gambopa gained extraordinary, hitherto unattained, Experiences in his Samādhi. Engrossed as he was with the thought of visiting Milarepa, the night [rapidly] passed.

The next morning Gambopa called the three paupers in and served them with meat and food far exceeding their expectations, making them completely satisfied and happy. He then said, "I wish to visit the Lama whom you mentioned yesterday. It seems that you know a great deal about him. I shall appreciate it very much if you will guide me to his place. I have sixteen ounces of gold and will give you half for studying the Dharma."

The two younger men replied, "We know very little about this Lama," but the older one said, "All right, I will guide you to him."

That evening Gambopa made offerings and said prayers to the Three Precious Ones. That night he blew a long, huge brass trumpet, the mighty voice of which reached to every corner of the earth. Even today, there is no trumpet anywhere in all Tibet, [in Weu and Tsang][7] with a greater or more far-reaching sound.

Gambopa then hung a drum in the air and beat a rhythm upon it, producing a solemn, pleasant, and overwhelming boom heard by numerous men and animals. On the same night, he had a vision: A girl, looking like a native of Mon, came to him and said, "You beat a drum for human beings, but many animals have [also] been blessed by the sound." She then handed him a skull-cup full of milk, saying, "Having blessed even the animals to such an extent, please drink this cup of milk. [Before long] not only all the animals here, but all living beings in the Six Lokas will come to you. I am now going to the West." She then disappeared.

Afterwards, Gambopa made this comment: "The human beings who heard the sound of my drum that night are those men of lesser capacity who must go through the successive stages of the Path in a gradual manner. Great, indeed, are the bounties given to us by the [Ghadamba] Lamas.[8] The animals who heard my drum are my great yogi disciples who pracice meditation in caves. This vision also indicated that I shall go to my Guru Milarepa and rely solely on his instructions in the Skillful Path and Mahāmudrā."

Gambopa and the old man then set out to find Milarepa. In the course of the journey Gambopa now murmured, now spoke, and now cried aloud, "Oh, when can I see my Guru?" His yearning to see the Jetsun was so great that tears never left his eyes, and the thought of obtaining rest and comfort never entered his mind.

When they arrived at New Place, in Upper Nyang, the old man fell sick. He said to Gambopa, "I do not know much about the way from here on. There is, however, a monastery called Sajya [nearby]; you can inquire there." He then left Gambopa to go on alone.

Gambopa walked on like a blind beggar wandering in no-man's land. When night fell, he covered his face with his hands, bent down to the ground, and wept bitterly. [Suddenly] the old man [appeared again] and said, "Do not weep so bitterly! I will show you the way." Later [Gambopa] realized that all three paupers were Milarepa's transformations.

Gambopa continued his journey, asking for directions along the way. When he reached Dronso Charwa, he met a number of tradesmen from the highlands and asked them about Milarepa. A merchant from Nya Non called Dawazungpo said, "The master of Yoga, the great Milarepa, the accomplished Guru whose fame is known all over Tibet, is now residing at Chu Bar of Drin." Hearing this, Gambopa became so excited that he thought the merchant was Milarepa Himself. In wild confusion he hugged the man and burst into tears.

With the newly acquired information, Gambopa now went towards Din Ri. When he reached the center of a big plain he became exhausted, and sat down to rest on a rock. But due to extreme hunger and fatigue his entire Prāna-system had become so unbalanced and disordered that he fell from the rock and fainted, lying unconscious for half a day. When he came to, there was not even a single hair of his entire body from his head down to his feet, which did not feel painful. He was desperately thirsty, but there was no one to bring him water. He remained there without food and water for two days and nights. Then he made this vow: "If I cannot see the Jetsun in this life, I swear that in the next life I will be born near him, and that my mind will be united and become one with his. In the Three Bardos after my death I will look only to him as my sole refuge." With the greatest sincerity, and in tears, he made this vow.

Before long, a Ghadamba monk from Sha Yul came by, and asked Gambopa, "Where are you going?"

"I am going to Drin to visit Jetsun Milarepa."

"I too am going in that direction. But aren't you very sick?"

"Yes, indeed, and I am also very thirsty. Could you give me a drink of water?" The monk gave him a bowl of water and after drinking it Gambopa was completely refreshed. Then, accompanied by the monk, he resumed his journey.

Meanwhile, the Jetsun, in a very happy mood, was preaching the Dharma at Fortune Hill. During the discourse, he would sometimes remain silent for a time and then laugh heartily. A very well-gifted lady patron from Drin, called Tsese, asked him, "Why, dear Jetsun, do you now laugh heartily and now remain silent? Do you laugh because you see the progress made by some well-gifted disciple, and sit in silence when you see the wrong thoughts of an incapable one?"

"I am thinking of neither the demerits of the bad disciples, nor of the merits of the good ones," replied Milarepa.

"Why, then, did you smile and laugh today?"

"This is because my son, the Monk from Weu, has now arrived at Din Ri. He fell fainting and in pain beside a rock. With tears pouring down his face and in great faith and earnestness, he called to me for help. Feeling pity for him, I blessed him in Samādhi; then I became very joyful and burst into laughter." As he said this, his eyes filled with tears.

Tsese asked again, "When will he arrive?"

"He will get here sometime between tomorrow and the day after."

"Do we have the Karma of seeing this man?"

"Yes. Whoever has the opportunity of preparing his seat upon his arrival will be sustained by the nourishment of Samādhi. Whoever has the opportunity of first seeing him will be guided to the happy Pure Land of Liberation."

When Gambopa and the Ghadamba Lama arrived at the center of the marketplace they saw a woman weaving. "Do you know where the great Yogi Milarepa lives?" asked Gambopa. "Where do you come from?", she asked.

"From the great sun-like province of Weu, to visit the Jetsun Milarepa."

"In that case please come to my house — I would like to offer you some food."

Tea, cakes, and other refreshments were served them. Then the lady patron said, "The Jetsun knew, yesterday morning, that you were coming. He also made a prophecy about your future. Knowing that you were tired and sick in Din Ri, he blessed you in Samādhi. I obtained permission from him to welcome you first."

Gambopa thought, "It was the grace of the Jetsun that saved my life. Judging from his predictions about me, I must be a well-gifted person." Thinking thus, Gambopa became a little proud of himself. Knowing of this self-conceit, Milarepa refused to see him for a fortnight in order to subdue his pride. During this time Gambopa was told to live alone in a rocky cave, and Sevan Dunba provided him with fuel and utensils for cooking.

[A fortnight having passed], the lady patron brought Gambopa to see the Jetsun. With his power of working miracles, Milarepa transformed both Rechungpa and Shiwa Aui into the appearance of his own form. As a result, Gambopa was unable to identify the real Jetsun. Then Rechungpa pointed to the central figure and said, "*This* is the real Jetsun."

Whereupon Gambopa, the Precious One, offered Milarepa sixteen ounces of gold as a Maṇḍala, together with a brick of tea, introduced himself, and related the story of his journey from Weu. Then he earnestly besought the Jetsun to recount his life story.

Milarepa looked straight ahead for a while, solemnly, and with his eyes fixed picked up a piece of gold from the Maṇḍala, tossed it into the sky, and said, "I offer this to Marpa Lho Draugwa." As he said this, heavenly music and light appeared [all around them], in magnificence beyond description. Milarepa took a full skull-cup of wine and drank half of it. Then he handed the remainder to Gambopa, and said, "Drink it up!"

Gambopa hesitated, thinking, "This is against the priestly rule, particularly in front of so many people."

"Do not think so much, drink it!" said Milarepa.

Being afraid of spoiling the good omen, Gambopa at once drained the skull-cup, proving [by this behavior] that he was a good vessel, capable of receiving the Pith-Instructions, and would become the holder of the Lineage.

"What is your name?" asked Milarepa.

"My name is Sudnam Rinchin [the Precious Meritorious One]."

The Jetsun then repeated thrice: "His merits were gained by accumulating a store of Virtues; he is truly Precious to all sentient beings!"

Milarepa thought to himself, "Whoever hears the name of this son of mine will be liberated from Saṃsāra, but I had better not speak of it now." [After a while] he said to Gambopa, "It is very wonderful that you have faith in me and come here to see me. I do not

need your gold or tea. As to my life story, I shall sing you a song."
Then, accompanied by Rechungpa and Shiwa Aui, Milarepa sang:

In the sky of Dharmakāya, beyond playwords,
Gathering the clouds of ever-flowing Compassion,
I bow down at the feet of gracious Marpa,
The shelter and refuge of all beings!

On my right sits my son Rechungpa,
On my left, sits Shiwa Aui;
Both join me in chorus, singing
A song for you, dear Physician!

In the holy land of India,
Though many teachers boasted much,
The two most famous Gurus were
The great Nāropa and Medripa [Maitṛpa],
Who like sun and moon lit up the world.
Their heart-son was Marpa, the Translator,
Who mastered Buddha's teachings,
Was the host to all Maṇḍalas, and
Attracted well-endowed disciples.
Hearing of the great Master, praised
By all Ḍākinīs, I yearned to see him.

I sought him with all my strength.
On seeing him I swooned in ecstasy,
Bowed at his feet, and sought profound Instruction
That in this life would lead to Buddhahood.
My father Buddha said,
"By the mercy of Nāropa
I have this knife-like teaching,
Sharp enough to cut Saṃsāra's chain."

Exerting my body, mouth, and mind,
A pauper, I worked hard to please him.
Looking at my fervor and devotion
With omniscient eyes, he said kindly:
"The Instructions of the Four Series⁰
Are not perfect today;
Some are deficient, some are overdue.
Though one may risk a headache
Imparting them to one's disciples,

Little profit can they bring.
In days of defilement such as these
People have little time for leisure,
While their activities are great.
Waste not your time in studies,
But practice the Essential Teachings."

To repay the bounty of my Guru
And conquer the fear of death,
I meditated hard and resolutely,
Converting into blessings my wrong thoughts.
Realizing what the Three Kleśas are,
I saw the Trikāya Omnipresent.
To my capable disciples will I transmit
The inner Experience and blessings; to you
Will I impart the profoundest Pith-Instructions;
With their practice, you will spread the Buddhist
    faith.
Bear this in mind, my dear Physician;
You soon will reach the State-of-Relaxation.
This in brief is my life story;
The details can wait until some other time.

I, the old man, do not want your gold,
I have no stove on which to brew your tea.
If you want the doctrine of the Whispered Lineage,
Follow my way and practice as I do.
Venerable Sir, in answer,
I have sung this song.

Milarepa then commented, "This is my reception of our revered Physician Priest." Then Gambopa brewed the tea and brought it to the Jetsun, saying, "Please accept this offering, this symbol of my veneration for you."

Milarepa accepted it with delight. He said to Rechungpa, "We should offer this monk some tea in return. Now go and collect a little from every Repa here." Accordingly Rechungpa [did so, and] prepared the tea. Milarepa continued, "Now we need some seasoning." Saying this, he made water into the pot, making the tea extraordinarily delicious.

The Ghadamba Lama then asked the Jetsun to bless him, and, for the sake of establishing a Dharmic relationship, to give him some instruction.

The Jetsun asked. "What do you have to offer me in return for receiving my blessing?"

The Lama replied, "I having nothing to offer."

"It is shameful to say that you have nothing to offer when I see that you have plenty of gold with you. After all, what is the use of blessing the faithless or giving the Pith-Instructions to the irresolute? I think it might be better for you to resume your business trip to Nepal without interruption."

"One cannot deceive the Jetsun," thought Gambopa, "One must be careful about what one thinks in front of him." Henceforth Gambopa was convinced that the Jetsun was identical with the perfect Buddha.

"Have you received any initiations before?" Milarepa asked Gambopa. "Yes," he replied, and then described in detail the initiations and instructions he had been given by his other Gurus, together with his Experiences and attainment of Samādhi.

The Jetsun laughed, saying, "One cannot extract oil from sand, for it is produced from seeds. First practice my Heat Yoga to see the Mind-Essence. By this I do not mean that your previous initiations are not good enough, I merely want to stress the importance of a correct Karmic relationship, and the absolute need for you to receive the blessing from my Lineage."

Thereupon Milarepa blessed Gambopa and initiated him into the Pagmo practice of the Whispered Lineage, in the Maṇḍala painted in cinnabar, and then he was given the Pith-Instructions. After practicing them for some time, Gambopa gained good Experiences. He compared Milarepa's teachings with those he had received before from other Gurus, and as a result many doubts arose in his mind. In order to uproot them, Gambopa went to Milarepa for the essentials of the View, Practice, and Action. Then, having cleared up all Gambopa's doubts, Milarepa sang a song relating the teaching of Tantra in accordance with the Ghagyuba traditions:

> My dear Physician Priest,
> The Ultimate View is to observe one's mind
> Steadfastly and with determination.
> If one searches for the View outside one's mind,
> 'Tis like a [blind] monster
> Seeking in vain for gold.
>
> My dear Physician Priest,
> The Ultimate Practice is not to consider
> Distractions and drowsiness as faults.

Doing so to stave them off is like
Kindling a lamp in bright daylight.

My dear Physician Priest,
The Ultimate Action is to cease
    taking and abandoning.
To take and to abandon is to be
Like a bee trapped in a net.

My dear Physician Priest,
The Ultimate Discipline is to rest
At ease in the View.
If one seeks the Discipline-Without-Rules
Outside [of one's own mind], it is like
Lifting the flood-gates of a dam.

My dear Physician Priest,
The Ultimate Accomplishment is the full conviction
    of one's mind.
If one seeks elsewhere the Accomplishment of
    Non-being,
It is like a turtle trying
To leap into the sky.

My dear Physician Priest,
The Ultimate Guru is one's mind.
If one seeks elsewhere a Guru,
It is like trying [in vain]
To get rid of one's own mind.
In short, my good Physician Priest,
You should know that all forms
Are nothing but the mind!

Gambopa thought, "What the Jetsun has just said is very true," so
with great diligence he persisted in his meditation. The first night he
practiced naked in a cave, but warmness and ecstasy arose within him
spontaneously. Before dawn he fell asleep, but his body still remained
upright, as firmly as a rock.

He continued to meditate thus for seven successive days, the heat
and blissfulness arising effortlessly. Then he saw the Five Buddhas in
the Five Directions. In commenting on this Milarepa said, "This experience is like a man pressing his eyes and seeing two moons in front

of him. What you have experienced is only due to your having controlled the five Prāṇas. It is neither good nor bad."

Although the Jetsun had told him that this experience was of no [significance or] merit, Gambopa was full of enthusiasm, and in a delighted mood continued the meditation for another three months. Then one morning at daybreak, he was [suddenly] overcome by a feeling that all the vast Three Thousand Great Millenary Worlds in the Universe were spinning round like a turning wheel. He vomited many times, and fell to the ground in a faint which lasted for a long time. He reported this to the Jetsun, who commented, "This was because the Tig Le [Bindu] in the Great Bliss Cakra [of your Head Center] is increasing. It is neither good nor bad. Just continue wtih your meditation."

Again, one evening, Gambopa saw the Black Spot Hell.[10] Because of this vision, his upper chest[11] became congested, and a strong current of Heart-Prāṇa arose [and stirred his entire body]. He reported this to the Jetsun, who said, "This was because your meditation-belt[12] is too short and binds the Nāḍīs too tightly, so loosen it. This experience was caused by a constriction of the upgoing Prāṇas. It is neither good nor bad. Keep on with your meditation."

One day Gambopa saw clearly the Deva-of-Desire[13] and all the other Devas of the Six Lokas; he saw that those in the higher Realms rained down nectar to feed those in the lower Realms, satisfying them all — [but Gambopa himself] was unable to drink the nectar-rain, and died under the blade of a knife [?]. Asking Milarepa about this vision, he was told, "The raining-down of the nectar was due to the Tig Le [Bindu] increasing in the Right and Left Channels [Roma and Jhunma] at the Throat Center. Your inability to drink the nectar was because your Central Channel has not yet opened. You should practice certain vigorous bodily exercises." Saying which, the Jetsun taught Gambopa a few forceful exercises [including those of leaping and tumbling].

Gambopa practiced for another month, then one day his body began shivering, trembling, and shaking incessantly. He thought, "What has happened? Am I possessed by demons?" He informed the Jetsun who said, "This was due to the Tig Le increasing in the Dharma Cakra at the Heart Center. It is neither good nor bad. You should now concentrate on your exercises, and do not stop them."

From then on, Gambopa needed little food. One day he saw both the moon and the sun, covered by the [dragon] Rāhu which had two thin tails. The Jetsun commented, "This was because the Prāṇas in Roma [Iḍā] and Jhunma [Piṇgalā] are now entering the Central Channel [Avadhūtī]; it is neither good nor bad." Then Milarepa repeated thrice: "He is a mighty vulture, now is the time, now is the time."

Gambopa practiced most industriously for another month, and then he saw a red Maṇḍala of the Hevajra before him. He thought, "Last time, the Jetsun said, 'Now is the time, now is the time.' That must have presaged this Maṇḍala of my Patron Buddha." He asked the Jetsun about this vision, who replied, "This is because the Red Tig Le[14] at the Dharma Cakra of the Heart Center, which was coming up from below, is now stabilized. It is neither good nor bad. You should now meditate in a relaxed and spontaneous manner."

Gambopa continued practicing for some time longer, and then one day he saw a skeleton-like Maṇḍala of Dem Chog Luyipa.[15] "This," the Jetsun explained, "was because of the increase of Tig Le in the Transformation Cakra at the Navel Center. It is neither good nor bad."

Gambopa again practiced diligently for fourteen days, then one night he felt that his body had become as vast as the sky. From the top of his head down to the tips of his toes, his whole body, including all the limbs, was full of sentient beings, most of them drinking milk. Some were drawing the milk from the stars, and drinking it. He also heard a roaring noise like that of a great storm, but knew not from whence it came. At dawn he loosened his meditation-belt, and the noise then stopped. Gambopa reported this experience to the Jetsun, who explained, "This was because the Karmic Prāṇas have driven all the Tig Le into the hundreds of thousands of Nāḍīs throughout your entire body. Now these Karmic Prāṇas have become transformed into the Wisdom Prāṇas." Whereupon Milarepa imparted to him the Superb Dumo Instruction[16] and set him to practicing.

One day the whole valley appeared to Gambopa to be full of smoke, so that in the afternoon all became dark to him. Like a blind man, he crawled and groped his way to the Jetsun's abode. The Jetsun said, "This does not matter at all. Just sit at ease and meditate." Then he taught Gambopa the method of clearing the hindrances in the upper part of the body; as a result, the smoke dispersed like [darkness at] the dawning of day.

Then one evening Gambopa's whole body appeared to contain neither flesh nor blood, but only bones linked together by numerous Nāḍīs. He asked the Jetsun about this experience, who said, "This is because you have worked too hard: your Prāṇa has become too rough, so practice more gently." Thereupon Gambopa practiced the Yoga of the Patron Buddha in the evening, and the Guru Yoga, with many prayers, at midnight. Before dawn he practiced with the Life Prāṇa, and at dawn he slept for a short while.

[After a time] twenty-four signs, which bore no relationship at all to

his previous habitual thinking, appeared in his dreams. Upon awaken-
ing he thought, "Were these dreams good or bad signs?" He became
doubtful, and hesitant. Then he thought, "My Guru is actually the
omiscient Buddha Himself; why don't I ask *him*?" Thinking thus, he
immediately arose and went directly to Milarepa, even forgetting to
put on his robe.

At that time the Jetsun was sleeping in a cave at Chu Bar with his
clothes bundled up for a pillow. Gambopa bowed down before him
and said, "Dear Jetsun, I have a very important matter to report to
you. Please do not sleep! Please get up!"

"It came to me this morning that some distracting thoughts had arisen
in your mind," said Milarepa. "Now tell me, what disturbs you so?"

Gambopa replied, "Oh my precious Guru! I had certain dreams last
night. I wonder whether they are good or bad omens. Please interpret them for me." Whereupon he sang:

> Oh wondrous Jetsun Yogi,
> The Cotton-clad, practicing ascetic deeds!
> To all beings you, the famous Mila,
> Are the glory, veneration, and adornment.
>
> The first time I heard your name
> I was filled with joy and inspiration.
> With great earnestness, and disregarding
> Hardships, I set out to seek you —
> As did the Ever-Crying Bodhisattva.[17]
>
> Throughout my rugged journey
> I cried with yearning heart:
> "When can I see my Jetsun Guru?"
> 'Twas like the Ever-Crying One.
>
> When I reached a place from here
> One-and-a-half days' journey,
> I came close to death — lying
> In the road like a discarded stone.
>
> Due to my unyielding will
> And indomitable faith,
> I was able to complete my journey
> To meet you, my Father Jetsun,
> In this wondrous place, Auspicious Hill.
> [This experience reminds me of]

The Story of Meeting the Holy Chupoa[18]
At the Fragrant Palace in the East.

When I saw you, my hair rose in delight.
Beyond description was my joy
As my longing was fulfilled at seeing you.

Little have I to offer you;
I am disgusted with Saṃsāra,
Frightened by the toil of life and death,
And abhor all worldly things.
From the bottom of my heart
This echo sounds:
"Go to practice! Go to meditate."

Pray, my Jetsun Guru, always remember me
And embrace me with your compassion!
Please listen to your servant,
Who has something to report this morning.

Last night I recited the Yidham's Mantra,
At midnight I prayed to you, my Jetsun Guru,
Then I practiced the Life Prāṇa.
Before dawn I fell asleep
And had these wondrous dreams,
Apparently not caused by my habitual thoughts.

I dreamt I wore a hat with silken brim
Beautified by fur along its edge;
Above it was the image of an eagle.

I dreamt I wore a pair of greenish boots
Well cut, embossed with brass
And fastened by silver buckles.

I dreamt I wore a white silk robe,
Red-spotted and adorned
With pearls and golden threads.

I dreamt of a belt around my waist
Made of cloth from Mon
And embroidered with fine flowers,
Silk tassels, and [many] pearls.

I dreamt of wearing round my neck
A white, uncut felt scarf
With jasmines made of silver.

I dreamt I held a Tsandar staff,
With seven precious stones adorned
And golden lattice-work design.

I dreamt that in my left hand lay
A skull brimful of golden nectar.
Then said I: "Let me use
This as my drinking bowl."

I dreamt of a many-colored sack
Filled with two loads of rice.
Then said I: "Let me use
This for my Dharma food."
And then I shouldered it.

I dreamt of a wild beast's pelt,
With head and claws attached.
Then said I: "Let me use it
As the cushion for my seat."
And then I shouldered it.

Looking to my right I saw
A fertile mead of golden flowers,
Where many sheep and cattle grazed.
I watched them closely like a shepherd.

Looking to my left I saw
A jade-green meadow full
Of many kinds of flowers,
Where many women bowed to me.

In the center of the meadow on a mound
Of golden flowers, a Bodhisattva sat
Crosslegged upon a Lotus Seat,
Golden and many-hued.

I dreamt that before the Bodhisattva
A fountain played, and from his back
A brilliant aura radiated

Surrounding him with blazing fire,
While sun and moon were shining from his heart.

These were the wondrous things of which I dreamt.
I know not if as omens they were good or bad.
Oh great Yogi, who sees the past, the present,
And the future, pray interpret them clearly for me.

The Jetsun replied, "Dear Physician-monk, my son, do not feel uneasy, but relax and set your mind at rest. Do not let distracted thoughts mislead you into the trap of ego-clinging. Let the knots of skepticism untie themselves, cut the string of dual clinging at its most subtle length, and pierce through the most delicate and subtle 'frame' of habitual thinking. Do not bestir yourself and think too much, but, putting your mind at ease in a state of naturalness, make no effort whatsoever. I am a yogi who has fully mastered this illusory body. With a full knowledge and direct realization of the very essence of all dreams as such, I can, of course, interpret as well as transform them. Today I, your old father, will explain their meanings to you. Now give me your full attention, and listen carefully to my song":

This, my dear Physician,
Is my answer. Hearken
Carefully to what I say!

My son, you have learned the teaching
Of Dem Chog in the tradition of Zung Ghar;
Also the teaching of Ghadamba, in Upper Weu.
You have mastered and stabilized
The good Samādhi. I have always thought
That you were wondrous and outstanding.

But now, in your great enthusiasm,
By your dreams you have been caught.
Is this due to lack of understanding,
Or merely a pretense? Have you
Not read Sūtras and many Tantras?
Dreams are unreal and deceptive, as was taught
By Buddha Himself, in the Final Truth of Pāramitā.
To collect, supply, and study them
Will bring little profit.
So Buddha used dream as one of the Eight Parables
To show the illusory nature of all beings.

Surely you remember these injunctions?
And yet, your dreams were marvelous —
Wondrous omens foretelling things to come.
I, the Yogi, have mastered the art of dreams,
And will explain their magic to you.

The white hat on your head indicates
That your View will go beyond the "high" and "low."
The fair trimming on the brim is a sign
That you will demonstrate the Dharma
Essence, subtle yet profound.
The lovely colors of the fur imply
That you will explain the various teachings
Of the Schools without mixing them.
The flying eagle on the top means that you
Will gain Mahāmudrā, the foremost View —
And will see the Essence of the Unborn.

The Mongol boots that you dreamt of wearing
Portray your climbing from the lower to the higher
        Vehicles.
Their green color and adorning bosses
Mean that you will attain Buddha's Four Bodies.
The "pair" shows increase of the Two Provisions.
The silver ring-strap on the boots
Is the absence of wrong practices;
Also it foretells that you
Will be like a son of Buddha —
Humble and self-restraining,
The exemplar of all Buddhist acts.

The silk robe you dreamt of wearing
Indicates that you will not be sullied
By any vice. The threads of gold
Symbolize a worthy and stable
Mind. The red spots foretell
Compassion and altruism.

The decorated belt you dreamt of wearing
Means that you will "fasten" the Three Realms.[19]
The jewels, white flowers, and silk ornaments
Show your adornment by Three Learnings[20]
And guidance over virtuous disciples.

The Tsandar staff you dreamt of holding
Proves that you have a perfect Guru;
The seven jewels on the staff
Symbolize the greatness of His merits.
The finery of golden lattice work
Foretells that you will nurture your disciples
With the Pith-Instructions of the Whispered-Lineage.
Holding the staff in your right hand
And striding forward with delight
Proves that you will dwell in the Pure Land.

The magnificent Vajra skull you dreamt of holding
Shows that you will illustrate the truth of Voidness.
The nectar, filling full the skull,
Means your enjoyment of great blissfulness.
The nectar's brilliant, golden light
Indicates you will brighten forms.
The thought of the skull as your drinking bowl
Signifies the merging of the three previous delights.
Holding the skull in your left hand shows that
The inner Experience will never leave you.

The varicolored bag of which you dreamt
Proves that you will bring all forms
        into the Path.
The two loads borne upon your shoulder
Foretell your march along the Mahāyāna Path
Through the practice of Wisdom and of Skill.
The rice therein — the thought
Of using it for sustenance —
Means that you will enjoy good health,
Long life, and Samādhi's food.

Your dream of the pelt on your left shoulder
Proves mindfulness, immune from wandering thoughts.
The head and four claws symbolize
Your ever-increasing Bodhi-Mind
And the Four Good Thoughts[21] with which
You will relieve the people's pain.
The thought of using the skin for cushion
Means you will realize the solidarity
Of Void-Compassion in your mind.

Your dream of golden flowers on your right
Shows the growth of your outer and inner merits.
The sheep and cattle grazing in the fields
Symbolize that refuge in the Dharma
Will fulfill the wishes of all beings.
The thought of herding them implies
That you will always be compassionate
To helpless and suffering men.

Your dream of a jade-green meadow on your left
Indicates that you will know Bliss-Wisdom
Through constant practice of Transcendental Samādhi.[22]
The blooming flowers of many kinds show how
The various experiences of different stages
Will grow step by step within you.
Many women bowing down before you
Presage that you will master all Dākinīs
Residing in all the Nādīs [Channels] and Tig Les.

The mound of golden flowers in the center
Indicates that with Realization, Samādhi,
And immaculate observation of the discipline,
You will attract around you many monks
Like clouds that gather in the sky.

The luxuriant golden leaves
Upon the lotus seat imply
That your mind will n'er be sullied by Saṃsāra,
Keeping like a lotus its head above the mud.
The Bodhisattva in the Lotus Posture
Signifies that you, the young Bodhisattva,
Will abide not in Nirvāṇa,
But with great compassion
Will transform your body into many forms to help
The mother-like sentient beings in Saṃsāra.

The fountain playing before you shows
That your fountain of Dharma will ever spout.
The aura radiating from behind you
Means that your virtues will purify Tibet.
The fire blazing from your body symbolizes
That the warm and blissful wisdom of Dumo-heat
Will melt the ice of wandering thoughts.

The sun and moon shining from your heart
Presage your e'er remaining in
The never-coming, never-going Realm of Great Light.

My dear son, your dream
Was very good, not bad.

To prophesy by judging signs correctly
Is a virtue allowed by the Dharma;
But 'tis harmful to be attached
And fond of dream interpretation,
Thereby incurring ills and hindrances.
Knowing that "dreams" are but illusions,
You can bring them to the Path.

How can you explain them
Without thorough knowledge?
Some evil dreams appear as good —
[But only an expert] sees they presage ill;
Only a master of the art
Can recognize good dreams
When they take on ominous forms.
Do not, good priest, attach yourself
To either good or evil signs!
Bear, dear monk, these words in mind!

Milarepa continued, "Physician-priest, my dear son, all your dreams predicted that the Dharma would grow to full bloom within you. I, your old father, with infinite knowledge and confidence, have explained to you in detail the symbolic meanings of your dreams. Do not forget my predictions, and see if they come to pass. When the time comes, and they are verified, a supreme faith toward me, unlike that which you have now, will arise in you. You will then realize the effortless Mind-Essence in an extraordinary way. Here and now you will gain liberation from both life and death.

Again, my son, if you want to be a devoted yogi you should never cling to dreams because, by doing so, you will eventually expose yourself to the influence of devils. If one disobeys the instructions of one's Guru, disregards the good advice of others, and clings to self-conceit, one will in the long run lose one's mind. Dear son, you should not look at the faults of your friends, nor raise vicious thoughts and bestir yourself in many activities. Failure is always a result of the ignorance of others' minds. Furthermore, you should know that this life is merely a part of the *Bardo of Birth-Death;* its experiences are unreal and illusory, a form of reinforced dreaming. Mental activity in the day-time [creates a latent form of] habitual thought which again trans-forms itself at night into various delusory visions sensed by the [semi-] consciousness. This is called the deceptive and magic-like *Bardo of Dream.*

"When habitual thoughts become deeply rooted, they drive one into good and bad activities, thus creating the *Bardo of Samsāra* and com-pelling one to experience pleasures and miseries. To purify this [vicious circle of Saṃsāra], one should practice the Dream Yoga and the Il-lusory-Body Yoga. He who can master these Yogas, can then realize the Sambhogakāya in the Bardo State. You should, therefore, prac-tice them diligently until you reach perfection."

Gambopa then besought the Jetsun for an easy and practical teach-ing on these different Bardos. In reply, Milarepa sang:

I bow down to all Jetsun Gurus!
Especially I take refuge in Him
Who bestowed upon me many bounties.
In answer to your request, my son,
I sing this song of Bardo for you.

Sentient beings in Saṃsāra
And all Buddhas in Nirvāṇa
Are in nature equal, and the same in essence.
Son, this is the *Bardo of View!*

The all-manifesting Red and White [Forces][23]
And Mind-Essence indescribable
Are but the true non-differentiated state.
Son, this is the *Bardo of Practice!*

The myriad forms of illusion
And the non-arising Self-mind
Are one, not two, in the Innate-Born.
Son, this is the *Bardo of Action!*

The dreams that arose last night through habitual
    thoughts,
And the knowledge of their non-entity this morning,
In the light of Maya are the same.
Son, this is the *Bardo of Dream!*

The five impure Skandhas and the pure
Buddhas in the Five Directions
Are one in the Perfecting Yoga —
The state of non-discrimination.
Son, this is the Bardo of Arising
And Perfecting Yoga, the *Bardo of Path!*

The Father Tantras that come from Skillfulness
And the Mother Tantras that arise from Wisdom
Are one in the Third Initiation of the Innate-Born.
Son, this is the *Bardo of Quintessence!*

Self-benefit is reflected in the changeless
　　Dharmakāya,
Altruistic deeds are done by the ever-manifesting
　　Body-of-Form,[24]
Yet, in the primordial state, they are but one.
Son, this is the *Bardo of Trikāya.*

The impure illusory body of the womb-gate
And the pure form of Buddha's Body
Are one in the great light of Bardo.
Son, this is the *Bardo of Accomplishment!*

The Jetsun then said to Gambopa, Rechungpa, and Shiwa Aui, "Remember your dreams tonight and report to me tomorrow. I will then interpret them for you."

The next morning Shiwa Aui came [to the Jetsun] first, and said, "Jetsun! Last night I had a very good dream. I dreamt that a warm sun shone forth in the East, and then it entered into my heart." Rechungpa followed, and said, "I dreamt that I arrived at three big valleys and shouted in a loud voice." Then Gambopa came in remorseful tears, saying, "I had a very bad dream." Milarepa replied, "We do not know whether it was good or bad; do not come to a conclusion about it too hastily. Now tell us about it."

"I dreamt that I slaughtered many people of different races, and stopped their breath. Oh, I must be a sinful person with bad Karmas!" Milarepa said kindly, "My dear son, do not cry so bitterly — give me your hand." Saying this, he held Gambopa's hand and continued: "Son! You will accomplish what you have longed for. Many sentient beings will put their hopes in you for their deliverance from Samsāra, and their wishes will be fulfilled. My son is born! Now the old father has done his share of serving the Dharma!" [Then, turning to the others,] he said, "Oh Shiwa Aui, your dream was only a fair one. Because your vow [to serve the Dharma] was not great enough, you cannot benefit many sentient beings. Nevertheless, you will be able to go to Buddha's Pure Land. Rechungpa, because you have violated my injunctions three times under evil influence, you will reincarnate thrice more, in three different valleys, as Buddhist scholars whose fame will be heard afar."

The Jetsun Gambopa, the Physician from Nyal, then meditated for another month with great diligence. At first he saw the Seven Healing Buddhas.[25] He needed to take no more than one breath in a whole day. After one exhalation the Prāṇa dissolved itself automatically. One afternoon he held his breath and saw the Sambhogakāya Buddha's Pure Land, with the infinite View of Wonders. Distracted and amazed by these marvelous scenes, he [had to] let out his breath —[and suddenly] he found it was already evening. He thought of telling his Guru, but being afraid of disturbing the Jetsun's meditation, he did not go to him that evening. In the meditation period at dawn he again held his breath, and saw Buddha Sākyamuni appear as the Chief among a thousand Buddhas.

At daybreak he went to the Jetsun and made obeisance to him. The Jetsun said, "There is no need for you to tell me your visions. I know them already. Now you have seen both the Nirmāṇakāya and the Sambhogakāya of your Patron Buddha. But you still have not seen the Dharmakāya. My son, although you would like to stay with me, because of your vows in past [lives], you must now go to Central Tibet. So go, and meditate there. The dangers that you have so far met [in your meditation] have been countered by me. Hereafter you will face another danger, that of miraculous power. [That is to say], when you attain these wonder-powers, the Devil of the Son of Heaven will come to you; and that is the time you should be extremely cautious, [and careful] in keeping these powers most secret. Generally speaking, the Secret Word Doctrine[26] [Tantrism] is an esoteric teaching. The Accomplishment is also brought about through secrecy. An extremely gifted person with highly developed capacity will not be affected by evil influences. You are one of this kind; therefore no devil can ever influence you. For the sake of benefiting all sentient beings you should gather disciples and teach them.

"You can start to teach and spread the Dharma when you behold and stablize the realization of Mind-Essence. In time you will see it more clearly, which will be quite a different experience from those you are having now. Then you will see me as the perfect Buddha Himself. This deep and unshakable conviction will grow in you. Then you may start to teach. He who can bring his Prāṇas to the tips of his fingers can then overcome all the Prāna-hindrances. Try and see whether you can do so now."

Gambopa then laid a heap of ashes on a slab of stone. Charging his fingers with the Prānas, he pointed at the heap. When midnight came,[27] the ashes began to disperse.

The next morning Gambopa informed the Jetsun of this happening, who said, "You have not yet mastered the Prānas, but have only partially controlled them. However, you will soon attain both the Common and Special Miraculous Powers, and perform transformations. As now you need no longer stay with me, go to Mount Gambo Dar, in the East. There you will find a hill resembling a king sitting on his throne, its top looking like an ornamental helmet similar to the one I am now wearing; its woods resemble a golden Mandala. In front of this hill lie seven others shaped like heaps of jewels; they appear like seven ministers prostrated before the king. On the neck of this hill you will find your disciples. Go there now and benefit them." Whereupon Milarepa sang:

> Oh Venerable Monk, my son!
> Will you go to Central Tibet?
> If so, you may think of delicious meals.
> Whenever such yearning arises,
> Eat the food of divine Samādhi
> And realize that food is but delusion.
> Bring, therefore, all experiences
> To the Realm of Dharmakāya!
>
> At times you may think of your native land.
> Whenever such yearning arises,
> Realize that your true home
> Is in the Dharma-Essence,
> And know that all countries are delusive.
> Bring, therefore, all experiences
> To the Realm of Dharmakāya!
>
> At times you may think of gems and money.
> Whenever such yearning arises,
> Consider the Seven Heavenly Jewels
> And realize that gems and wealth are but illusions.
> Bring, therefore, all experiences
> To the Realm of Dharmakāya!
>
> At times you may think of companionship.

Whenever such yearning arises,
Think of Self-born Wisdom as your consort.
Remind yourself that all companions
Are temporal and deceptive.
Bring, therefore, your experiences
To the Realm of Dharmakāya!

At times you will think of your Guru.
Whenever such yearning arises,
Visualize Him upon your head
And for His blessing pray.
Visualize Him sitting
In the center of your heart,
And forget Him never.
But you should know that even your Guru
Is delusory and dream-like,
That all things are unreal and magical.

The Gambo Dar Mount in the East
Is like a king upon his throne,
The hill behind is like a floating scarf,
The hill before's a heap of gems,
Its top a jeweled helmet.
Surrounding it are seven small hills
Bowing like ministers before the king,
While the woods are like a golden Maṇḍala.

On the neck of this mountain
You will find disciples.
Go there — you will help sentient beings!
Go there — you will accomplish altruistic deeds!

Milarepa continued, "I now give you the name of World Glory Vajra-Holder Bhikṣu." Whereupon he initiated Gambopa, giving him all the Instructions, and blessed him. Then the Jetsun bestowed upon him a golden Ahrura[28] and blessed it with his tongue and saliva. A tinder-pouch was also given as a farewell gift. Then Milarepa said, "Now you may go to your destination and meditate there."

Upon Gambopa's departure for Central Tibet [Weu], Milarepa escorted him as far as Shamboche. When they came to a stone bridge the Jetsun said, "Venerable Monk from Weu, as a good omen, let us not cross the river [together]. Now put down your load, and let us, father and son, talk for a while. Oh Monk from Weu, renounce pride and egotism, cut the strings of affection and attachment, and abandon all worldly desires of this life as a good Buddhist should do. Merge all the teachings into one practice. Always pray to me; never associate with wicked persons, those whose avarice, hatred, and ignorance are great, lest you be contaminated by their shadows of sin. There are people who see nothing but others' faults and take all to be their enemies. They vilify others, criticize the Dharma, and bring bad influences to all, for in the depths of their hearts the fires of hatred are always burning. To give an example, the snake has neither wings, legs, nor hands — logically it should be a feeble, meek creature; but as soon as one sees it, one is seized by abhorrence. This reflects the great hatred existing within the snake. He who cherishes hatred within, will see all men as his enemies. Again, some people are very mean — they grasp and store up everything, even if it be a piece of wood or a basket of stones. They say, 'When we become old we will need a means of livelihood; when we die, we will need food for sacrifice in the cemetery.' They say that one cannot practice the Dharma without money, that even a Bodhisattva needs money to accumulate his Spiritual Provisions. Then they indulge in usury and all forms of profit-seeking. Their blood is always boiling with greed. Again, some people will say, 'Now is not the time for us to practice the transcendental teachings. He who does not cultivate his compassion, will fall into the path of Hīnayāna. One should never stick to one teaching, otherwise he will be possessed by bigotry and narrow-mindedness.' These people are veiled with great ignorance — you should never associate with them or pay attention to their babblings. If you talk to them, they will ask you who your teacher is and what kind of Dharma you practice. But your answers will eventually lead them to anger. Because of their narrow-mindedness, good advice will never do them any good, but only incur their vituperation. As a result they will lose their refuges and be damned. In other words, one's good advice causes other people to sin. This is why you should not associate with men who are dominated by the ever-increasing Three Poisonous Desires. [The Holy Tantra says]:

> 'To stay seven days in a Hīnayāna temple
> [Brings a Tantric yogi harm, not benefit.]
> Like a tiny, cautious sparrow, watch
> Your conduct with the greatest care!'

"My son, do not take pride in your continence and discipline. Be in harmony with all; be patient, persevering, virtuous, and noble; and bridle your wandering thoughts. Always talk less and restrain yourself from distractions. Constantly dwell in hermitages and spend all your

THE HUNDRED THOUSAND SONGS OF MILAREPA

time in furthering your Three Learnings. You may have realized that
your Self-mind is Buddha Himself, yet you should never abandon your
Guru. You may have known that all deeds are intrinsically pure, yet
you should never abandon even the smallest virtue. You may have
realized that all causes and Karmas are void, yet you should abstain
from committing even the smallest transgression. You may have realized that self and others are one in the Great Equality, yet you
should not denounce the Dharma and forsake sentient beings. Son, in
the Year of the Rabbit, the Month of the Horse, and on the fourteenth day of that month, you should come to see me. Now listen to
my song:

> My son, when the Realm that is beyond
> Playwords in your mind appears,
> Do not let yourself indulge in talk
> Lest you become proud and garrulous,
> Carried away by worldly claims.
> It is important to be humble and modest.
> Do you understand, Venerable Monk from Weu?
>
> When Self-liberation appears within,
> Engage not in logic and speculation
> Lest meaningless activities involve you.
> Son, rest yourself without wandering thoughts.
> Do you understand, Venerable Monk from Weu?
>
> When you behold the void nature of Mind,
> Analyze it not as one or many
> Lest you fall into the void-of-annihilation!
> Son, rest at ease in the sphere beyond all words.
> Do you understand, Venerable Monk from Weu?
>
> When you practice Mahāmudrā,
> Practice not virtuous deeds with mouth or body
> Lest your Wisdom of Non-distinction vanish.
> Son, rest at ease in the non-doing state.
> Do you understand, Venerable Monk from Weu?
>
> When revelations and prophesies are disclosed,
> Be not conceited or overjoyed
> Lest you be deceived by devilish presages.
> Son, rest at ease in the non-clinging state.
> Do you understand, Venerable Monk from Weu?

When you observe your mind with penetration,
Stir not ardent passion or attachment
Lest the devil of desire possess you.
Son, rest at ease and without hope.
Do you understand, Venerable Monk from Weu?

Then Milarepa placed his feet upon Gambopa's head and said, "Venerable Monk from Weu! I have just imparted to you all the Four Initiations. Now be happy and joyful." Thus [in this one act], the Jetsun gave Gambopa, [first,] the Initiation of the Divine Body, blessing his body to become Buddha's Maṇḍala; [second,] the Initiation of Divine Speech, blessing his words to become Mantras; [third,] the Initiation of Dharma, enlightening his mind to the Dharmakāya. The very act of putting his feet upon Gambopa's head symbolized that Milarepa had given his disciple the Initiation of Vajra-Guru, ordaining him as a full-fledged Teacher of Tantra. Again the Jetsun gave Gambopa the Initiation of Expression-Samādhi and said, "I have an unusually profound pith-instruction, but it is too precious to give away. Now you may go!"

Milarepa then sent Gambopa on his journey, himself remaining where he was. When Gambopa had crossed the river and reached a distance from whence he could barely hear the Jetsun's voice, Milarepa called him back, saying, "Who else but you would deserve to receive this most precious pith-instruction, even though it is of too great a value to be given away? Now come here, and I will impart it to you." In great joy Gambopa asked, "Should I now offer you a Maṇḍala?" "No, it is not necessary to offer me one. I only hope that you will cherish this teaching and never waste it. Now look!" *Saying this, Milarepa pulled up his robe, exposing his naked body covered with lumps of callus.* "There is no profounder teaching than this. See what hardships I have undergone. The most profound teaching in Buddhism is 'to practice.' It has simply been due to this persistent effort that I have earned the Merits and Accomplishment. You should also exert yourself perseveringly in meditation."

[This unforgettable sight] made an indelible impression upon Gambopa, who, in obedience to his Guru's instruction, began his journey to the East.

As for the account of Gambopa's life-story, and his great achievements in spreading the Dharma and benefiting sentient beings, the reader is advised to refer to Gambopa's own Biography in which detailed information may be found.

Then the Jetsun Milarepa went to Chu Bar, gathered all his disciples together, and said, "This physician-monk will benefit a great many sentient beings. Last night I dreamt that an eagle flew from here to Weu and alighted on the top of a precious gem. Then many geese flocked round it. After a short while, they dispersed in different directions, each goose again gathering about five hundred more companions. Thus all the plains and valleys became full of geese. This dream indicates that although I am a [lay] yogi, numerous followers in my Lineage will be monks. I am happy beyond words that I have now completed my service to the Dharma!" Milarepa spoke with deep feeling and great joy.

This is the story of Milarepa's foremost heart-son — His Holiness, Gambopa.

NOTES

1 In order to predict the future growth of the Ghagyuba, Marpa one day told his disciples to remember their dreams that night and report to him the next morning. Milarepa dreamt of four huge pillars in the Four Directions, upon which four animals performed different acts. Marpa gave this dream a detailed interpretation in which he predicted the various accomplishments of his four great disciples and the coming of Gambopa. See W. Y. Evans-Wentz' "Tibet's Great Yogi, Milarepa," 2nd ed., 1951, pp. 149-155.

2 The Great Compassion Lotus Sūtra: T.T.: sÑin.rJe.Chen.Po.Padma.dKar. Pohi.mDo.; Skt.: Mahākaruṇāpuṇḍarīkasūtra.

3 Tsa Tsa: See Story 45, Note 10.

4 It is believed that a truly compassionate Bodhisattva is immune from the attacks of insects or beasts. Tibetan lamas even use this as a yardstick to judge and measure the compassion of their fellow lamas.

5 The Golden Light Sūtra: T.T.: gSer.Hod.Dam.Pahi.mDo; Skt.: Suvarṇa-prabhāsottamasūtra.

6 This is a free translation. Literally, " . . . ask him to impart to you a recitation (T.T.: Luñ.) of the [Mantra] of the Immovable White [Goddess]." The Immovable White Goddess seems to be the Goddess gDugs.dKar.

7 Weu (T.T.: dWus.): Central Tibet; Tsang (T.T.: gTsañ.) Southwestern Tibet.

8 The translator suspects that some printing errors may have crept into the text here. It seems more appropriate in this instance for Gambopa to remind himself of the bounties he received from the Ghadamba (T.T.: bKah.gDams.Pa.) Lamas, though the text reads " . . . bKah.sDom.Gyi.bLa.Ma. . . . ," meaning the Lamas who are bound by Injunctions. Ghadamba is an independent School of Tibetan Buddhism, founded by Atīsha and his disciples, and Gambopa was formerly associated with this School before he met Milarepa."

9 Lit.: "The Instructions of the Four Directives" (T.T.: bKah.Babs.bShi.). The translator presumes this implies the Four Tantras.

10 Black Spot Hell: T.T.: dMyal.Wa.Thig.Nag.

11 Upper Chest, literally, the upper portion of the heart (T.T.: sÑiñ.sTod. Du.).

12 Meditation belt: a soft cloth belt fastened about the yogi's body in order to help him keep his posture erect and balanced during meditation.

13 Deva-of-Desire (T.T.: hDod.lHa.): This refers to the Devas or heavenly beings in the Realm of Desire (hDod.Khams.).

14 Red Tig Le (T.T.: Thig.Le.dMar.Po.): the Essence of the female, or negative, force.

15 Dem Chog Luyipa (T.T.: bDe.mChog.Lu.Yi.Pa.): a form of the Tantric deity Samvara.

16 The Superb Dumo Instruction (T.T.: mChog.Ge.gTum.Mo.): This seems to be a special instruction imparted only to the most advanced yogis, not included in the over-all Dumo practice.

17 The Ever-Crying Bodhisattva (T.T.: rTag.Du.Ñu.): a Bodhisattva who longed for the teaching of Prajñāpāramitā but could not obtain it. In his long search for the teaching he traveled through many lands and underwent many trials. The repeated extraordinary distresses and disappointments that he encountered during his journey made him cry all the time. The full story is related in the Mahāprajñāparamitāsūtra.

18 The Holy Chupoa: T.T.: Chu.nPhags.

19 The Three Realms, or the Three Kingdoms (T.T.: Khams.gSums.), i.e., the Realms of Desire, of Form, and of Non-form, which include all realms in the cosmos. See Story 5, Note 21.

20 The Three Learnings: The Learnings of Precepts, of Dhyāna, and of Wisdom.

21 The Four Good Thoughts, or the Four Immeasurable Good Wills (T.T.: Tsad.Med.bShi.): They are (1) to wish that all sentient beings may gain happiness and cultivate the "seeds" of happiness, (2) to wish that all sentient beings may be separated from all sufferings and their causes, (3) to wish that all sentient beings may attain pure happiness — that which involves no sufferings of any kind, and (4) to wish that all sentient beings may be freed from gain and loss, desire and hatred, hope and fear, and may abide in the Realm of Equality.

22 Transcendental Samādhi, literally, Leakless Samādhi (T.T.: Zag.Med.Tiñ. hDsin.). "Zag.Pa.," though literally signifying "leak," here means desires or Kleśas. "Zag.Med.," therefore, means the desire-free, or, transcendental Samādhi.

23 Red and White (T.T.: dKar.dMar.) here imply the positive and negative forces.

24 Body-of-Form (T.T.: gZugs.sKu.): This implies both the Nirmānakāya and the Sambhogakāya.

25 Seven Healing Buddhas: T.T.: sMan.bLa.mChed.bDun.

26 The Secret Word Doctrine (T.T.: gSuñ.sÑags.), or the teaching of Vajrayāna.

27 This is a rather important account of the sign of a yogi's mastery of Prāna, but unfortunately the text does not specifically mention the time when Gambopa first started the test. Here the text reads, "... Nam.Phyed.Tsam.Na.Thal.Wa. Bun.Bun.hDug." "Nam.Phyed" usually means midnight; however, in this case it could possibly be interpreted as "a half day." Thus, it could mean that it took Gambopa half a day to disperse the ashes.

28 Ahrura (T.T.: A.Ru.Ra.): a universal medicine which supposedly can cure all illnesses, probably myrobalan. See Story 27.

THE CONVERSION
OF THE SCHOLAR, LODUN

Obeisance to all Gurus

WHEN the Jetsun Milarepa was staying in the Small Tamarisk Forest,[1] he was visited by a monk named Lodun Gedun, a follower of Rechungpa and Sevan Repa, but formerly an associate of Monk Dhar Lho, who once disputed with the Jetsun.[2] After making many obeisances to Milarepa, he said, "Most precious Jetsun, when I first saw you I admired you greatly and I witnessed how my friend [Dhar Lho] died; yet, I could not then decide whether the Dharma that we practiced was right or wrong. Nevertheless, when I left I greatly respected you. I now come to you for instruction. Pray be kind enough to teach me."

The Jetsun replied, "The Dharma practice of a man who indulges in diversions but not in remembering death, will be of little use, because he can neither reduce his wrongdoings nor increase his virtues. Now listen to my song":

> Our Lord Buddha preached the Dharma
> To conquer worldly wishes,
> Yet those conceited scholars
> Are slaves to their desires.
>
> The Buddha instituted priestly rules
> So that the world could be renounced,
> Yet those restrained and "virgin" monks
> With the world are fully occupied.
>
> Buddha praised the recluse's way of living
> So that worldly ties should be renounced,

Yet many "hermits" of today
Are more attached to worldly ties.

If you forget that death will come, your Dharma
Practice means little and helps nothing.

"To my regret, I have always been like that," said Lodun. "From now on I shall ever remind myself of the coming of death. Now pray give me some instructions to practice." The Jetsun, thinking "I shall see whether he can really devote himself to meditation," replied, "Whoever has little desire for this life, can reach Buddhahood by practicing scholastic Buddhism, although it may take a longer time." He sang in elaboration:

I bow down to all Gurus.

Listen to me, Venerable Monk!
The basic Priestly Rules are the
Great pillars of the Buddhist Hall.
One should rect them straight,
Keeping them from leaning.

Study in logic and the Sūtras is
A precious cleanser of Buddhist teaching,
Removing the rust of wrong ideas.

The disciplines of the Three Learnings[3]
Are of Buddhism the friends;
They should not as foes be treated.

The logic and views of Mahāyāna
Conquer the disputes of fools,
Enlightening those in darkness.

But Lodun said, "Hitherto I have only practiced verbal Dharma. Pray grant me the quintessential Teachings." Thus, with great earnestness, he continued to petition the Jetsun.

Knowing that Lodun's time for initiation had come, Milarepa at first sat quietly and pretended to frown. Whereupon Lodun besought Rechungpa, Sevan Repa, and the other disciples to intercede for him. Milarepa, very pleased by their sincere petitions, finally gave his consent, saying, "The persuasion of two Repas is too strong for me to resist. Our venerable monk is also a gifted man capable of genuine practice." [Then, turning to Lodun Gedun, he continued], "Under these circumstances, I will give you the instructions, and I sincerely hope you will practice them diligently! If one only knows but does not practice the Dharma, the results will be like this": Whereupon he sang,

I pay homage to all Gurus!

Both you, the priest, and you yogis, have pled
    with me.
The peititioner is our venerable monk,
A learned man, renowned in three valleys.
He asks for instructions to enter the Path;
Of good will are he and his assistants.

I am the Yogi Milarepa,
Beloved son of Buddha Marpa.
I speak not from hearsay, nor with pomp,
My words are sensible and from the heart,
They will stand criticism and analysis.
So with care listen to what this old man says:

He who practices not the Dharma with devotion,
Can at most become a sky-going Preta.[4]
These sky-going creatures are
Well-versed in rhetoric and logic.
Knowing much of Tantra, they possess
Magic powers and work wonders.
Living in comfort, they enjoy all pleasures.
But since they do not truly practice Dharma
Nor take heed of their minor faults,
They can never free themselves
From worldly desires and self-conceit.
Thus the Compassion-Voidness will ne'er arise
    in them,
Nor will the buds of pain within them wither.
In Saṃsāra's sea they will forever flounder.

Much knowledge, sharp intelligence, and mighty magic —
These powers are like fire and wood, scorching one's mind.
One can be sure that unhappiness
Will result from his own sinful deeds. Practice
Of the Dharma is the unmistaken way.

The Death-reviving Drug[5] is a life-saver,
But 'tis useless of not taken.
If a sick man wants to be cured
He should take the right medicine.

The heavenly nectar of long life
Is at hand for the Asuras. If they fail
To drink it, they suffer from untimely death.
What good can the elixir do them?
To protect yourself from untimely death, pour
The nectar in your mouth and drink it.

In Yama's treasury much food
Is stored of a hundred flavors.
But many Yamas fail to eat it,
And from starvation die.
What does this food benefit them?
He who would relieve his hunger should
Put the food in his mouth and eat it.

With great faith Lodun said, "Each word of yours impresses me with deep conviction. Your preaching is indeed most profound. Now please be kind enough to instruct me in the essence of the Six Pāramitās." In response, the Jetsun sang:

I am not well-versed in words,
Being no scholar-preacher,
Yet this petitioner is sincere and good.

The Six Pāramitās contain all Buddhist teachings.
To those who practice Dharma,
Wealth is but a cause of diversion.
He who gives his all away,
Will be born a prince of Heaven.
Noble is it charity to practice!

Moral Discipline is a ladder to Liberation
Which neither monks or laymen can discard.
All Buddhist followers should practice it.

Buddhist Patience, by Drang Sung[6] exemplified,
Is the virtue which the Buddha cherished most.
It is a garment difficult to wear,

Yet all merits grow when it is worn.

Diligence is the short path to freedom
And a necessity for Dharma practice.
Without it nothing can be done.
Ride then the horse of diligence.

These four Dharmas bring merit to men,
Being indispensible for all.
Now I will speak of Wisdom.

Meditation is a teaching between these two,
As it applies to both Wisdom and Merit practice.
By it all distractions are overcome,
For all Buddhist practice it is most important.

Wisdom-Pāramitā is the teaching of Final Truth,
The dearest treasure of all Buddhas.
Enjoy it then without exhaustion;
It is the wish-fulfilling gem of Heaven,
Fulfilling the hopes of all sentient beings.
To those who can renounce activities,
Wisdom-Pāramitā will bring final rest.
This Provision of Wisdom is most precious;
By it one will reach perfection step by step.

This is my reply, Venerable Monk.
Remember and practice it with joy!

Having heard this song, many of the disciples gained great progress. The Jetsun then said to Rechungpa and Sevan Repa, "Prepare the offerings; I am going to initiate our venerable monk." The Initiation and Pith-Instructions were thus given to Lodun.

After meditating for some time, Lodun had many Experiences. One day he came to Milarepa while a number of disciples were also assembled there, and said, "[During my meditations] too many wandering thoughts and wild visions came to me. No matter how hard I tried, I could not keep my mind quiet and restful. I do not know whether this is good or bad; if it is bad, please teach me how to overcome it; if it is good, please show me the way to further it."

"He has really been practicing hard," thought Milarepa, who then remarked, "You may have had many wandering thoughts and wild visions, but [in essence] they are all one. It matters not whether they are good or bad. What you should do is to concentrate your effort on practicing the *View*. Now hearken":

Obeisance to all Gurus!

Listen to me, Lodun and you others.
Know you what mind-projection is?
It creates and manifests all things.
Those who do not understand,
Ever wander in Samsāra.
To those who realize, all appears as the Dharmakāya.
They need search no more for another View.

Know you, Venerable Monk,
How to set your mind at rest?
The secret lies in letting go —
Making no effort and doing nothing,
Letting the mind rest in comfort
Like a child asleep at ease,
Or like the calm ocean without waves . . . .
Rest, then, in Illumination
Like a bright and brilliant lamp.

You should rest your mind in peace,
Corpse-like without pride.
Rest your mind in steadfastness;
Like a mountain, do not waver.
For the Mind-Essence is
Free from all false assertions.

Know you, Venerable Monk,
How all thoughts arise?
Like dreams without substance,
Like the vast rimless firmament,
The moon reflected in water,
The rainbow of illusion — like all these they arise.
Never consciously deny them,
For when the light of Wisdom shines
They disappear without a trace
Like darkness in the sun.

Know you, Venerable Monk,
How to cope with wavering thoughts?

Versatile are flying clouds,
Yet from the sky they're not apart.
Mighty are the ocean's waves,
Yet they are not separate from the sea.
Heavy and thick are banks of fog,
Yet from the air they're not apart.
Frantic runs the mind in voidness,
Yet from the Void it never separates.
He who can "weigh" Awareness
Will understand the teaching
Of Mind-Riding-on-the-Breath.[7]
He who sees wandering
Thoughts sneaking in like thieves,
Will understand the instruction
Of watching these intruding thoughts.
He who experiences his mind wandering *outside*,
Will realize the allegory
Of the Pigeon and the Boat at Sea.[8]

Know you, Venerable Monk, how to act?
Like a daring lion, a drunken elephant,
A clear mirror, and an immaculate
Lotus springing from the mud, thus should you act.

Know you, Venerable Monk,
How to achieve the Accomplishments?
The Dharmakāya is achieved through Non-discrimination,
The Sambhogakāya through Blissfulness,
The Nirmanakāya through Illumination,
The Svābhāvikakāya[9] through Innateness.
I am he who has attained all these four Kāyas,
Yet there is no flux or change in the Dharmadhātu.

The View, Practice, Experience,
Remedy, Act, and Accomplishment,
Are the six essential things
A yogi faces in his devotion;
Learn and apply them in your practice!

Following his Guru's instructions, Lodun continued to meditate with great diligence and perseverence. As a result, he gained superb Experiences, which he presented to the Jetsun in this song:

I pay homage to all Father Gurus!

Beyond creation and extinction
Is this illuminating Self-mind!
Riding on the moving Prāṇas it runs
In all directions to all places.
Since the mighty animation of the mind
Is in itself beyond all knowing,
Everything that I desire is found
In the mind-treasury within.

Devoid of form and color,
Excelling the sense realms,
Is this wondrous mind
Out-reaching words and phrases.

By practicing the profound Instruction,
Heat and bliss spring forth without;
As a result, deep understanding grows within;
Then one is forever freed from all adulteration.

Accomplishment can never be attained
When off the Path of Skillfulness;
Wondrous are these instructions
Of the Whispered Lineage.
By following this profound Path of Skill,
Realization have I, the Yogi, gained.
These wondrous teachings are good indeed to practice!

Milarepa advised Lodun: "Venerable Monk, do not fasten your mind to any 'ground,' do not close it to any contact, do not fall into bigotry or extremes. Your mind is something that can never be described, explained, or designated, yet you may call it anything you like, when you have fully realized this truth."

Lodun then continued to meditate in the mountains and gained [further] Realization. By study he cleared away all outer doubts, and through actual practice he wiped out all inner misconceptions until, a yogi monk, he became the snow-lion-like intimate son of Milarepa.

This is the story of the monk, Lodun.

NOTES

1 The Small Tamarisk Forest (T.T.: Hom.Chuñ.dPal.Gyi.Nags.): literally, the Small Tamarisk Meritorious Forest.

2 See Story 34.

3 The Three Learnings (T.T.: Slobs.gSum.): The Learnings of Precepts, of Meditation, and of Wisdom, are the three main topics of Buddhist studies.

4 Sky-going Preta: Here, the word "Preta," (T.T.: Yi.Dags.), does not imply the Preta or Hungry Ghost generally known as a denizen of one of the three lower miserable Realms. It is used here in a very loose sense to denote certain sky-going spirits.

5 Death-reviving Drug (T.T.: Çi.Sos.sMan.Gyi.bDud.rTsi.): literally, the Death-reviving Drug Nectar.

6 T.T.: Drañ.Sroñ.; Skt.: ṛsi: This refers to the story of Kṣāntyṛsi who patiently endured insult and injury, i.e., Śākyamuni in a former life suffering mutilation to convert Kalirāja.

7 The teaching of Mind-Riding-on-the-Breath: According to the central teaching of Tantrism, namely, the theory of the Identicalness-of-Mind-and-Prāna (T.T.: Rluñ.Sems.dWyer.Med.), mind cannot function without relying on, or "riding upon" the breath or Prānas. It is the Prāna that makes the mind move. See the translator's Foreword to "Tibetan Yoga and Secret Doctrines," W. Y. Evans-Wentz, Ed., 2nd ed., Oxford University Press, London, 1958.

8 Flying off from a boat in the sea, a pigeon cannot fly very far before it is forced to return to the boat because no landing-place is in sight. This metaphor alludes to the fact that wandering thoughts, no matter how wild and uncontrollable they are, will eventually return to the Mind-Essence, as there is nowhere else to go.

9 The Svābhāvikakāya, known as the "Fourth Body" of Buddha. Actually it is the unification aspect of the Trikāya.

ༀ།

43

SONG OF THE
EIGHT WONDROUS JOYS

Obeisance to all Gurus

WHEN the Jetsun Milarepa was staying at the Red Rock Height of Drin, a monk of the Dre Tribe, who had never seen the Jetsun before but was greatly impressed by his fame, came in great faith to visit him. Reaching Milarepa's abode, he saw only a cooking pot in the cave and thought, "There is nothing here — not a single page of Buddhist scripture, not a Buddha-image, not even a small symbol of the Dharma, let alone the necessary supplies for amusement and livelihood! [Since there is no holy symbol] such as a Sūtra or image of Buddha on which he can put his whole reliance,[1] I wonder what will happen to him when he dies?"

The Jetsun knew his thought at once and said, "Venerable Monk, you need not worry about that. I do have my Holy Scriptures, images, and reliance on the Dharma. I shall have no regret, but shall rejoice when I die. Now listen to my song":

I bow down to all Father Gurus!

My body is the Holy Maṇḍala itself,
Wherein reside the Buddhas of all Times.
With their blessings I am freed
From all needs and attachments.
By day and night I offer to them;
Happy am I to do without material things.

Knowing that all beings in the Six Lokas
Are latent Buddhas, and all Three Realms
The Self-creating Beyond-measure Palace,

507

Whate'er I do is a play of Dharmadhātu;
Whoe'er I am with is the Patron Deity;
Where'er I stay is the Buddha's abode.
With my great wisdom I clearly see them all.
Happy am I to forego outside help and symbols!

On the "paper" of the Red and White
Forces I use the "ink" of Wisdom,
Writing the words of the Five Senses.
All forms then becomes the Dharmakāya.
Happy am I without those foolish books.

All sentient beings in Saṃsāra
Have "Thatness," but realize it not.
Applying the Profound Instructions, I absorb myself
In the Samādhi of the Three-in-One Trikāya.

Oh, whenever death may come
I shall feel nought but joy!

The monk thought, "It is indeed correct that he has telepathic
power; this also proves that the other claims concerning him must be
true." His faith irrevocably confirmed, he besought Milarepa with
great earnestness to accept him as a disciple.

Recognizing that this monk was well-endowed, Milarepa gave him
the Initiation and verbal instructions, and then sent him to meditate.
[After a time] he gained excellent experience of blissfulness. One day
he came to the Jetsun while many disciples were also gathered there
and said, "In the past I had no experience of joy within, therefore
my craving for wealth and material things was very great. But you, the
Jetsun who has no attachments whatever, have a great joy within
you all the time. From now on I shall follow your way, meditating
for the rest of my life in a hermitage so that I may always be joyful
too."

Milarepa was exceedingly pleased. He replied, "This is very true.
He who keeps to the hermitage will always be happy and can even-
tually become a good guide [on the Path of Dharma]." Whereupon
Milarepa sang of "The Eight Wondrous Joys":

I bow down to you, the King of Kings,
The Buddha's wish-fulfilling Nirmāṇakāya,
The glowing torch that dispels the darkness
        of ignorance,

To you, Translator Marpa, I pay sincerest homage.

The sky keep of Red Rock Heights
Is where Ḍākinīs meet,
A place of delight that brings
Much inspiration to me.
Oh wise and persevering disciples,
Pay attention to the song
This old man sings in joy.

In this quiet hermitage
Where no sectaries are found
Resides a guide ever in Samādhi.
He knows the Path, a happy man
Realizing his own body as the Holy Temple.
Oh, how marvelous it is to know
That Mind-nature like the sky is pure!

A firm and steady faith is the guide
That can lead you from Saṃsāra.
Is there one here who has this guide?
Oh, happy it is to see that both
Saṃsāra and Nirvāṇa are self-liberating;
Oh, marvelous it is to realize
That the Four Bodies of Buddha
Ever exist in one's own mind.

The [non-clinging] contact with objects
By the Six Senses, is the guide
That turns all hindrance into help.
Is there one here who has this guide?
Happy it is to reach the shore of No-desire,
And wondrous to be freed from all duality.

An upright Guru with a [genuine] Transmission is
The guide who clears away your doubts and ignorance.
Is there one here who has this guide?
Oh, happy it is to be the man
Who serves his Guru as a Buddha.
'Tis wondrous to behold the Self-face of the mind!

This cotton clothing is the guide
That protects me in snow mountains

From both cold and heat.
Is there one here who has this guide?
Oh, wonderful it is to lie naked in the
        mountain snow,
Happy it is to fear neither heat nor cold!

The instruction of Identifying,
Transforming, and Uniting[2] is the guide
That can crush all fears of Bardo.
Is there one here who has this guide?
Oh, marvelous it is to reach the home of Reality,
Happy it is to be a man with nor life nor death.

The Skillful Path of the Whispered Lineage
        is the guide
That can distinguish the pure and the adulterated
        mind.
Is there one here who has this guide?
Oh, marvelous it is to feel the Life-Prāṇa
Coursing through the Central Channel!
Happy it is to have a mind and body
Always at ease and in Bliss!

The yogi who practices Voidness and Compassion
Is the guide who cuts off jargon and playwords.
Is there one here who has this guide?
Oh, happy it is to be surrounded by enlightened
        beings
And marvelous to win disciples through transformations!

This is the Song of the Eight Joys,
Sung for you with delight by this old man.
To clear the minds of my disciples,
I chant these words with cheer; forget
Them not, but hold them in your hearts!

Hearing this song, Dre Dun and the other disciples were all greatly
cheered and inspired. Dre Dun then said to the Jetsun, "All you have
said is most marvelous. Now please grant me an instruction on the
View, Practice, Action, and Accomplishment that is easy to understand, to practice, and to 'carry.' "
In reply Milarepa sang:

I pay homage to all Father Gurus.

When you deepen the View through thought profound,
Be not misled by verbal knowledge.

Before you have realized Awareness in itself,
Chatter not about the View of Voidness!

All that which manifests
Is unreal as an echo,
Yet it never fails to produce
An effect that corresponds.
Karmas and virtues therefore
Should never be neglected.

Revile not others with
Your bigotry and egotism,
Cling not to self-fixed ideas without
An understanding of the Supreme Truth.
First, fully realize Self-nature
And root up all errors from within!

Before the great Illumination
Shines forth in your mind, cling not
To sweet ecstasy and Voidness.
Though all things are Void-manifesting,
Never wallow in pleasures, nor expect
Your troubles to vanish without effort.

Things in themselves are void,
So never cling to Voidness
Lest you stray in formalism.

When, in the tide of mundane bliss
One's crude, wandering thoughts subside,
An ecstasy will then arise. But he
Who is attached to it, will go astray.

Before Realization shines forth within,
Or one can bless all objects and appearances,
Before all five sense-experiences turn into
        great bliss,
Or all delusory thoughts come to an end,

Engage not in anomalous acts at will,
Lest you go astray in practicing the Equal Acts.[3]

In bringing into being the last Accomplishment,
One should not seek Buddhahood elsewhere.
Before the essence of Self-mind is clearly seen
Beware of falling into hopes and fears.

Should you disciples think your body to be Buddha's,
Never deem it to be the real Nirmāṇakāya.
Should your wavering thoughts vanish in the Dharmakāya,
Never think of them as real entities
Now extinguished into nought.

The great Merits, Acts, and Pure Lands
Are natural manifestations of pure Wisdom;
Never should one regard them
As real things in the outer world.

Having heard this song, Dre Dun gained a decisive understanding.
For a long time he meditated in a hermitage and eventually gained
superior Experiences and merits. He was then known as Dre Dun Drashi
Bar, and became one of the intimate sons of the Jetsun among the
ranks of those senior Repas, such as Dungom Repa.

This is the story of Dre Dun.

NOTES

1 Reliance (T.T.: rTan.): any Dharmic Symbol upon which one puts his
trust. This can be a Sūtra, a Buddha-image, or the relics of a Buddhist saint.

2 This refers to the teaching of identifying all manifestations as Māyā, transforming all manifestations into pure forms, and uniting all manifestations with
the Dharmakāya. If one can do this, he will be able to overcome all fears in the
Bardo.

3 Equal Acts (T.T.: sPyod.Pa.Ro.sÑoms.): In the advanced stage, Tantric
yogis practice many anomalous actions in order to eradicate all their conventional
thoughts and habits, thus equalizing all their antithetical and dualistic ideas.

ༀ༈

44

MILAREPA CONVERTS
THE UNBELIEVERS
THROUGH MIRACLES

Obeisance to all Gurus

O NE DAY Jetsun Milarepa made up his mind to visit a temple where the monks were extremely hostile to him, accusing him of being a nihilistic heretic. All his disciples implored him not to go, but he paid no heed. As he was approaching the gate of the congregation hall, all the monks saw him coming. They rushed at him, beat him savagely, dragged him into the hall, and tied him to a pillar. But after awhile Milarepa appeared again outside the temple! The monks gathered round once more, beating him severely, dragging him into the temple again, and smiting and chastising him in every manner possible. But strangely enough, no matter how fiercely they struck him or how forcefully they tugged and pulled at him, Milarepa remained still as an image, and they could not move him an inch.

More monks were then called, and every way of shifting him was tried, but in vain. Finally they bound his body with ropes — attempting to drag it from before and push it from behind. Yet it stood firm like a great, heavy rock. The monks, thoroughly exhausted by all this, gave up in bewilderment and frustration.

Some of them began to implore Milarepa to go away, while others asked him, "When we detained you inside the temple you suddenly appeared outside; when we tried to force you out, you stubbornly remained within. How could this happen?" Milarepa replied, "I am a nihilistic heretic, so if I am killed, I keep nothing; if I am beaten, I suffer nothing. When I was detained in the temple or chased out of it, I still retained nothing. Since I have annihilated clinging to both Saṃsāra and Nirvāṇa, I can, of course, do all these things!"

513

The elders among the monks then said, "Because of our ignorance we failed to recognize you as an accomplished yogi. Please forgive our misconduct, and leave us." The Jetsun replied, "I do not know whether or not I am an accomplished yogi. Nor do I know where such a yogi may be found, or what he would do now. But you monks should not be so proud of yourselves and wrong others to such an extent. You should know that to revile and wrong the innocent is even worse than to commit the Ten Vices, while to indulge in self-conceit is the very sign of ego-clinging and the cause of falling into Saṃsāra."

"We are fully convinced that you are an accomplished being," replied the monks. "Please tell us why you came here today and spoke as you did."

In answer, Milarepa sang:

> Like the transparent, crystal mind of Bardo,
> Nothing can wreck or hinder me,
> Catch me, or release me.
>
> Striking like a shooting star,
> I, Milarepa, have today worked wonders
> To convert all unbelievers.
> I shall work no more miracles,
> For I am sure that all impieties
> And misconceptions are destroyed.

Some monks then asked, "This is indeed wonderful, but why do you say that you will not work any more miracles?"

"There are only three occasions when miracles should be performed," replied the Jetsun, and sang:

> To convert the impious, to better
> Meditation Experiences, and to
> Identify the Three Accomplishments
> Should miracles and wonders be performed.
> At other times they should be concealed.
> This was what my Jetsun Guru decreed.

A monk said, "With such a [profound] understanding of the Manifestation-Void, one can surely study the Buddhist teachings with ease and delight." Milarepa replied, "When I studied these teachings, I never held my head high. Well, I may have studied much, but now I have forgotten it all! I think it is perfectly right for me to have done so. Now listen":

Forgetfulness of kinsmen comes
To him who realizes Equality.
Fitting is it then for him
To forget desires and attachment.

Forgetfulness of this and that will come
To him who realizes Wisdom beyond thought.
Fitting is it then for him
To neglect all pains and joys.

Forgetfulness of meditation practice comes
To him who realizes non-thought and non-consciousness.
Fitting is it then for him
To disregard all gain and loss.

Forgetfulness of the Gods of Arising Yoga[1] comes
To him who realizes the self-nature of Trikāya.
Fitting is it then for him
To ignore all conceptual teachings.

Forgetfulness of striving for accomplishment comes
To him who realizes the Fruit inherited within.
Fitting is it then for him
To forget all lesser dharmas.[2]

Forgetfulness of all words and talk comes
To him who practices the instructions of the
        Whispered Lineage.
Fitting is it then for him
To forget prideful studies.

Forgetfulness of black-printed books comes
        of itself
To him who realizes that all things are holy
        scriptures.
Fitting is it then for him
To forget Buddhist books.

Another monk then said, "Before one reaches Buddhahood, one is expected to encounter many hindrances, deviations, and doubts. It is not advisable then to forget the [regular] Buddhist teachings!" In reply Milarepa sang:

He who understands that all confusions
Are mind-made and is convinced about
Non-being, will stop making efforts,
Happily enjoying Truth immutable.

He who realizes Ultimate Reality,
Discriminates no more between the dharmas;
In joy he then experiences
The overthrow of ignorance!

When one realizes the truth of Non-extinction,
Hope and fear will in his mind arise no more;
In joy he then experiences
The departure of confusion!

Through ignorance one wanders in Saṃsāra,
But through the Pith-Instructions of an accomplished
    Guru
One can be freed from attachment and desires.
This is the supreme glory of the Saṅgha!

Philosophies are made by mind
And speculative words mean little,
For of no use are they
In conquering the passions.
Try to subdue your self-conceit,
My dear priests and scholars.

In Enlightenment one sees that the essence
Of perceiving and confusing is the same.
Oh followers of Dharma,
Abandon not Saṃsāra,
But rest your mind
Effortless, at ease.
Then with the vast Void you will
Identify yourself.
This is the teaching of all Buddhas!

Thereupon all the monks were filled with new faith toward Milarepa, and ceased cherishing impious and pernicious thoughts about
him.

Among the priests, there was a distinguished monk called Ligor

Sharu whom Milarepa accepted as a servant-disciple and initiated with the Pith-Instructions. After meditating for some time, Ligor Sharu gained good Experiences. Then he thought, "If the Jetsun, with such great power and blessing, could adapt himself slightly to people and conventions, many more outstanding scholars in Weu and Tsang [Central and Western Tibet] would come to him. As his fame and prestige increased he would be able to benefit more people and to serve the Dharma on a greater scale." So thinking, he came to Milarepa and told him of his ideas. But the Jetsun replied, "I will only act in accordance with my Guru's injunctions; other than that, I will do nothing in this life. Those who take heed of worldly affairs may do what they like, but I am not interested in their plans. Now listen":

I bow down to Marpa, the Translator.

Realizing that fame is unreal as an echo,
I abandon not the ascetic way of life,
Throwing away all cares and preparations.
Whatever reputation I may have,
I shall always be happy and contented.

Realizing that all things are illusion,
I cast away possessions;
For wealth obtained by strife
I have not the least desire!
Whatever my means and prestige,
I shall always be happy and contented.

Realizing that all followers are phantoms,
I have no concern for human relationship
And travel where I please —
Unlike those artificial scholar-priests
Who act with discretion and restraint.
Whatever the status I may have,
I shall always be happy and contented.

Realizing that desires and sufferings
Are themselves the great Equality,
I cut the rope of passion and of hatred.
With or without associates,
I shall always be happy and contented.

The nature of being is beyond playwords;

Attachment to any doctrine or concept
Is merely a matter of self-confusion.
Unshackling the fetter of the knower-and-the-known,
Whatever I become and wherever I remain,
I shall always be happy and contented.

In the great Illuminating Mind itself,
I see no pollution by wandering thoughts.
Throwing away all reasonings and observations,
Whatever words I hear or say,
I shall always be happy and contented.

Ligor Sharu, the monk-disciple, then said, "Dear Jetsun, for you, of course, this is quite enough. But I asked for the sake of benefiting inferior sentient beings and propagating the teaching of the Ghagyu-ba." Milarepa replied, "In the beginning I made a solemn vow to live in this way; I have done so up till now, and I will do so in the future. I am quite sure that by living thus I can benefit many sentient beings and serve the Dharma well."

"What vow did you make?" asked the monk. "This," replied Mila-repa, "and I hope that you, my disciples, will also make another like it." Whereupon he sang:

Because of my fear of Saṃsāra, and the grace of
my Guru,
I vowed that I would never pursue things in
the outer world
Before I had enjoyed the supreme taste of the
Holy Dharma.

I vowed that I would never seek food for myself
Before I had carried out my Guru's injunctions.

I vowed that I would ne'er display the Tantric Acts
Before I had mastered fully the Skillful Path.

I vowed that I would never shoulder the Ghagyuba Doctrine
In defiance of Nāropa's admonishments.

I vowed I would never practice Dharma for
self-benefit;
This was the oath I took when first I stirred
the Bodhi-Mind.

I vowed that I would never try to spread Marpa's
     teachings
[In an artificial way], for He would act in
     secret
To spread the teaching throughout Tibet.

To please my Guru is to practice and meditate
     right now!
Other than this, I know of no way to please him!

Through the blessing of the Jetsun, Ligor Sharu changed his views
and, following the example of his Guru, also made the same vow.
With great determination he meditated continuously in the hermitage,
and as a result, he gained the extraordinary Merits of the Path and
Bhūmi.[3] Eventually he became one of the intimate sons of the Jetsun among the priest-yogi disciples, and was known as Ligor Sharuwa.

This is the story of Ligor Sharu.

*The foregoing [collection of] stories are those concerning Mila-
repa and his well-endowed disciples, those who became the Jetsun's
great intimate sons.*

NOTES

1 In the practice of Arising Yoga the yogi strives to remember and sustain
the vision of the Self-Buddha at all times. But since this is done with a conscious effort through the mundane mind, this Yoga practice is not of a transcendental
nature, being designed merely as a preparatory practice for higher Yogas.

2 Lit.: "To forget the mundane dharmas."

3 Bhūmi (T.T.: Sa.), literally means the earth, but this term is used in most
Mahāyāna scriptures to denote the advanced stages of the Path. Generally ten
major stages, or Bhūmis, are given. See Story 54, Note 2.

PART THREE

MISCELLANEOUS STORIES

VARIOUS SHORT TALES

Obeisance to all Gurus

W HEN Jetsun Milarepa was living in the solitary place called Ku Ju,
Rechungpa besought him for a teaching through which he could
practice his devotion with body, mouth, and mind. In response Milarepa sang:

> To practice devotion with your body
> Is to observe the discipline of Non-distinction;
> To practice devotion with your mouth
> Is to keep it shut like the dumb buffalo;
> To practice devotion with your mind
> Is to see the nature of Non-existence.

Rechungpa asked again:

> Because of my ignorance,
> I still do not understand
> How to observe the discipline of body,
> How to control my mouth,
> And how observe Mind-Essence.

The Jetsun replied:

> To observe the discipline of body
> Is to keep the Rules of the Three Learnings,[1]
> To observe discipline with the mouth
> Is to keep it silent and at ease,
> To behold Mind-Essence is to observe
> It in a way that's free from clinging.

In expounding his Guru's instruction, Rechungpa sang:

In the innate-born Dharmakāya, free in itself,
Is the concept of the Sambhogakāya.
[Thus] can the Nirmāṇakāya serve innumerable beings.
The Foundation is the spirit of Renunciation,
The Path is the Bodhi-Mind and Bodhi-Acts,
The Fruit is the observance of Samaya rules.

Renounce the Eight Desires of the world,
Abandon all this life's affairs,
Forswear pleasures and wealth, abjure
Dishonesty and evil living.
Like a madman, pay no attention to your body;
Like a mute, keep your mouth shut at all times;
Like a child, free your mind without clinging;
These are the ways to practice one's devotion.

The Jetsun then commented, "But he who knows not the vital
points is liable to err like this":

He who strives for Liberation with
The thought of "I" will ne'er attain it.
He who tries to loosen his mind-knots
When his spirit is neither great nor free,
Will but become more tense.
He who has no Realization
Wanders in the dark like a blind man.
He who cannot keep the discipline
Has no true spirit of renunciation.
Without a Bodhi-Mind,
Others one cannot help.
If there is no Tantra, there
Will be no Teachings that guide.
The Eight Dharmas are the temptations of this world.
Desires and passions cause one to destroy the
        virtues;
By cunning and clinging, in Saṃsāra one is confined.
If thoughts arise, so does the "dual." Words
By talking cannot be transcended.
A teaching without Lineage is broken. Failure
To observe the discipline brings Yama.
If you become entangled with relatives
And foes you fall into confusion.
With the thought of "being," comes

The idea of taking and rejecting.
From the conception of "existence,"
Follows clinging. Without
Genuine Enlightenment, one's
Mind is obsessed by wishful-thinking.
All talking will become sheer nonsense
If one cannot elucidate the Truth!

. . .　　. . .　　. . .

At another time, Jetsun Milarepa covered his head and face while sitting on his meditation seat. A junior Repa came to him and asked, "Father Jetsun, how is it that you appear to be falling asleep?" In answer, Milarepa sang:

When I cover my head and face
I can see places far away,
But worldly beings nothing see
With their eyes wide open.
When I sleep with my body naked
I carry out the Dharma.

The Eight Worldly Desires
Are causes of distraction.
All acts are completed
Within one's mind. How
Wonderful is this experience
Of unceasing ecstasy!

I, the Yogi who has completed his devotion,
Ever feel joyful in whate'er I do!

. . .　　. . .　　. . .

On another occasion, when Jetsun Milarepa was staying at Tsiba Gonti Tson, Rechungpa asked him, "If a yogi's power, Experiences, and Realization are great enough, must he also make a secret of his accomplishments, or may he demonstrate them if he wishes?" In response the Jetsun sang:

The lion on the snow mountain,
The tiger in the forest,
And the whale in the ocean —

These are the three leading animals.
If they could conceal themselves
It would be wonderful for them,
For they would then avoid their foes.
These are my three outer parables.
Now listen to the inner ones:

The physical body of the yogi,
The Skillful Path of Tantra,
And the Accomplishment through Devotion,
[These are three precious things].
If a yogi could conceal them
It would be wonderful for him,
For he would then meet fewer foes.
Alas, few yogis in Tibet
Can now conceal these things.
Therefore, few accomplished
Beings can here be found.

. . .   .

At another time, Shangon Repa came and told the Jetsun that he had many doubts in his mind. The Jetsun answered him in detail, and sang in conclusion:

Without realizing the truth of Many-Being-One,
Even though you meditate on the Great Light,
You practice but the View-of-Clinging.
Without realizing the unity of Bliss and Void,
Even though on the Void you meditate,
You practice only Nihilism.
If you cannot meditate
At any time and anywhere,
Your non-thought meditation is merely a delusion.
If you do not realize your plain-mind,[2]
Your practice on the Not-two
Cannot transcend effort and exertion.
If you do not realize self-mind as non-existent,
Your practice of Non-distinction
Cannot transcend strife and effort.
If a deep renunciation has
Not yet arisen in your heart,
Your actionless actions are

Still bound by hopes and fears.
Virtuous deeds turn into vices if
You know not [what is] beyond rejection and
    acceptance.
All you do will enmesh
You in the toils of Saṃsāra
If you know not [what is] beyond life and
    death.

. . .   .

Later, a serious drought occurred while the Jetsun Milarepa was
staying at the Water Wood Crystal Cave[3] beside the River of Benevolence, known as the Neck of the Goddess of Long Life. Because of the
scarcity of water some patrons of Drin quarreled, and fought one another over the water-rights. Finally, they all came to the Jetsun for
arbitration. He said to them, "I know nothing about worldly affairs.
The rain will come — you do not have to fight among yourselves."
Rechungpa, however, still urged the Jetsun to reconcile them, to which
Milarepa replied, "We yogis have nothing to do with worldly arbitration. Now hearken to my song":

You are the treasure of perfect virtues,
A source fulfilling all desires;
To you, the great Translator Marpa,
I bow down with deepest reverence.

The advisor, the mediator, and the go-between —
These three cause discord and pain.
He who wants to be free and neutral should remain
Silent like a mute and take no sides.

Properly, kinsmen, and one's native land —
These three imprison one in Saṃsāra's realms.
He who would cross the river of wretchedness
Should cut relentlessly attachment's chain.

Self-conceit, trickery, and pretense —
These three drag one down to lower Realms.
He who would reach a higher plane and the Path
    of Liberation,
Should keep his mind upright and straightforward.

Talking, discussion, and scholarship —
These three cause jealousy and pride.
He who would practice holy Dharma,
Should humble and modest be.

The kitchen, [household] work, and cares —
These three spoil a yogi's meditation.
He who would uphold his innate Wisdom,
Should strengthen his self-respect.

The Master, the disciple, and the learning —
These three burden and distract the mind.
He who would meditate in solitude,
Should avoid them all.

Sorcery, magic, and To Tse[4], these three
Doom a yogi to evil influence.
He who would consummate the Dharma practice,
Should remember the singing bird of Jolmo,[5]

I have now sung of the seven
Demerits against the Dharma
And their seven antidotes,
Acquired through my own experience.
With this merit I hope that soon
You will attain Buddhahood.

Then Milarepa prayed to the Precious Ones; whereupon heavy rain fell, and all disputes were calmed. The son-disciples and monks there assembled then besought a blessing from the Jetsun, asking him to vouchsafe them the essential teaching of Mahāmudrā and of the Six Yogas. He replied, "If you can practice without fail, I will teach you. These are extremely important points which you should all bear in mind":

Though, Father Guru, you appear
To have entered into Nirvāṇa,
In truth you dwell in the Pure Land of the
    Sambhogakāya,
Doing benevolent deeds for all
Sentient beings in the Three Realms.

To you, Translator Marpa, I pay
Sincerest veneration.

Dewashun, Shiwa Aui, Ngan Tson Dunba,
And my well-endowed disciples here assembled
Who are dear to me as my own sons,
Have asked me for instructions on meditation.
In reply I sing of the Ten Essentials.

It is important to know
That the rainbow Buddha-Body
Is void yet manifesting.

It is important to know
That devils and ghosts are non-existent;
Their magic forms are merely
Conjurations of one's mind.

It is important at all times to have
The greatest veneration
For the gracious Jetsun Guru.

It is important to know
That one should renounce
Endless worldly affairs.

It is important to work hard without distraction
For the warm and blissful Experiences
Of the Prāṇa and Nāḍī practices.

It is important to have a strong will to unite
The combining practice of Dream Yoga
And the Yoga of Illusory Body.

It is important to work on the Beyond-symbol
    meditation
For the naked, illuminating Essence.

It is important to note the Cutting-through
    instruction[6]
For the All-manifesting Voidness.

It is important to have pity and kindness

Toward unenlightened sentient beings.

It is important to have a free-from-fear-and-hope
    conviction
Of the non-arising Dharmakāya of Self-mind.

My dear sons, these are
The important things that you
Should bear in mind and practice.

All the disciples were greatly inspired. Rechungpa then besought
the Jetsun to elaborate on the teaching called "Pointing-out the Wisdom of the Four Blisses." This request was granted, and in conclusion Milarepa sang:

In a solitary place, like a forest,
The yogi should practice all Four Actions[7]
And balance the Four Inner Elements.
Thus, the Wisdom of Four Blisses
Will in his mind appear.

. . .   .

On another occasion Jetsun Milarepa went to Phuyagzha of Drin
for alms. A patron said to him, "Near the temple called Lhaze there
is a very delightful cave. If you would like to live there I will serve
you, but I do not know whether the local she-devil will be friendly
to you." Milarepa asked, "What sort of a cave is it, and who is this
devil?" The man replied, "The cave is very cozy and delightful but
the trouble is, that she-devil will just gulp down whoever stays there.
You may, if you think you can, stay in the cave and keep her com-
pany."
    Milarepa then went to the cave and remained there. At midnight
a woman appeared and thundered in a threatening voice, "Who is
staying in my home?" Milarepa paid no attention, but remained in a
mood of compassion. The she-devil then cried, "Damnation! It looks
as if he intends to stay here for good!" So she called a great army
of demons to throw rocks and hailstones at the Jetsun and conjured
many fearful visions to frighten him. But they could not even scratch
his skin because he was in Samādhi. The demons then all cried, "We
want to have our place and our beds for sleeping. Whatever reason
may have brought you here, go away now, go back where you be-
long! If you do not go, we shall call many more armies to come here

to drink your blood and eat your flesh!" But with great compassion
the Jetsun sang in reply:

> Listen carefully, you demon army,
> You malignant and vicious Hungry Ghosts,
> Do you know that you are being
> Punished by your own Karma,
> That the greater the malignant thoughts
> The greater the sufferings one undergoes?
> Do you know that fortune
> Will vanish with ill-will,
> That the greater your greed,
> The harder is your food to find?
> You are by pressing hunger
> Deprived of opportunities,
> Through too great love of moving
> You have lost your home and beds.
> Because you try too hard
> You cannot finish what you do.
> Because of your evil Karma
> You can hardly accomplish anything.
> Because you talk too much,
> Your foes you cannot conquer.
> The malicious visions that you conjured
> Are to me most welcome and amusing.
> To your sordid, delusive sorcery
> I, the Yogi, have much to say.
> You should beseech me with compliments
> If you would have back your home and beds.
> If you have any argument to make
> Consult together and present it.
>
> This is the stumbling place of many yogis;
> I now come here solely to discipline you!
> This is where I and you foregather.
> But I am the one whose wishes are fulfilled.
> You ghosts assembled here,
> Depart not, but remain
> And call your friends to join you!

The she-devil, leader of the specters, then said to Milarepa, "Because you wear the armor of Void-Compassion, you cannot be harmed in any way that we have tried!" Saying this, she and all the demons prostrated themselves before the Jetsun, offering him their lives and hearts, together with a solemn pledge [to reform]. Milarepa then preached the truth of Karma and the law of virtue to them.

Upon the Jetsun's return, the patron asked him, "Was the she-demon subdued?" Milarepa replied, "Yes indeed; now please listen to my song":

> In the Lhaze Temple at Drin
> I sat with this phantom body,
> Crossed-legged, absorbed in Non-dual Dhyāna. Without
> Distraction I contemplated on the truth of
>   non-being,
> Converting the vicious she-devil to Bodhi.
> Renouncing malice, my disciple she became.
> From now on, whoever meditates
> Will meet no trouble there,
> Whoever stays there will progress.
>
> That place has become an auspicious Cave of
>   Goddesses;
> The hostess there is now a lay-Buddhist —
> One of my faithful followers,
> A helpful friend to all.
> Whoever stays there is assured
> Of health, long life, and Accomplishment.

Hearing this song, the patrons were all delighted. With sincere faith they served the Jetsun with great hospitality during his half-day sojourn there. A faithful shepherd [among them] besought Milarepa to give him some Buddhist teachings that would be helpful to his mind. Milarepa said, "It is easy for me to preach the Buddhist teachings, but it is difficult to find people who can really practice them."

> Though grief in the Ocean of Saṃsāra
> Is preached, and its renunciation urged,
> Few people are really convinced
> And renounce it with determination.
> Though knowing life will ever turn to death,
> Few feel uneasy or think that it will end.
> Though their life is blessed with good prospects,
> Few can practice abstention for a day.
> Though the bliss of Liberation is expounded
> And Saṃsāra's pains are stressed,

Few can really enter the Dharma Gate.
Though the profound Pith-Instructions
Of the Whispered Lineage are given without stint, few
Without fail can practice them.
Though the teaching of Mahāmudrā is expounded
And the Pointing-out demonstration exercised,
Few can really understand the Essence of Mind.
To the hermit's life and Guru's wish
One may always aspire, but few
Can put them into practice.
The profound Skillful Path of Nāropa
May be shown without concealment,
But those who can really follow it
Are very, very few. My dear lad,
You should follow in my footsteps
If in this life you want to do
Something that is worthwhile.

His faith toward Milarepa firmly established, the shepherd followed him as a servant and was initiated with the Pith-Instructions. After meditating for some time, he eventually became a yogi with good Realizations.

. . .   .

At another time, for the benefit of sentient beings, Jetsun Milarepa went out for alms. Coming to a village in the center of a plain, he saw many people enjoying themselves. Some were playing dice, chess, and different games, while others were throwing stones and shooting arrows, and some women were weaving wool. Milarepa approached them and asked for alms. A young girl said, "My dear Lama, have you any kinsmen — father, mother, brother, or sister? Have you a house or land?" The Jetsun replied, "Yes, I have them all, and mine are better than most."

"In that case, they will provide you with all things needed for devotion," replied the girl. "But tell me something about your kinsmen." In answer, Milarepa sang:

My home is the Perfection Paradise,
My farm good will for all,
My house the great Compassion,
And my father's lineage the Tathāgata.
My uncles are missionaries

Who spread the Dharma everywhere.
My forefathers are Tilopa and Nāropa,
My father is the King of Skills,
My mother, the Fair Lady of Wisdom;
My elder brother is pure discipline,
My younger brother, stern diligence,
My sister is firm faith, and I myself
Am the offspring of spontaneity.
My body's elements are Merits,
And I meditate on Reality.
My sole visitors are deities.
As for my planting, I plow
Nothing but the Dharmakāya.

All the players in the party swarmed round Milarepa while he was singing. The girl then said, "Dear Lama, what you have sung is very wonderful. Since you are very rich, I would like to invite you to stay here as my spiritual teacher, one in whom I can confide my trust during misfortune and place my hope for present and future happiness. I will provide you with all things needed for the service of the deities and their holy symbols. You look, indeed, like a man with great blessing powers."

Some young men then said, "Dear Yogi, our delightful games and the pleasant work of the girls are signs of our joy and happiness. Do the heavenly beings have the same pleasures? You seem to have a very good voice. Please sing a song of comment for us on these things." The Jetsun replied, "Your joys are not the same as those of the heavenly beings. I shall tell you the differences in my song":

In the houses of you evil persons, gods
And holy symbols are like the roots of sins.
The oil lamps that flame in your stingy hearts
Are like bonfires before greedy tax-men.
The owners of much livestock
Are like meat-eaters' teeth.
The parents of many children
Are like pieces of boiled meat
In the grasp of a hungry man.
The worn-out elders, the forsaken
Housecleaners, resembles lonesome flies
Scenting scum amidst the ruins.
The owner of a great fortune
Is like the demon guard, Gordag.[8]

The games of throwing stones and shooting arrows
Are like fierce battles between gods and Asuras.
The games of chess resemble
Sordid intrigues between kings.
Those who play at shooting dice and throwing water
Are like demons grasping sacrificial food.
The burdens and tangles of your business
Resemble cobwebs on the trees.
Your singing and your dancing
Are the foolish play of gnomes.
The spectators of your games
Are ignorant animals
Gazing attentively at mirages.
The commentators on your games
Are writhing snakes without a head.
Those who crave for games and diversions
Are like hungry ghosts, the Fragrance-eaters,
Greedily sniffing at their hunted food!

Hearing this song, the listeners all prostrated themselves before the Jetsun with faith and veneration. Then the young girl invited Milarepa into her house and served him hospitably. Later, she practiced the instructions received from him and was able to enter the Path at the time of her death.

. . .　　. . .　　. . .

On another occasion, when Jetsun Milarepa went out [again] for alms, he reached the middle of a great plain and saw many people working on a house. He then lay down on the ground [near by as if nothing were going on there]. The hostess said to him, "My dear Yogi, you seem to be unoccupied — here are some tools, please use them to work for us a little and I will bring you some hot food." After a while she returned, and seeing that Milarepa was still lying there, said, "No wonder they say that some people deserve to be treated as good-for-nothing trash! You have plenty of time on your hands, yet you won't do *anything*, not even a little patching work. You are useless!" Saying which, she went off and left Milarepa alone.

Then Milarepa followed her into the house where the workers were having their dinner, and begged for some food. The hostess said, "One who does not work with his lazy body should not bother to eat with his lazy mouth." The Jetsun replied, "I did not help you to patch the walls because I was occupied on other business much more important than yours." The patrons then asked him what this important business was that had drawn away his attention. In answer, Milarepa sang:

> I bow down to all Gurus. Above all,
> I take refuge in the Gracious One!
>
> You see me as though I were doing nothing,
> But I see myself doing something all the time.
>
> On the plain of the uncreated Beyond-Extremes,
> I was building busily the Dhyāna Wall;
> I had no time to patch clay walls.
> On the Northern Plain[9] of Voidness,
> I was taming the wild goats of my desires;
> I had no time to plough my father's land.
> In the realm of Not-two and the Word-beyond,
> I was subduing the demon Ego;
> I had no time to fight with bitter foes.
> In the Palace of Beyond-measure —
> The Non-dual Mind-Essence —
> I was busily attending my affairs;
> I had no time to do household work.
> In the Buddha's Maṇḍala of my own body
> I was feeding my little child, "Awareness";
> I had no time to feed others and wipe their noses.
> In the courtyard of Great Bliss,
> I was gathering the Dharma wealth;
> I had no time to make money in this world.
> On the mountain of the immutable Dharmakāya,
> I was herding the steeds of Self-awareness;
> I had no time to tend other sheep and cattle.
> With the clay of my flesh and bones,
> I was building the Stūpa of Immanence;
> I had no time to make the Tsa Tsas.[10]
> On the triangular Heart Center,
> I was kindling the lamp of Illumination;
> I had no time to offer butter lamps[11] to deities.
> In the chapel of the Bliss-Void,
> I was offering Immortality
> To the Buddha of Dhyāna-Mind;
> I had no time to make material offerings.
> Upon paper of Immaculate Mind

I wrote the words of conquering desires;
I had no time to bother with worldly script.
In the Drinking-Skull of Śūnyatā
I was mixing the Three and Five Poisons;[12]
I had no time for priestly rules.
Filled with love and pity,
I was guarding all in the Six Realms;
I had no time to attend my kinsmen.
Before my Father Gurus,
I was brooding over their instructions;
I had no time for worldly actions.
In a quiet hermitage in the remote mountains,
I was practicing the Bodhi teachings;
I had no time to indulge in sleep.
With my triangular, shell-like mouth,
I was singing the song of Dharma;
I had no time for idle talk.

Hearing this song, all the attendants were converted. Then they asked, "Are you, by any chance, the Jetsun Milarepa?" "Yes," replied the Jetsun. "We are indeed fortunate!" they all cried. Whereupon they bowed down to him, circumambulated him many times, praised him, and served him with perfect offerings. The hostess also acknowledged her repentence.

A young man then said to Milarepa, "We would like to come to you for instructions; please tell us where your temple is and who provides your sustenance." In answer Milarepa sang:

I bow down to all Father Gurus.

My temple is an unnamed hermitage,
My patrons are men and women everywhere,
No one can tell where I go or stay.
In the caves where no man comes
I, the Yogi, am lost to view.
[When I travel] I carry
Only my Guru's instructions — lighter
Than feathers, I shoulder them with ease;
More handy than gold, I conceal them where I please;
Stronger than a solid castle,
In all perils they stand firm.
In the Three Winters I dwell happily in forests;

In the Three Summers I stay cheerfully on snow
       mountains;
In the Three Springs I live with pleasure in
       the marshes;
In the Three Autumns I wander joyfully for alms.
In the teaching of my Guru, my mind is always happy;
Singing songs of inspiration, my mouth is always happy;
Wearing cotton from Nepal, my body's always happy.
In delight I accomplish all and every thing —
To me there is but cheer and joy.

Milarepa accepted this young man as his servant, and later on he
become a yogi with good Realizations. Everyone in the assembly also
vowed to do a specific virtuous deed.

                    . . .   .

[Yet again] the Jetsun Milarepa went out for alms and came to a
place where men and women were having a beer-drinking party. They
were all followers of the Dharma in either the Tantra or Sūtra schools.
Milarepa asked them for food, but was derided and ridiculed, especially
by those who sat in the upper row. The leader of the group then said,
"Dear Yogi, where did you come from and where are you going?"
    "I am just a person who never mingles with the crowd, but spends
his life in no-men's mountains," replied the Jetsun.
    "You talk as if you were Milarepa; are you?"
    "Yes, but since I know nothing about the Eight Worldly Dharmas,
I never mingle with any Buddhist group."
    "This may be very true," replied the leader, "But if you are really
he, you should be able to preach the Dharma through songs. As we all
know, the Jetsun Milarepa is a yogi who has completely opened the
Nāḍīs of the Throat Center, and is thus capable of preaching any Dharma without the slightest hesitation or difficulty. To inspire those attending this meeting, therefore, please now sing for us."
    In response, Milarepa sang a song, "The Ocean of Saṃsāra":

       The peerless Guru always sits upon my head.

       Alas, is not Saṃsāra like the sea?
       Drawing as much water as one pleases,
       It remains the same without abating.
       Are not the Three Precious Ones like Mount Sumeru,
       That never can be shaken by anyone?

Is not Samaya like a feather
That's been shed and for which no one cares?
Are not the pure priestly rules
Like a leper's corpse abandoned
By the roadside, which none will touch?
Are not badgers' skins laid over seats
Full of thorns that prick the buttocks
Of eminent priests?
It is not true that many people think
It meaningless to keep the priestly rules?
Is it not true that many monks ignore their
    disciplines?

Are there Mongol bandits invading yogis' cells?
Why, then, do great yogis stay in towns and villages?
Are not people craving for rebirth and Bardo?
Why, then, do they cling so much to their disciples?
Are woolen clothes in the next life more expensive?
Why, then, do women make so much of them here?
Do people fear that Samsāra may be emptied?
Why, then, do priests and laymen hanker after
    children?
Are you reserving food and drink for your next life?
Why, then, do men and women not give to charity?
Is there any misery in Heaven above?
Why, then, do so few plan to go there?
Is there any joy below in Hell?
Why, then, do so many prepare to visit there?
Do you not know that all sufferings
And lower realms are the result of sins?
Surely you know that if you now practice virtue,
When death comes you will have peace of mind and
    no regrets.

By this time the whole party had become aware that the singer was
the real Jetsun Milarepa. Imbued with deep faith and veneration,
they served him with great hospitality. Milarepa then preached the
Dharma for them. By practicing these teachings, some of the group
were able to enter the Path at the time of their death. If these cases
were all recounted, it would make many more stories.

. . .   .

In this story [which actually contains a number of tales], Milarepa answered various questions asked by his close disciples as well as by his general patrons, in different places and at different times. Therefore, it cannot be ascribed to any one specific group.

NOTES

1 Three Learnings: See Story 42, Note 3.

2 The plain-mind (T.T.: Thal.Ma.Çes.Pa.): This term, which one very often sees in the literature of Mahāmudrā, is surprisingly similar to, or rather identical with, the Zen phrase, "P'ing Ch'ang Hsin" (the plain, or ordinary mind) which is the natural, spontaneous, straightforward, and naked mind. A monk asked Zen Master Chao Chou, "What is Tao?" Chao Chou replied, "The ordinary mind is Tao." Reading the literature of Zen and Mahāmudrā one finds many similiar expressions, but this phrase, "the plain-mind," is perhaps the most outstanding one.

3 Water Wood Crystal Cave: T.T.: Çel.Phug.Chu.Çiñ.rDsoñ.

4 To Tse (T.T.: Tho.Tshe.): the magic of producing hail and storms.

5 The singing bird of Jolmo (T.T.: hJol.Mo.): This refers to a Tibetan legend, but as the source is not available to the translator at this time, he is unable to give it.

6 Cutting-through Instruction (T.T.: gShi.rTsa.Chod.Pahi.gDams.Nag.): A more literal translation of this phrase would be: "The clear-cut instruction that clarifies the basis, or the core, of the issue."

7 The Four Actions: walking, sitting, standing, and lying.

8 Gordag (T.T.: dKor-bDag.): "The owner of property. It generally signifies the spirit of a demigod who is supposed to be the custodian of the images of all Buddhist deities, scriptures, symbols; in short, of all church and sacerdotal properties." (Quoted from Chandra Dass' "Tibetan-English Dictionary.")

9 Northern Plain (T.T.: Byañ.Thañ.): the vast, grassy land of Northern Tibet.

10 Tsa Tsa (T.T.: Tsha.Tsha.): a miniature Stūpa-shaped oblation, made out of clay in a specially designed mold. It is widely used in Tibet.

11 Butter is the only oil supply available for lamps in Tibet.

12 The Three Poisons are lust, hatred, and ignorance; the Five Poisons are lust, hatred, ignorance, pride, and jealousy.

THE PREACHING
ON MOUNT BONBO

Obeisance to all Gurus

WHEN the Jetsun Milarepa was dwelling in the Nirmāṇakāya Castle at Chu Bar, he cleared up the peerless Gambopa's doubts and misgivings concerning the Pith-Instructions. Then he proceeded toward the East, but heavy rain fell for many days and nights, and Milarepa's disciples were much wearied by it.

One day the sky began to clear, and the sun shone pleasantly warm upon the hills. Milarepa and his seven disciples went for a walk to refresh their bodies and minds. They all felt very comfortable and happy at such a beautiful day.

As they walked to the mountain peak of Bonbo, some of the Repas who were not familiar with the region saw the Snow Mountain of the Lady of Long Life, and asked the Jetsun, "What is the name of this snow mountain?" He replied, "It is called the 'Blue Heights of the Fair Goddess'." Whereupon he sang:

> To the neck of the Mountain of Blue Heights,
> To the peak of the rocky Bonbo Hill,
> Come we, eight visitors at leisure.
>
> Do you not feel happy, my dear sons?
> I, your father, feel wonderful today.
> Here in this joyful gathering of Master and
> disciples,
> I, the old man, cheerfully sing this song
> Of joy and pleasure, that will bring
> Auspicious luck and fortune.

541

Come, Dewashun and Shiwa Aui!
Come and join me in the singing;
You other Repas sit and listen.
Know you which this mountain is?
This is the Mount of the Auspicious Goddess
     of Long Life.
The triangular, sharp-edged peak looming above
     its waist
Is like a dumpling on a shell;
Flowing round its neck are silver-netted streams.

The high crystal peak that mirrors the first
     beams
Of sunlight in the morning is the crown,
Beautified by white hanging clouds.

Clinging to the lower Mount
Is perpetual mist and fog;
All day long the drizzle gently falls,
While rainbows brightly shine.
Here autumn flowers bloom
In different colors,
And thrive potent herbs
In great varieties.
This is the paradise of cattle,
This homeland of animals!
This is the Snow Mountain
The gods talk most about,
This is where I often meditate.
In answer to you Repas' questions
I sing this song, describing
This mountain vividly.

The Repa disciples were all pleased by this song. With great interest
they asked, "How powerful is this goddess? Does she follow the holy
Dharma, or evil?" In reply, the Jetsun sang:

The Lady of Long Life,
The five good sisters,
Lead the Twelve Goddesses.
They are worldly Ḍākinīs
With power to conjure.
Hostesses of the River Drin,

They speak Tibetan and Nepalese;
They assist all Buddhists
And protect their worshippers.
In chief they execute my orders,
And help you, my son-disciples.
Through my efforts and theirs Tibet
Will be led to the virtuous path,
And great Accomplishments will follow
In our Ghagyu Lineage.

The Repas all said, "It is wonderful that these goddesses have been converted as your disciple-servants. Please tell us what Dharma you preached for them and how they have served you?" In answer Milarepa sang:

Upon the neck of this Snow Mountain
I, Milarepa, once preached the Dharma
To the benevolent local deities.

I taught them how to distinguish good from evil,
I preached for them the Sūtra's Expedient Truth
Of the Law of Cause and Effect.
The savage beasts and Nāgas of
The Four Divisions came to listen.

The five revengeful Ḍākinīs were the hostesses
Who invited the preacher.
The five formidable sisters were the hostesses
Who attended on the guests.
Many noble visitors gathered round,
While Devas and ghosts enjoyed the feast.

All who were there, I guided to the Dharma
And converted them, not by great power
But by compassion and by love.
With skill I converted those formless ghosts
      and Devas,
With sincerity I preached to them the Dharma of
      peace.

I have no regrets for my past deeds.
Now I am old why should I be regretful?
When I die I shall have no fear, but only joy.

> Dear Repas, who stay here to renounce the world,
> You should practice with determination,
> With a happy-to-die feeling when you meditate.

They again asked, "Between human beings and Asuras, which are better endowed to practice the Dharma, and which serve sentient beings better?" The Jetsun replied, "Human beings are superior in practicing the Dharma, and more powerful in helping others than the Asuras. But the Lady of Long Life is a semihuman goddess.[1] She will devote herself with great power to serving my Doctrine. I have resigned from public life and renounced the Eight Worldly Claims for devotion. I have now forgotten many gods and deities and lost contact with them. Following my steps, you should also renounce the Eight Worldly Desires and devote yourselves to undistracted meditation. Listen to my song":

> My Guru's power of blessing
> Descended from above,
> Assuring me of freedom
> From the bonds of Dualism.
>
> As a vagabond I wandered in all lands
> Until fate brought me to the Gracious One.
> I renounced the world as he bade me,
> Meditating without diversion.
> All evils and misfortunes
> Are now Paths for me.
>
> In humbleness, I have practiced in solitude;
> Near death, I have exerted myself in devotion.
> I have been meditating all my life
> Till this old age.
> Bliss and warmness thus grow within me.
>
> I am a yogi who disregards good fortune,
> I am a yogi who abjures worldly happiness —
> One who remembers the pains of lower Realms.
> I am a yogi who never ingratiates his patrons —
> One who clings to the hermitage for meditations.
> By the blessing of my Guru
> I was "blown to the top" by a wind of love.
> Sitting near the edge, I arrived at the center;
> Adhering to humbleness, I cam to nobility.

In departing from men, one meets Buddha;
In undergoing sufferings, one attains happiness;
By exerting oneself in devotion, compassion
       grows within.
By remaining in solitude, one acquires more
       followers and disciples;
By practicing the Ghagyuba teaching,
The transmission of the Dharma spreads afar.

With my gracious Guru Marpa
Sitting e'er upon my head,
Like an old tiger, without fear of death,
I am well advanced in age.
With good cheer I sing this happy song!
My Repa sons, fritter not your lives away,
But determined and persevering,
Strive on in your devotions!

Milarepa and his disciples remained there for half a day and performed an offering ritual with the provisions they had brought. Then
some of the disciples expressed their intention to enter different hermitages, others to go for alms to various places, and yet others asked
the Jetsun for permission to stay with him. On their behalf, Rechungpa [and Gambopa] asked him to give some admonishments for all. In
response, Milarepa sang a song for Rechungpa and the other disciples
called "The Six Essentials":

On behalf of all Repas here,
My son Gambopa, the learned scholar,
And son Rechungpa, the unswerving yogi,
Have asked me to sing to you.
If you are wise, you will now listen
To this old man's song.

A bird knows when and where
To spread and close its wings;
The true rich man is e'er content;
A good agnostic e'er plays safe.
These are my metaphors.

After this Holy Offering on the tenth day,
Some of you say they will visit different
       countries,

Some that they will stay in various hermitages,
Others that they will follow and stop with me.
But as for me, if a great yogi
Aspires to fame and profit,
He will soon be trapped by devils.

It is therefore wise, my sons,
To seek protection from your Father
And listen to advice and criticism.

Do not hear my song as a sweet melody,
But listen carefully to its instructions;
Forget them not, inscribe
Them deeply in your heart.

He who has mastered his Tig Le
And gained the Power of Attraction,
Without relying on a qualified Rig Ma,[2]
Should never practice Karma Mudrā.
It is as dangerous to do so
As to climb a steep, rugged mountain.

Unless with a great, flowing compassion
One practices the vivid Yidham Samādhi
For the sole purpose of furthering
The Dharma and the welfare of all men,
One should never use the malicious Mantra
Or practice the Cursing Yoga,
Lest by Karma he will be
Reborn a malignant ghost.

Even if one has mastered his Prāṇa-Mind,
Unless he can work miracles through his bodily
        power,
And transform himself into beasts and snakes
With full realization of Māyā and of Voidness,
He should never bring corpses from cemeteries,
Lest he provoke the hatred
Of flesh-eating Ḍākinīs.

Except to one's own Vajra Brothers
And to Gurus thrice qualified,[3]
One should ne'er reveal his meditational Experience —

Even to men who deeply understand the Dharma —
Nor to devotees of other Lineages
Of different Practices and Views,
Let he lose the Power of Blessing
From the Practice-Succession.

Give not the Instruction of the Whispered Lineage
To him whose talent you have not observed;
Give it not without permission from
Ḍākinīs, nor for the sake of wealth
Or expediency to those who ask,
Lest by sins and transgressions you be shadowed.

Before one has the power of crushing others'
        doubts
Or can convert fault-finding unbelievers,
One should not perform the profound Secret Festival,
Or demonstrate Tantric Acts in villages
And towns, lest one be slandered;
These should only be performed
In hermitages and in solitude.

This little song of Six Guides to Devotion
Is a precious gem for Dharma followers;
Bear them, my Son-disciples,
Deeply in your hearts.

These words were imprinted profoundly on the minds of the heart-son disciples. Those junior Repas who wanted to stay with the Jetsun then said to him, "We are now in an age of defilement. For the sake of inferior and slow-witted persons like us, please preach something appropriate to our needs." In response, Milarepa sang:

Hearken further, my Son-disciples!

At this time of defilement
That shadows the Dharma of Śākyamuni,
One should strive with perseverance,
And carve upon his mind-stone
The word, "Diligence."

When you feel sleepy during meditation, try

To pray hard with your awakened body, mouth,
  and mind.
When the fire-spark of Wisdom dims, try
To inflame it with the wind of mindfulness.
If you want to be freed from Saṃsāra's prison,
Practice hard without diversion.
If to Nirvāṇa you aspire,
Abandon then this world.
If from the depths of your heart
You want to practice Dharma,
Listen to my words and follow in my footsteps.
If you want to consummate the [Supreme]
  Accomplishment,
Never forget that death will come.
If hard and long you meditate, all Buddhas
In the past, the present, and the future
Will be well pleased. If you are ever
Straightforward and upright in the Dharma,
You will receive the grace of your Guru.
If without error you understand these words,
You can be sure that more happiness
And joy will come your way,
For such is my experience.

With gratitude and delight, the disciples made up their minds to renounce all things of this life, and to strive for their devotions.

This is the story of Mount Bonbo.

NOTES

1 Semihuman goddess (T.T.: Mi.Ci.Rigs.Cig.): This is a free translation — a literal translation of this term is difficult. It seems to imply a goddess who has a portion of human inheritance.

2 Rig Ma: well-gifted and qualified females who aspire to the Tantric practice.

3 Lit.: "with three qualifications." Presumably the three capabilities of a Guru: (1) giving proper instructions to the individual disciple, (2) guiding him in his devotion, and (3) dispelling hindrances that he may encounter on the Path.

THE MIRACLE
OF THE VASE INITIATION

Obeisance to all Gurus

ONCE when the Jetsun Milarepa was staying at the Belly Cave of Nya Non, the Holy Vajra Ḍākinī revealed herself in person and explained to him the hidden meaning of some abstruse passages in certain Pith-Instructions in the Tantra of the Whispered Lineage of the Ḍākinīs.[1] Then she told him that this teaching could be imparted to a few well-endowed disciples.

[Before long] Milarepa gave Rechungpa, Ngan Dson Dunpa, and other heart-like son-disciples the Vase Initiation[2] of the Whispered Succession. [During the ceremony] Milarepa said to the vase, "I am now too old, please initiate them yourself." Thereupon, the vase flew up into the sky, and initiated all the disciples one by one.

During this, [they all] heard heavenly music in the sky and smelled a fragrance they had never smelled before; also, they beheld flowers falling down from the firmament, and many other wondrous, auspicious signs. All the disciples came to a full realization of the wise meanings of the Initiation.

Seeing that they were all amazed by these wonders, the Jetsun sang:

> In the immaculate Maṇḍala of the Whispered
>   Lineage,
> The oblation of Non-desire is made.
> During the precious Vase Initiation —
> A pointer to the Buddha's Wisdom —
> We heard [heavenly] music
> And saw deities in the Maṇḍala
> Receiving the celestial offerings.
> The vase flew up to give initiation,

And wondrous Wisdom rose within you all.
The reason for all this was through
The grace of the Ghagyu Gurus.

Milarepa then told the disciples that they should keep this teaching very secret for some time.

. . .   .

One day Rechungpa completed his painting of the Vajra Yoginī. Bringing it to the Jetsun, he asked him to sanctify it. Milarepa replied, "This old man does not know how to perform an elaborate ritual of sanctification. But I will try to pray the Wisdom-Sattva [the Divine Power][3] to descend and sanctify your picture of the Samaya-Sattva [the object to be sanctified]."[4] So saying, he threw a flower into the picture [as if bringing the true Wisdom-Sattva to dissolve in it]. Whereupon the picture shook and vibrated [as a sign of receiving the blessing power of the Wisdom-Sattva]. Meanwhile, the symbols of Buddha's Body, Word, and Mind — the brilliant light of rainbows — shone from the sky and entered and dissolved into the picture. Heavenly flowers also fell down like rain. Milarepa received them on his head, as if using a blessing-skull [in a Tantric initiation], and all the flowers then dissolved into his body and united with him. As the disciples stood wonder-struck, Milarepa sang:

The pictorial form of the Samaya-Sattva
Is blessed by the holy light of Body, Word,
      and Mind;
This is the embodiment of the Wisdom-Sattva,
The Body of the Real.
When the light [of Wisdom] enters the picture
And dissolves, it completes the blessing.

Though Mila is old and did not rise,
The Wisdom Dākinīs have brought divine
Flowers from the Land of Dharmakāya,
Which merged into the Patron Buddha's [picture].
When I performed this sanctifying rite
These wondrous flowers adorned my head and body;
Then the Patron Buddha entered and united with me.
You who have witnessed this great miracle
Are indeed well-gifted and well-destined.

Thus, Rechungpa and the other disciples all witnessed the fact that the Jetsun was no different from the Vajra Yogini Herself.

This is the story of the [Vase] Initiation and of the sanctification of [Rechungpa's picture of the Vajra Yogini].

NOTES

1 Whispered Lineage of the Ḍākinī (T.T.: mKhah.hGro.sÑan.brGyud.).

2 Vase Initiation (T.T.: Bum.dWañ.): This is the first initiation among the four Anuttara Tantra Initiations. The disciple is given the instruction of the Arising Yoga, which includes all Mantra and Maṇḍala practices.

3, 4 Wisdom-Sattva (T.T.: Ye.Çes. Sems.Pa.), and Samaya-Sattva (T.T.: Dam. Tshig.Sems.Pa.): In sanctifying an object or symbol, such as a Buddha's image, figure, or Stūpa, a consecration rite called Rab.gNas. is held. The sanctified object is called Dam.Tshig.Sems.Pa. or Dam.Tshig.Pa., and the divine consecrating power, embodied in a form identical with the object, is called Ye.Çes.Sems.Pa., or Ye. Çes.Pa.

48

THE STORY OF SHINDORMO AND LESEBUM

Obeisance to all Gurus

SHINDORMO and Lese were a [married] couple who had had great faith in the Jetsun from early days. At one time they invited him to Tsar Ma. As soon as Shindormo saw him coming, she [went to him] at once and held his hands, saying, "Now that we are growing old and death is approaching, we are afraid, and sorry that we have not been able to practice the Dharma with you." Saying this, she cried mournfully for a long time. Milarepa said to her, "My dear patroness, except for advanced Dharma practitioners, the pains of birth, decay, illness, and death descend upon everyone. It is good to think about and fear them, because this enables one to practice the Dharma when death is approaching." Whereupon he sang:

> In the river of birth, decay, illness,
> And death we worldly beings are submerged;
> Who can escape these pains on earth?
> We drift on with the tide. Amidst
> Waves of misery and darkness
> We flow on and on. Seldom in
> Saṃsāra can one find joy.
>
> More miseries come by trying to avoid them;
> Through pursuing pleasures one's sins increase.
> To be free from pain, wrong
> Deeds should be shunned.
>
> When death draws near, the wise
> Always practice Dharma.

"I do not know how to observe the suffering of birth," said Shindormo, "Please instruct me how to meditate upon it." In answer, the Jetsun sang:

> My faithful patroness, I will
> Explain the suffering of birth.
>
> The wanderer in the Bardo plane
> Is the Alaya Consciousness.
> Driven by lust and hatred
> It enters a mother's womb.
>
> Therein it feels like a fish
> In a rock's crevice caught.
> Sleeping in blood and yellow fluid,
> It is pillowed in discharges;
> Crammed in filth, it suffers pain.
> A bad body from bad Karma's born.
>
> Though remembering past lives,
> It cannot say a single word.
> Now scorched by heat,
> Now frozen by the cold,
> In nine months it emerges
> From the womb in pain
> Excruciating, as if
> Pulled out gripped by pliers.
> When from the womb its head is squeezed, the pain
> Is like being thrown into a bramble pit.
> The tiny body on the mother's lap,
> Feels like a sparrow grappled by a hawk.
> When from the baby's tender body
> The blood and filth are being cleansed,
> The pain is like being flayed alive.
> When the umbilical cord is cut,
> It feels as though the spine were severed.
> When wrapped in the cradle it feels bound
> By chains, imprisoned in a dungeon.
>
> He who realizes not the truth of No-arising,
> Never can escape from the dread pangs of birth.
>
> There is no time to postpone devotion:

When one dies one's greatest need
Is the divine Dharma.
You should then exert yourself
To practice Buddha's teaching.

Shindormo asked again, "Please preach for us the sufferings of old age." In response, the Jetsun sang:

Listen, my good patrons, listen
To the sufferings of old age.

Painful is it to see one's body
Becoming frail and quite worn out.
Who can help but feel dismayed
At the threat of growing old?

When old age descends upon one,
His straight body becomes bent;
When he tries to step firmly,
He staggers against his will;
His black hairs turn white,
His clear eyes grow dim;
His head shakes with dizziness,
And his keen ears turn deaf;
His ruddy cheeks grow pale,
And his blood dries up.

His nose — the pillar of his face — sinks in;
His teeth — the essence of his bones — protrude.
Losing control of tongue, he stammers.
On the approach of death, his anguish and debts
     grow.
He gathers food and friends,
But he cannot keep them;
Trying not to suffer,
He only suffers more;
When he tells the truth to people,
Seldom is he believed;
The sons and nephews he has raised
And cherished, oft become his foes.
He gives away his savings,
But wins no gratitude.

Unless you realize the truth of Non-decay,
You will suffer misery in old age.
He who when old neglects the Dharma,
Should know that he is bound by Karma.
It is good to practice the Divine
Dharma while you still can breathe.

Shindormo then said, "What you have just told us is very true; I have experienced these things myself. Now please preach for us the sufferings of sickness." In reply, Milarepa sang:

Dear patrons, you who know grief and sorrow,
Listen to the miseries of sickness.

This frail body is subject e'er to sickness,
So that one suffers excruciating pain.
The illnesses of Prāṇa, mind, gall, and phlegm[1]
Constantly invade this frail human body,
Causing its blood and matter to be heated;
The organs are thus gripped by pain.
In a safe and easy bed
The sick man feels no comfort,
But turns and tosses, groaning in lament.
Through the Karma of [past] meanness,
Though with best of food you feed him,
He vomits all that he can take.
When you lay him in the cool,
He stills feels hot and burning;
When you wrap him in warm cloth,
He feels cold as though soaked in sleet.
Though friends and kinsmen gather round,
None can relieve or share his pains.
Though warlocks and physicians are proficient,
They cannot help cases caused by Ripening Karma.
He who has not realized the truth of No-illness,
Much suffering must undergo.

Since we know not when sicknesses will strike,
It is wise to practice Holy Dharma —
The sure conqueror of illness!

"I hope to practice [more] Dharma when death draws near," said

Shindormo, "Now please preach for me the suffering of death." In answer, Milarepa sang:

> Listen, my disheartened patroness:
> Like the pain of repaying compound debts,
> One must undergo the suffering of death.
> Yama's guards catch and carry one
> When the time of death arrives.
> The rich man cannot buy it off with money,
> With his sword the hero cannot conquer it,
> Nor can the clever woman outwit it by a trick.
> Even the learned scholar cannot
> Postpone it with his eloquence.
> Here, no coward like a fox can sneak away;
> Here, the unlucky cannot make appeal,
> Nor can a brave man here display his valor.
>
> When all the Nāḍīs converge in the body,
> One is crushed as if between two mountains —
> All vision and sensation become dim.
> When Bon priests and diviners become useless,
> The trusted physician yields to his despair.
> None can communicate with the dying man,
> Protecting guards and Devas vanish into nought.
> Though the breath has not completely stopped,
> One can all but smell the stale odor of dead flesh.
> Like a lump of coal in chilly ashes
> One approaches to the brink of death.
>
> When dying, some still count the dates and stars;
> Others cry and shout and groan;
> Some think of worldly goods;
> Some that their hard-earned wealth
> Will be enjoyed by others.
>
> However deep one's love or great one's sympathy,
> He can but depart and journey on alone.
> His good friend and consort
> Can only leave him there;
> In a bundle his beloved body
> Will be folded and carried off,
> Then thrown in water, burned in fire,
> Or simply cast off in a desolate land.

Faithful patrons, what in the end can we retain?
Must we sit idly by and let all things go?
When your breath stops tomorrow
No wealth on earth can help you.
Why, then, should one be mean?

Kind kinsmen circle round
The bed of the dying,
But none can help him for a moment.
Knowing that all must be left behind,
One realizes that all great love
And attachment must be futile.
When that final moment comes,
Only Holy Dharma helps.

You should strive, dear patroness,
For a readiness to die!
Be certain and ready; when the time
Comes, you will have no fear and no regret.

Whereupon, Shindormo besought the Jetsun for instructions. Practicing them [for some time, she gained such great progress that] at the time of her death she entered the initial stage of the Path.

. . .   .

About the same time [another patroness], Lesebum, invited Milarepa to stay with her. She said, "Although you, Jetsun Father and Sons, cannot stay with us long, remain at least for a few days." Upon this earnest request, Milarepa and his disciples stayed with her for seven days.

During this period, the people of Nya Non gathered in large numbers to make Tsa Tsa [miniature images of Buddha]. All the villagers helped with the work. Lesebum then asked Milarepa, "Would you, Jetsun Father and Sons, care to come to this meeting to enjoy yourselves?" "No," replied Milarepa, "I do not care to go." "Then," said Lesebum, "since this is a day-for-merit, I hope your Reverence will be kind enough to make offerings in my prayer room, and mold some Tsa Tsa for me. For the sake of sentient beings, please also look after my baby son, my sheep, and my household during my absence."

Well-dressed and adorned, she then went to the gathering. But Milarepa and his disciples let the time pass by and did nothing she had requested. As a consequence, the sheep trampled the field and ate up all the crops [and, worst of all,] when Lesebum entered the house on her return, her baby was crying at the top of his lungs. She thus became aware that the Jetsun had done nothing she had asked.

She then said, "It is understandable that you did not do the other things I asked you, but a Buddhist should have great compassion; is it not then a fault, and a great shame, that you disregarded the child and the sheep when they were in need?" In reply, the Jetsun sang:

> On the pasture of the Great Bliss,
> I was herding Immortal Sheep;
> I had no time to watch
> Those of blood and flesh.
> I leave them, Lesebum, for you!
>
> As a mother of Love and Great Compassion,
> I was tending Illumination's child;
> So I had no appetite
> To tend the nose-wiping boy.
> I leave him, Lesebum, to you!
>
> On the firm mountain of No-change
> I was making Tsa Tsa of Mindfulness;
> I had no time to mold clay images.
> I leave them, Lesebum, for you!
>
> In the prayer-room of my upper body
> I was lighting Illumination's lamp;
> I could not erect the pole
> For hanging prayer-flags.[2]
> I leave that, Lesebum, to you!
>
> In this shabby house of my phantom body,
> I was cleansing the dirt of normal thoughts;
> I had no time to clean your house.
> I leave it, Lesebum, to you!
>
> Among the many forms of life,
> I was watching Māyā's play;
> I could not wash the cups and dishes.
> I leave them, Lesebum, for you!

Lesebum replied, "Oh Jetsun, please do not look down upon the good deeds that we worldly beings try our best to do. I have also served many other Lamas [besides you]." In answer, Milarepa sang:

> To serve a Lama without compassion
> Is like worshipping a one-eyed demon;
> He and patron will misfortune meet.
>
> Practicing the Dharma without Bodhi-Mind
> Is the self-delusion of a fool;
> It but intensifies desire and greed.
>
> To give alms with partiality
> Is like paying back a feast;
> It will only fortify more hopes.
>
> To make offerings to the wrong person
> Is like giving an imposter money;
> It only brings more trouble and confusion.
>
> To give charity without compassion
> Is like tying oneself to a pillar
> With a strong leather strap;
> It only binds one tighter [in Saṃsāra's prison].
>
> Bearing a high view without taming the mind,
> Is like a swaggerer bragging about
> Nonsense through a worn-out throat;
> One only violates the virtues.
>
> To meditate without knowing the way
> Is like a juggler conjuring a magic
> House. Its falsehood will soon be exposed.
>
> To engage in various [Tantric] acts
> Without a real sign of Karma, is like
> A madman from a hot spring drinking;
> The more he drinks, the thirstier he gets.
>
> If, from wordly desires,
> One has lead a solemn life,
> It is like wrapping filth
> In a pretty dress of silk —
> Beautiful and grand without,
> Within stinking and rotten.

"Accomplishment" that is joined
With desires and self-conceit,
Is like a doll of clay.
It will soon break in pieces
When tested by striking.

Hearing this song, Lesebum became very remorseful. Taking a fine jewel from among her ornaments she offered it to the Jetsun, and besought him for the Instructions. Milarepa then sang, "The Words of the Gem":

Hearken, my rich Lesebum
With sparkling intelligence!
When you turn back and look into your body,
Meditate without craving for pleasures.
When you turn back and look into your mouth,
Meditate in silence and in quiet.
When you turn back and look into your mind,
Meditate without wavering thoughts.
Keep body, mouth, and mind from distractions,
And try to practice *without* practicing.

Following these instructions in her meditation, Lesebum gained some experience. She then sang a song to the Jetsun as her Seven Offerings:[3]

To you, the wondrous [yogi] clad in cotton,
Who has indomitable courage,
A man assured of freedom,
Beyond both greed and fear,
To you, ascetic Repa, I pay homage,
To you, great Repa, I present my offerings.

I now repent all my wrongdoings before you
And take sympathetic joy in all your deeds.
I pray you to turn the Wheel of Dharma,
I beg you, Nirvāṇa ne'er to enter.
To all beings I now dedicate my merits.

When I watch my body, and try
To stop craving for pleasure,
The craving oft arises.

When I observe my mouth, and try
To subdue the wish for talking,
Alas, the longing still prevails.

When I watch my mind, and try without
Wandering thoughts to meditate,
Wandering thoughts always arise.

When I concentrate my body, mouth,
And mind to practice the Non-practice,
The effort-making practice is still there.

To overcome these difficulties
And to further my progress,
Pray grant me more instructions.

In response to her request, the Jetsun sang:

Listen, listen, Lesebum, with care.
If you are harassed by craving for pleasure,
Leave all your associates,
Giving all away in alms;
Rest yourself at ease without
Yearning or attachment.

When you feel like talking, try
To abjure worldly desires.
Beware of your pride and egotism,
And rest yourself at ease in humbleness.

If wavering thoughts keep on arising,
Catch hold of your Self-mind with alertness.
Be attached not to Saṃsāra nor Nirvāṇa,
But rest yourself at ease in full Equality.
Let what arises rise,
Take care not to follow.

If in meditation you still tend to strive,
Try to arouse for all a great compassion,
Be identified with the All-Merciful.

Always think of your Guru as sitting on your head,
And meditate with perseverance on the Void.

Then dedicate to all your merit.

On my words ponder, Lesebum,
And practice with zeal the Dharma.

In accordance with Milarepa's instructions, Lesebum continued her meditation. Eventually she became a yoginī, and reached the initial stage of the Path.

This is the story of Shindormo and Lesebum.

NOTES

1 The Prāṇa, gall, and phlegm illnesses: According to Tibetan pathology, these are the three major sicknesses of man, i.e., the sickness of Prāṇa (T.T.: rLuñ.), of gall (T.T.: mKhris.Pa.), and of phlegm (T.T.: Bad.Kan.).

2 Prayer-flags: Certain Mantras and prayers are printed on specially designed flags made of thin cloth, which are then hung on high poles as a symbol of blessing and good will.

3 Seven Offerings (T.T.: Yan.Lag.bDun.Pa.): This is the famous and widely practiced "Seven Offerings" exemplified by Bodhisattva Samantabhadra as described in the Avataṃsaka Sūtra. The prayer of the Seven Offerings is included in almost every ritual and ceremony of Tibetan Buddhism; they are: (1) to pay homage to all the Buddhas and sages in the infinite universes; (2) to make offerings to them; (3) to confess one's sins; (4) to delight in all virtues of others, or to feel sympathtic joy over others' merits; (5) to beseech Buddhas and sages to preach the Dharma; (6) to implore Buddhas and sages not to enter Nirvāṇa; and (7) to dedicate all merits that one has accumulated to the attainment of Buddhahood.

The original Samantabhadra's Vows — the exemplars of "the Bodhisattva's Act," are not seven as stated in the Avataṃsaka Sūtra, but ten; three are omitted in the so-called Seven Offerings.

49

MILAREPA AND
THE DYING SHEEP

Obeisance to all Gurus

A T ONE time when the Jetsun Milarepa and his heart-son Rechung-pa were living in the Belly Cave of Nya Non, Rechungpa was still harboring a slight craving for worldly pleasures, which the Jetsun had often admonished him to give up. But Rechungpa thought, "I have already renounced my native land and the Eight Worldly Desires, yet the Jetsun considers this insufficient — merely halfway in the practice of the Dharma. Can this really be true?" Full of doubt, he questioned Milarepa, who answered, "In a general sense what you have said may be true, but by itself it is not enough. Now listen to my song":

> He who sits upon my head
> In the Palace of Great Bliss,
> Is the Immaculate One —
> The glory of all merits.
> He [Marpa], is the essence of the Lineage Gurus,
> The source of my perpetual inspiration.
> To Him I pay sincerest homage,
> To Him I send my heart-felt praise!
>
> Though you renounce your native land
> Living far away alone,
> You must still observe the precepts.
> He who cares for his good name,
> Will fall into the world once more.
>
> Though you renounce good food and care,

Be careful in receiving alms.
He who still yearns for tasty food,
Will fall into the world again.

Though an elegant garment is far superior to
    a plain dress,
It must be made according to the principle of
    tailoring.
Yogis who cling to fine, soft clothes
Will fall into the world once more.

If you've forsaken home and land,
Modest be and persevering.
He who aspires to fame and eminence,
Will fall into the world again.

When you forsake the "big" estate
And till your own small land [of self],
You must obey the rules of farming.
Should you expect big harvests quickly,
You will fall into the world once more.

Saṃsāra in itself is groundless and unreal;
When you look you find it hard
To define, ungraspable.
Yet when you realize it,
It is Nirvāṇa itself.
All things in themselves are void;
A yogi is attached to nothing.

Rechungpa asked, "Since I am following the Path of Tantric Skill, may I take some comfort and enjoyment to increase my devotion?" The Jetsun answered, "If you can really advance your devotion by means of enjoyments and pleasures, you may use them, but not if they only increase your [worldly] desires. I was enjoined by my Guru, Marpa, to renounce all worldly desires for an ascetic life of devotion. As a result of following his words throughout my life, a little merit has now grown within me. You, also, should renounce all Eight Worldly Desires and meditate hard while you still have the chance. Now hearken to my song":

Remember how your Guru lived
And bear in mind his honeyed words.

He who wastes a chance for Dharma,
Will never have another.
Bear, then, in mind the Buddha's teaching
And practice it with perseverance.
By clinging to things of this life,
In the next, one suffers more.
If you crave for pleasures
Your troubles but increase.

One is indeed most foolish
To miss a chance for Dharma.
Practice hard in fear of death!
Committing sins will draw
You to the Lower Realms.
By pretending and deceiving,
You cheat and mislead yourself.
Merits diminish with
The growth of evil thoughts.
If you are concerned with future life,
Diligently practice your devotions.
A yogi longing for good clothes
Will soon lose his mind;
A yogi yearning for good food
Will soon do bad deeds;
A yogi loving pleasant words
Will not gain, but lose.
Renounce worldly pursuits, Rechungpa,
Devote yourself to meditation.

If you try to get a patron
Who is rich, you will meet a foe.
He who likes to be surrounded
By crowds, will soon be disappointed.
He who hoards much wealth and money,
Is soon filled with vicious thoughts.
Meditate, my son Rechungpa,
And put your mind into the Dharma.

Realization will be won
At last by he who practices;
He who cannot practice
But only talks and brags,
Is always telling lies.

Alas, how hard it is to find
The chance and time to practice long.
Rechungpa, try to meditate without diversions!

If you merge your mind with the Dharma,
You will e'er be gay and joyful;
You will always find it better
If you dwell oft in solitude.
Son Rechungpa, may the precious
Illuminating-Void Samādhi
Remain forever in your mind!

Milarepa then thought, "Because of my urging, Rechungpa's desires
for worldly pleasures may have lessened to a certain extent, yet he
still cannot overcome [all of] his wrong inclinations. I shall try to
further his spirit of renunciation." So he took him to the market of Nya
Non for alms.

Many butchers had gathered there. The meat was piled up like
walls, animals' heads were stacked in huge heaps, skins were scattered over the ground, and blood ran together like water in a pond.
In addition, rows of livestock were fastened to stakes for slaughtering.
An old man from Mon with a crippled arm was butchering a big
black sheep, pulling out its entrails while it was still alive. Fatally
wounded, it managed to escape and staggered moaning toward the
Jetsun for help. Watching this pitiful scene, Milarepa shed many tears.
He immediately performed the Transformation Yoga for the sheep
and delivered its soul [consciousness] to the Bodhi-Path. Whereupon,
with overwhelming compassion, Milarepa sang:

How pitiful are sentient beings in Saṃsāra!
Looking upward to the Path of Liberation,
How can one but feel sorrow for these sinful men.
How foolish and sad it is to indulge in killing,
When by good luck and Karma one has a human form.
How sad it is to do an act
That in the end will hurt oneself.
How sad it is to build a sinful wall
Of meat made of one's dying parents' flesh.
How sad it is to see meat
Eaten and blood flowing.
How sad it is to know confusions
And delusions fill the minds of men.
How sad it is to find but vice,

Not love, in people's hearts.
How sad it is to see
That blindness veils all men
Who cherish sinful deeds.

Craving causes misery,
While worldly deeds bring pain.
With this in mind one feels sorrowful,
Thinking thus, one searches for a cure.

When I think of those who never
Take heed to their future lives,
But indulge in evil deeds,
I feel most disturbed and sad,
And deeply fearful for them.

Rechungpa, seeing all these things,
Don't you remember Holy Dharma? Don't
You in Saṃsāra lose all heart?
Rouse the spirit of renunciation, go,
Rechungpa, to the cave to meditate!

Heed the bounty of your Guru
And avoid all sinful deeds;
Casting worldly things aside
Stay firm in your practice.
Keep your good vows and devote
Your life to meditation.

Rechungpa was filled with sadness, and a fervent desire for renunciation arose from the depth of his heart. Shedding many tears, he vowed, "Dear Jetsun, from now on I shall renounce all worldly desires and pleasures, and devote myself to meditation. Let us, Master and servant, go to the remote mountains; but tell me where." In answer, Milarepa sang:

Alas, trapped by evil Karmas, in the dark
Sentient beings wander in Saṃsāra.
The robber, wandering thoughts,
Drives them wild, thus depriving them
Of the chance for cultivation.
Wake up, meditate now, everyone!
Let us two Repas go to the Snow Lashi mountain.

Long and hazardous is Saṃsāra's road, pressing
And pernicious is the bandit of Five Poisons,
But Son Rechungpa, hold tight your Child-
Of-Awareness, seek Wisdom's Escort.
Sinful men seldom think that death will come;
To Snow Lashi we two Repas
Will go now for meditation!

High is the Mountain-of-Faults,
Fearful the hounds and hunters.
The "Dyāna-beast" is e'er exposed
To the danger of being captured.
Be wise, then, escape to the Land of Peace.
Sinful men seldom think that death will come;
To Snow Lashi we two Repas
Will go now for meditation!

This house of the human body
Is falling down and, weathered
By seepage of food and drink, is
Decaying with the months and years;
'Tis dangerous to live in it.
Escape then to safety,
Ready to die with joy.
Sinful men seldom think that death will come;
To Snow Lashi we two Repas
Will go now for meditation!

Deep and full of perils is Saṃsāra's sea;
It is wise to cross it now
In the boat of Awareness.
Fearful is confusion's rolling tide;
Escape from it now,
To the "Not-Two Land."
Sinful men seldom think that death will come;
To Snow Lashi we two Repas
Will go now for meditation!

Wide is the marshy bog of lust,
Harassing the muddy swamp of family life;
Be wise, escape from it, riding
Renunciation's Elephant.
Be wise and escape to safety,

In the dry land of Liberation!
Sinful men seldom think that death will come;
To Snow Lashi we two Repas
Will go now for meditation!

Great is the danger now of falling
Into Hīnayāna's views and deeds;
Only the ignorant make
About nothing much ado.
Sinful men seldom think that death will come;
To Snow Lashi we two Repas
Will go now for meditation!

On this occasion, many people in the bazaar were spontaneously confirmed with great faith in the Jetsun and his son. They all wanted to offer them much food and service, but Milarepa told them that their food was the food of sin [directly produced] through the Eight Worldly Desires, and refused to accept it. He and Rechungpa then set out on their journey to the Snow Mountain of Lashi.

This is the story of Milarepa's admonishments on the importance of being ready to die.

THE BEER-DRINKING SONG

Obeisance to all Gurus

A T ONE time when the Jetsun Milarepa and his son Rechungpa
were living in the Great Conquering Demon Cave¹ on Lashi Snow
Mountain, the frightful conjurations created by the Asuras became
so great that Rechungpa [had to] hide in the back of the cave and
absorb himself in Samādhi.

One day a great number of Devas and specters arrived, and dis-
playing many dreadful forms, threw numerous weapons at Milarepa to
frighten him. With threatening voices, they shouted, "Let us grab him,
eat his flesh and drink his blood!" But [undaunted] Milarepa sang:

> I pray all Gurus to subdue
> All hatred and malignance!
>
> Pitiable are you ghosts and demons.
> Accustomed to evil thoughts and deeds,
> With joy you afflict sentient beings.
> Addicted to flesh-eating,
> You crave to kill and strangle!
> Born as hungry ghosts
> Ugly and repulsive,
> You commit more sinful deeds.
> You are doomed to go to Hell.
> Since you forget the seed of Liberation,
> You find the door to freedom ever shut.
> Alas, how pitiable and sad this is!
>
> Sitting on Compassion-Voidness' seat,
> I can perform all miracles.
> If you ghosts can grab and eat me,

I shall be most pleased and happy.
With compassion's Bodhi-Mind
I rejoice to see you here!

Whereupon Milarepa entered the Water-Samādhi.[2] Before long more demon and Deva armies arrived. Among them was an extremely fearful demoness who said, "Who is this man?" A demon replied, "Let us first move to [the safe side] near the water, and see." In doing so he kicked loose a few pebbles [with a clatter], and at that very moment Milarepa suddenly appeared, saying, "I am here!" He also showed his naked body to the demons who, surprised and panic-stricken, all ran away.

After a while they returned and once more vainly attacked Mila-repa with their magic. Finally they gave up, crying, "Let us all be reconciled!"

In a state of great compassion Milarepa then sang:

Listen carefully, you Non-men,
You army of ill-Karm'd demons.
Your evil deeds will harm none but yourselves!

Since to me all forms are but the Dharmakāya,
Even a demon army is my glory.
Hearken, Devas and demons all. If you
Will take refuge in the Triple Gem,[3]
You will be reborn in a good place.
If you stop eating flesh and drinking blood,
You will attain high birth and freedom.
If you stop harming others, then
You will soon enter Bodhi's Path;
If you withdraw from sinful deeds,
You can embrace the Buddhist Doctrine.

Only by practicing Ten Merits
Can you understand the meaning
Of your Guru's [firm] instructions!
Only when you have removed
Confusions of body, word, and
Mind can you join the order of
Illumination-holders. Only when
You vow to keep the disciplines can we

> Agree as friends. Only when you keep
> Samaya's precepts can you be my disciples.

In repentence, the demons were all converted. They said, "From now on we will obey your orders. Please teach us the Dharma." Milarepa then preached for them the truth of Karma, the teaching of Taking-in-Refuge, and the Growth of the Bodhi-Mind. Confirmed with faith, the demons all offered their lives to Milarepa as a pledge of their solemn vows and departed.

The next morning Milarepa went to Rechungpa and asked, "Did anything happen to you last night?" "I was in the [Samādhi of] Illumination," said Rechungpa, "and had an amusing vision: someone came and threw a pebble at you while you were lying on your bed. Did it hit you?" Milarepa replied, "In great joyfulness, my body turned into water last night.[4] I am not sure whether that pebble hit me or not, but my chest feels a little uncomfortable. You may check on it for me." So saying, he again transformed his body into water, wherein Rechungpa found a small pebble and removed it. After that the Jetsun felt comfortable once more.

At that time many disciples came to visit Milarepa. One day he suggested that they all take a walk to the [top of the] high mountain in front of Lashi. But the disciples said, "It will be too strenuous for you because of your age. We advise you not to go." The Jetsun replied, "I think I can manage it easily." Whereupon he sang:

> I bow down to all Gurus!
>
> Milarepa wants to climb that
> Mountain peak, but he is now too old;
> His body is worn out and frail.
> Shall he lie still and restful
> Like you, my brother Mountain?

Milarepa had hardly finished singing when he suddenly appeared on the top of a cliff — his feet set firmly on the rock. Then he ascended higher until he reached the top, sitting there comfortably for some time [clothed] in a rainbow-shroud. He then flew back to the cave and said to the disciples "I need someone to pour beer for me when I am up there." "But please tell us how do we get there and how we can serve you beer?" they asked. "If you want to reach the mountain peak," replied, Milarepa, "you should practice like this":

> Hearken, my sons! If you want

To climb the mountain peak
To enjoy the view,
You should hold the Self-mind's light,
Tie [it] with a great "Knot,"
And catch it with a firm "Hook."
If you practice thus
You can climb the mountain peak
To enjoy the view.

Come, you gifted men and women,
Drink the brew of Experience!
Come "inside" to enjoy the scene —
See it and enjoy it to the full!
The incapable remain outside;
Those who cannot drink pure
Beer may quaff small-beer.
He who cannot strive for Bodhi,
Should strive for superior birth.

Rechungpa said, "I can practice the Dharma and aspire to drink the beer. But please show me how." The Jetsun replied, "The best way to drink the 'beer' is to follow the good advice of Marpa." Then he sang:

I bow down to the Translator Marpa
Who in primordial Reality
Abides, Master of the essential truths.
It is not easy to describe him.
Like the sky, he is bright and clean,
Omnipresent as the sun and moon;
He never discriminates between
"High" and "low," like bushes in a swamp.
He is my Lord Buddha,
Sitting upon my head,
My glory and adornment.

In the Six Realms the chief
Actors are human beings
Who use their poorer crops to brew
Beer in the autumn and the spring.
But to brew for ourselves,
The Dharma's followers,
Build a fireplace with Three Gates, prepare

A cauldron of Śūnyatā, and then fill it
With grain of the pure White Element[5]
And the water of Compassion.
Then light the fire of Wisdom
And boil well the mash.

In the Central Plain where all is equal,
The flag of the Great Bliss is raised.
When the yeast of instruction has been added
[To the cauldron] one then may sleep at ease
On the bed of the Four Infinities.

The fermented barley of One-in-Many
Is taken out and put into a jar.
Strengthened by non-dual Wisdom-Skill,
The beer of Five Prajñās is matured;
At the entrance of the Wish-fulfilling
House, the beer of pure nectar is purified.
The Pure Heruka[6] causes it, by the
Heruka of Totality is it conditioned
And by the Lotus Heruka colored.
Its smell is the Heruka of Variety;
Its taste, of Vajra; and its touch, of Gaiety.

I am a yogi who drinks beer, because
It illumines the Dharma Body,
Completes the Body of Sambhoga,
And gives form to all Nirmāṇakāyas.
From Non-cessation's pulp
Only men with hardened heads
Can drink this nectar beer.

Here is another parable:

From the brew of Dharma-Essence
Comes precious and stimulating beer;
To Gurus and Buddhas of the Three Perfections
It is a superb oblation!
Along the middle way of Skillful-Wisdom
The rules of Samaya are observed;
Thus the Maṇḍala's deities are pleased.

With the brew of common and special instructions

[Mystical] sensations are obtained;
One thus fulfills one's wishes
And those of other men.

Whoever in the cup of Six Adornments[7]
Drinks the pure beer of the Whispered Lineage,
In him will the Great Bliss flame up.
Of this Bliss a single sip
Dispells all griefs and sorrows.
This is the beer a yogi drinks —
A special Dharma shared by few,
An act most wonderful and splendid,
An act superb and marvelous.

Hearing this song, the disciples all gained firm understandings.

This is the story of Milarepa conquering demons in the Great Cave and singing a Drinking Song while strolling [with his disciples].

NOTES

1 Great Conquering Demon Cave (T.T.: bDud.hDul.Phug.Mo.Che.).

2 Water-Samādhi: Literally this should be, "Exhaustion-of-the-Elements Water-Samādhi" (T.T.: Zad.Par.hByun.Wa.Chuhi.Tin.ne.hDsin.). This rather enigmatic term denotes a Samādhi in which the yogi manipulates his power to "exhaust" or subdue all the other four elements — Earth, Fire, Wind, and Space — thus preventing their manifestation and activity, and bringing the Water Element alone into manifestation. It is said that a spectator will not see the yogi's physical body, but a vision of water when he is engaged in this Samādhi. Likewise, the proficient yogi can also apply his power to manipulate the other four elements; thus we have the Exhaustion-of-the-Elements: Earth-, Fire-, Wind-, and Space-Samādhis.

3 The Triple Gem: the Three Precious Ones, i.e., Buddha, Dharma, and Saṅgha.

4 See Note 2.

5 The Pure White Element (T.T.: dKar.Po.Dan.Wa.): This seems to imply the white Tig Le — the Essence of male semen, a symbol of positive energy.

6 Heruka: the general name for Tantric deities, usually of a fierce form.

7 The Six Adornments: (1) the tiara of human skulls, (2) the necklace of human heads, (3) the bone armlets and wristlets, (4) the anklets, (5) the breastplate Mirror-of-Karma, and (6) the cemetery-dust ointment.

HEARTFELT ADVICE
TO RECHUNGPA

Obeisance to all Gurus

A	T ONE time the Jetsun Milarepa was staying at Ramdin Nampu with his son-disciples, Rechungpa, Drigom Repa, and others. One day, while Rechungpa and Drigom Repa were having a long debate about the teachings of Nāropa and Medripa, the Jetsun commented, "First listen to my song, then continue your discussion."

> My gracious Guru always sits upon my head,
> The Realization is always in my mind.
> Oh how can one describe this joyful feeling!
>
> Listen you two, one Repa and one priest,
> Who still linger in the realm of action.
>
> If you do not understand *within*,
> Your noisy bark will but inflate
> Your pride and egotism.
>
> Is not the clearance of misunderstandings
> Within called the "Endless View" — a yogi's glory
> Confirming reasons and the Scriptures?
>
> Is not Nhamdog dissolving in the Dharmakāya
> Called spontaneous practice — a yogi's glory
> Confirming meditation principles?
>
> Is not self-purity of the Six Senses
> Called the Action-of-One-Taste — a yogi's glory

Responding freely to times and changes?

Is not the Experience of the Bliss-Void
Called the fruition of the Whispered Lineage —
A yogi's glory conforming with
The *Four Initiations?*

Is not the art of brightening Śūnyatā
Called the Stages and Bhūmis of the Path —
A yogi's glory witnessing
The sign-posts on the Way?

Is not the consummation of Self-mind[1]
Called the attainment of Buddhahood
In one life — a yogi's glory
Confirming the Four Bodies?

Is not a possessor of the Pith-Instructions
Of Reason and the Scriptures called
A Guru with Lineage — a yogi's glory,
Embodiment of Love and of Compassion?

Is not one with compassion and great faith
Called a disciple-with-capacity —
A yogi's glory embodying
The merit of veneration?

One must observe the mind to gain a decisive
View. To win progress one must meditate;
One must act to reach the consummation.

Perfection of Mind is the Accomplishment;
The Fourfold Body of Buddha is
A presence and Realization.
He who knows one, knows all.

Hearing this song, their misunderstandings were all cleared. Then the Jetsun told Rechungpa that if one determines to practice the Dharma, he should practice like this; whereupon he sang:

Listen, my son, the Illumination-Holder.
To practice the Dharma you should know these things:
That your Guru who produces merit,

The embodiment of all the Buddhas,
Is the Dharmakāya in Itself.
Rechungpa, are you thus convinced?

You should know his instructions
Are superb, nectar-like antidotes
That cure the Five Poisonous Desires.
Rechungpa, are you thus convinced?

His deeds and acts are those
Of the Nirmāṇakāya.
Son, are you thus convinced?

The mind's ever-flowing thoughts are
Void, intrinsically groundless;
[They seem] to rise, and yet they n'er exist.
In unwavering mindfulness
You should have a firm belief.
Rechungpa, are you thus convinced?

The pleasures that heavenly beings love
Are subject to change and transience.
Firmly believe that in Saṃsāra
True happiness can ne'er be found.
Rechungpa, are you thus convinced?

All things with form are momentary and fleeting,
Like flowing water and incense smoke, like lightning
In the sky. Know that leisure in this life is rare.
Rechungpa, are you thus convinced?

That all on earth will die is certain —
There's no escape: for Beyond-death strive.
Rechungpa, are you thus convinced?

Hearing this song, all the son-disciples gained further understanding.

One day some patrons of Nya Non arrived. They invited Rechung-pa to accept hospitality in their village for a time, and the Jetsun gave him permission to sojourn there for a fortnight. Other Repas also went to the village for alms.

In the meantime Tsese, Ku Ju, and other patrons from Drin came to visit Milarepa. When they saw him sitting there with his penis freely exposed, they were shamed and horrified, and feared to go near him. Finally Tsese approached and offered him a covering-cloth. Whereupon all the visitors gathered round him and said, "Oh Jetsun, the manner in which you expose your naked body and organ makes us worldly men feel very embarrassed and ashamed. For our sake, please be compassionate and considerate enough to cover it."

When he heard this request, Milarepa suddenly stood up naked and sang:

> Through wandering long in many places,
> I have forgotten my native land.
> Staying long with my Holy Jetsun,
> I have forgotten all my kinsmen.
> Keeping for long the Buddha's teaching,
> I have forgotten worldly things.
> Staying for long in hermitages,
> I have forgotten all diversions.
> Through long watching of monkeys' play,
> I have forgotten sheep and cattle.
> Long accustomed to a tinder-box,
> I have forgotten all household chores.
> Long used to solitude without servant or master,
> I have forgotten courteous manners.
> Long accustomed to be carefree,
> I have forgotten worldly shame.
> Long accustomed to the mind coming and going
> By itself, I have forgotten how to hide things.
> Long used to burning Dumo-heat,
> I have forgotten clothing.
> Long accustomed to practice non-discriminating Wisdom,
> I have forgotten all distracting thoughts. Long used
> To practicing the Two-in-One Illumination,
> I have forgotten all nonsensical ideas.
> These twelve "oblivions" are the teachings of this Yogi.
> Why, dear patrons, do you not also follow them?
> I have untied the knot of dualism;
> What need have I to follow your customs?
> To me, Bodhi is spontaneity itself!
>
> The Dharma of you worldly people
> Is too difficult to practice.
> Caring for nought, I live the way I please.
> Your so-called "shame" only brings deceit

And fraud. How to pretend I know not.

The patrons then made fine, bountiful offerings to Milarepa, and left. Meanwhile, Rechungpa remained in the village, and though he only stayed one day in each patron's house, it was many days before he could return to the hermitage. When he finally came back, he found that the door was shut. Rechungpa thought, "Was it because I stayed too long in the village that the Jetsun became displeased?" And he sang:

> In the immanence of Dharma
> There's no need to read the stars;
> Those who consult the stars
> Are far from Immanence.
>
> The Great Perfection[2] has no dogmas;
> If an obstinate creed arises,
> It is not the Great Perfection.
>
> In the Mahāmudrā there is no
> Acceptance or rejection. If there
> Be, it is not the Great Symbol.
>
> In the Experience of Great Bliss
> There is neither light nor shade.
> If either of the two arises,
> It is not Great Bliss.
>
> The great Middle Way cannot be described;
> Nor can it be defined, for if it could,
> It would not be the Middle Way.
>
> I, Rechungpa, have just returned;
> Are you, my Father well today?

From over the top of the door Milarepa sang in reply this song:

> There is no Buddha other than one's mind; there is
> No faster Way than Prāna and Nādī practice;
> There is no cruelty or vengeance in the Three
>   Refuges;
> There is no experience greater than that of the
>   Bliss-Void;

No grace is higher than the Jetsun Guru's —
The refuge and glory of all men.

By practicing the correct instructions
Conviction will grow in one's mind.
With complete Realization,
Those instructions are fulfilled.
Once a firm resolution has been made,
Experience and conviction blossom.
When in one's heart kindness grows,
One through love can help all others.
He who sees his Guru as the Buddha,
Will then receive the great blessing power.

Rechungpa, the quotations
You have made are excellent.
If you understand them,
You will find the Dharma
There. If not, your remarks
Are babble and jabber.

How have you been, my son Rechungpa?
Your old father is well and healthy.

The Jetsun then opened the door and Rechungpa went in. Milarepa said, "We will take a rest today, and have a talk. I see now that
you still have great desires for worldly things. You should renounce
them and meditate alone in the mountains. Now listen":

Through my Guru's grace I have been
Able to stay in the mountains.
Pray enable me e'er to remain in solitude.

Listen attentively, well-gifted Rechungpa.
When you dwell in solitude,
Think not of whispered accusations
Lest you stir your mind with anger.
When you meditate with your Guru,
Think not of religious affairs
Lest you fall into confusion.
When you give Dormas[3] to spirits,
Expect not assistance from them
Lest you, yourself, become a demon!

When engrossed in meditation,
Meet no friend or companion
Lest they interfere with your devotions.
When ascetically you persevere,
Think not of meat and wine lest
You be born a hungry ghost.
When you practice the Whispered Successions'
Skillful Path, yearn not for learning
Lest to the wrong path you stray.
When in the hills you dwell alone,
Think not of leaving lest
Evil thoughts arise.

My son, it is through perseverance
That the Holy Dharma is attained.
It is through hard work that the pains
Of Saṃsāra are relieved.
My son, my vowed disciple,
Let your father help you to bring
Forth the true Enlightenment!
Let me help you to the Last Realization
That the Dharmakāya and all forms are one!

His song struck [to the root of] Rechungpa's hidden faults. Whereupon Rechungpa prostrated himself before the Jetsun and sang:

I have through your blessing
The chance to practice Dharma.
When for good I left my parents,
Your grace was written in my heart.
Though long ago I left my home,
I still long for companionship,
Thinking of food, and dress, and wealth.

An ascetic, I have lived and dwelt in caves,
Far from temptations in the world.
Yet the thought of gathering
And gaining still rises in my mind.

What I now see is the accomplished being,
What I possess are the Whispered Pith-
Instructions. I have meditated long and hard,
Yet I still think of seeing other Gurus

To learn more teachings from them.

I have tried to serve my Guru,
I have strived to reach
Buddhahood in this life,
I have stayed in lonely places,
Yet I still think of doing this and that.

My Jetsun Guru, the Immutable Essence,
Dorje-Chang, pray help, bless, and convert your son!

Milarepa then gave Rechungpa many verbal instructions, and as a result he made great progress. After this incident, the patrons of Nya Non invited Milarepa and his son to dwell in the Belly Cave.

This is the story of Ramdin Nampu.

NOTES

1 The text reads: "Rañ.Sems.Zad.Sar.sKyol.Wa.La." More literally, "Is not the exhaustion of Self-mind called the attainment of Buddhahood . . .?" Mahāyāna Buddhism holds that the phenomena of exhaustion and of consummation seem to be always inseparable; exhaustion of something, such as the desires and ignorance, implies the simultaneous consummation of something else, such as transcendental Wisdom and Compassion. The "exhaustion of Self-mind" here seems to be used in a more positive, rather than in a negative sense.

2 The Great Perfection (T.T.: rDsogs.Pa.Chen.Po.; Skt.: Mahāsampanna): This is the "teaching-on-the-mind" of the Ningmaba School, or the Ningmaba's version of the Mahāmudrā teaching. Mahāmudrā, Mahāsampanna, and Ch'an Buddhism are all one teaching under different names.

3 Dormas: See Story 30 Note 7.

RECHUNGPA'S
JOURNEY TO WEU

Obeisance to all Gurus

B Y THE invitation of his patrons in Nya Non, who provided perfect food and service, Jetsun Milarepa dwelt in the Belly Cave,
while Rechungpa stayed in another cave above it. At one time the
Gurus, patron Buddhas, and Ḍākinīs all revealed themselves to Rechungpa in his dreams, persuading him to ask the Jetsun to relate his
life story. After Milarepa had done so, Rechungpa yearned to go to
Central Tibet [Weu].

At that time some patrons said, "Compare the father [Milarepa]
with the son [Rechungpa]; the son seems to be far superior because
he has been in India." Then the younger people all went to Rechungpa, while the older ones came to the Jetsun. One day many patrons
arrived. They brought Rechungpa fine and bountiful food, but gave
Milarepa only meager offerings. [Not knowing this], Rechungpa
thought, "Since they have brought me such good food, they must have
made even better offerings to the Jetsun." He went to Milarepa and
said, "Dear Jetsun, haven't we received fine offerings today? With all
this food we can hold a sacramental feast with all the Repas. Shall we
do so?"

"Very well," replied Milarepa, "you will find my share under that
slab of stone. Take and use it." But Rechungpa found only a portion
of rotten meat, a bottle of sour beer, and a small quantity of barley
flour. On his way back, Rechungpa thought, "Is this fitting of those
patrons? Compared with my Buddha-like Guru, I am nothing. I cannot match a single hair of his head, even with my whole body. But
now these ignorant patrons are doing this foolish thing. Hitherto I
have been living with my Guru and receiving all the Instructions from
him. My intention was to go on living with him so that I could serve
and please him. But as things stand now, if I stay with him too long

I will only become a hindrance and stand in his way. Thus, instead of being a helper I will become a competitor. I ought to ask his permission to leave."

Very early next morning, Rechungpa went to see the Jetsun. He noticed that Milarepa was sleeping with his head hidden [under his arms, like a bird]. Megom Repa was also asleep in his bed. Rechungpa thought, "Concerning self-achievement, my Guru has completely realized the Dharmakāya. And as to altruism, does he not at times practice it like a bird?" Knowing what Rechungpa was thinking, the Jetsun sang a song called "The Four Activities":

> Listen with care, my son Rechungpa!
> Your old father, Mila, sometimes sleeps,
> But in sleeping he also practices,
> For he knows how to illumine Blindness;
> But not all men know this Instruction.
> I shall be happy if all can share this teaching.
>
> Your old father, Mila, sometimes eats,
> But in eating he also practices,
> For he knows how to identify
> His food and drink with the Holy Feast;
> But not all men know this Instruction.
> I shall be happy if all can share this teaching.
>
> Sometimes your old father, Mila, walks,
> But in marching he also practices,
> For he knows that walking
> Is to circle round the Buddhas;
> But not all men know this Instruction.
> I shall be happy if all can share this teaching.
>
> Rechungpa, you should also practice in this way.
> Get up, Megom, it is time to make some broth!

In asking the Jetsun's permission to leave, Rechungpa gave many reasons for going to Weu. At the end of his petition, he sang:

> To visit different places
> And journey to various lands,
> To circumambulate holy Lhasa,
> See the two divine faces of Jo Shag,[1]
> Visit the saintly Samye Temple,

Circle round the Yuru Kradrag,
Visit the seat of Marngo,
"Sightsee" at Nyal and Loro,
And to beg for alms,
I must go to Weu.

Milarepa replied, "My son, although you will have disciples in Weu, the time has not yet come for you to go there. Please do not go against your Guru's injunctions, but listen to this song":

Born for the Supreme and Skillful Path of Secret
    Words,[2]
He is the Jetsun Buddha disguised in human form,
Possessing the divine Four Bodies,
The embodiment of Blisses Four.
To Him, the great Marpa,
I pay sincerest homage.

On this early morning
Of the auspicious eighth,
The dawning sun, like a crystal ball of fire,
Radiates its warm and brilliant beams.
I, the Yogi, feel very well and happy.

Son Rechungpa, as people have well said,
You are the spear-holder
Of a hundred soldiers.
Please do not talk like this,
But control your mind.
Try to cleanse it as a mirror bright,
And lend your ear to this old man.

When you live in a quiet hermitage,
Why think about staying in other lands?
Since you meditate on your Buddha Guru,
Why need you circle Lhasa?
While you watch your mind at play,
Why need you see Samye Temple?
If you have annihilated doubts within,
Why need you visit Marngo?
Since you practice the Whispered Lineage teaching,
Why need you "sightsee" at Loro and Nyal?
If you observe with penetration your Self-mind,

Why need you circumambulate the Kradrag?

But Rechungpa still kept on pressing his request. Whereupon the Jetsun sang:

It is good for you, the white lion on the mountain,
To stay high, and never go deep into the valley,
Lest your beautiful mane be sullied!
To keep it in good order,
You should remain on the high snow mountain.
Rechungpa, hearken to my words today!

It is good for you, the great
Eagle on high rocks to perch,
And never fall into a pit,
Lest your mighty wings be damaged!
To keep them in good order,
You should remain in the high hills.
Rechungpa, hearken to your Guru's words.

It is good for you, the jungle tiger,
To stay in the deep forest;
If you rove about the plain
You will lose your dignity.
To keep your splendor in perfection,
In the forest you should remain.
Rechungpa, hearken to your Guru's words.

It is good for you, the golden-eyed
Fish to swim in the central sea;
If you swim too close to shore,
You will in a net be caught.
You should remain in the deep waters.
Rechungpa, hearken to your Guru's words.

It is good, Rechungdordra of Gung Tang,
For you to stay in hermitages;
If you wander in different places,
Your *Experience* and *Realization* will dim.
To protect and cultivate devotion
You should remain in the mountains.
Rechungpa, hearken to your Guru's words!

"Dear Guru, if I stay too long with you, I shall become a hindrance rather than a help," countered Rechungpa. "It is also for the sake of *furthering* my Experience and Realization that I want to go to different countries!" And he sang:

Hear me, my Father Jetsun!
If I, the white lion on the snow
Mountain, do not rise up and act,
How can I glorify my splendid mane?
Rechungpa wants not to remain, but to visit Weu.
I beg your permission to depart today.

If I, the great eagle, king of birds,
Do not fly high into the firmament,
How can I magnify my mighty wings?
Rechungpa wants not to remain, but to visit Weu.
I beg my Guru's permission to depart today!

If I, the great tiger, the jungle lord,
Do not rove in the deep forest,
How can I better my grand smile?
Rechungpa wants not to remain, but to visit Weu.
I beg your permission to depart today!

If I, the fish in the deep ocean,
Swim not to the ocean's edge,
I can never sharpen my golden eyes.
Rechungpa wants not to remain, but to visit Weu.
I beg my Guru's permission to depart today!

If I, Rechungdordra of Gung Tang,
Travel not to different countries,
I can ne'er improve my Experience and Realization.
Rechungpa wants not to remain, but to visit Weu.
I beg your permission to depart today!

The Jetsun then said, "Rechungpa! Before you have reached the Ultimate Realization, it would be far better for you to stay with me and not go away. Now listen to this song":

Listen, Rechung Dorjedrapa,
The well-learned Buddhist scholar.
Listen, and think with care on what I say.

Before faith and yearning arise for Dharma,
Beg not alms for mere enjoyment.
Before you have realized primordial
Truth, boast not of your sublime philosophy.
Before you have fully mastered the Awareness
Within, engage not in blind and foolish acts.
Before you can feed on the Instructions,
Involve not yourself in wicked occultism.
Before you can explain the profound Teaching,
Be not beguiled by partial knowledge.
Before you can increase your merits,
Dispute not over others' goods.
Before you can destroy your inner cravings,
Treat not charity as if it were your right.
Before you can stop projecting habitual thoughts,
Guess not when you make predictions.
Before you have gained Supreme Enlightenment,
Assume not that you are a venerable Lama.
Before you can master all virtues and practices,
Consider not leaving your Guru.
Son Rechungpa, it is better not to go, but stay!

[In spite of the Jetsun's attempted dissuasion], Rechungpa was still bent on going. Milarepa then said, "It seems that you will not take my advice, but have made up your mind to leave. Well, although once I promised our patrons not to let you go to Weu, and swore to it, all oaths are like phantoms and dreams. So I will now grant your request and let you go. You may make your preparations at once."

Rechungpa was so delighted that he almost cried. He then stayed with the Jetsun for a few more days to learn more Pith-Instructions and to copy some scriptures.

At the time of his departure, Rechungpa dressed very simply in a cotton robe. He put the Ahru [drug?] of Bhamen and the trident on his back, put the Scripture of the Whispered Succession under his arm, and came to the Jetsun for his farewell blessing.

Milarepa thought, "Rechungpa has lived with me for such a long time! After this separation we may never meet again." [With this thought in his mind] he escorted Rechungpa for a distance. When they came to the crest of a hill, he asked, "How will you walk on your way?" Rechungpa sang in answer:

Using the Dharma View as a simile,

I walk forward in the Manifestation-Void.
With no thought of Nihilism or Realism, I walk ahead;
Following the immutable Path, I walk straight on.
Though my understanding may be poor, I have no regret.

Using the Dharma Practice as a simile,
I march forward in the Bliss-Illumination.
Neither drowsy nor distracted, I march ahead;
Following the Path of Light, I march straight on.
Though my practice may be poor, I have no regret.

Using the Dharma Action as a simile,
I walk forward in the Discipline.
Without foolish talk, I walk ahead;
Following the Path of Non-clinging, I walk straight on.
Though my action may be poor, I have no regret.

Using the Dharma of Samaya as a simile,
I walk forward in Purity. Without
Hypocrisy and circumvention, I walk ahead;
In the Path of Straightforwardness, I walk straight on.
Though my discipline may be poor, I have no regret.

Using the Accomplishment of Dharma as a simile,
I march forward in Immanence.
Without fear and hope, I march ahead;
In the Path of the Four Bodies, I march straight on.
Though my accomplishment may be small, I have no regret.

Using the Jetsun Marpa as a simile,
I walk forward in the Whispered Lineage.
Without talk and words, I walk ahead; following
The Path of Pith-Instruction, I walk straight on.
Though my spiritual provision is meager, I have
    no regret.

Using my Guru Milarepa as a simile,
I march forward in Fortitude. Without
Laziness and sloth, I march ahead;
In the Path of Diligence, I march straight on.
Though my perseverance may be small, I have no regret.

Using myself, Rechungpa, as a simile,

I walk forward in the way of the Gifted Ones.
Without deviation and wrong thoughts, I walk ahead;
In the Path of Veneration, I walk straight on.
Though my prayer may be feeble, I have no regret.

"Your understanding is very good," Milarepa replied, "But you should know that a child grows better with its mother, an egg ripens quicker in a warm place, and a yogi will never go astray if he lives with his Guru. Now you will not listen to my advice but insist upon going away. With my pity and love I will never forsake you. You should also pray constantly to me."

When Rechungpa heard these words, he shed many tears. Then he said, "I shall never, at any time, lose the faith and conviction that my Jetsun is Buddha Himself; so far, I have had no other Guru but you; hereafter, before I attain perfect Buddhahood, I will look to no other Guru. In the state of Bardo after this life, please also protect and escort me." Whereupon he sang:

Pray, my Buddha Guru, the e'er compassionate one,
Pray escort your son, Rechungpa!

When I climb the mountain of the *View*,
I see the traps of Realism and Nihilism,
The bandits of bigotry in ambush,
And the "twin roads" steep and perilous.
Pray, my Father Guru, Buddha's Nirmāṇakāya,
Pray escort and protect me
Until I reach Perfection's Road.

When I climb the mountain of *Practice*, I see
The snares of drowsiness and distraction,
The perilous passage of constraint,[3]
And the danger of misleading, wandering thoughts.
Pray, my Father Guru, Buddha's Nirmāṇakāya,
Pray escort and protect me
Until I reach Non-being's Plain.

When I climb the mountain of *Action*,
I see my old companion, desire,
Debauchery's perilous path,
And the strong robber, frivolity.
Pray, my Father Guru, Buddha's Nirmāṇakāya,
Pray escort and protect me until I reach

The pass of Freedom and Spontaneity!

When I build the Castle of Samaya,
I see my knowledge is insufficient,
That my assistant is incompetent,
And that great are the dangers of discordance.
Pray, my Father Guru, the Buddha's Nirmāṇakāya,
Pray escort and protect me until I reach
The pure base of Non-existence!

When I reflect on the Accomplishment,
I can see the long road of Saṃsāra,
The perilous passage to Nirvāṇa,
And the savage bandits of hope and fear.
Pray, my Father Guru, the Buddha's Nirmāṇakāya,
Pray escort and protect me until
I reach the home of the Four Bodies.

Great is Rechungpa's wish for travel,
Great his desire for pleasure and for comfort.
People in Tibet are impious;
The thief of hypocrisy
Is ready now to act.
Pray, my Father Guru, Buddha's Nirmāṇakāya,
Pray escort and protect me until
I return home from my journey!

"For your auspicious and successful trip," said the Jetsun, "I shall
sing you in farewell":

Do you know what my Transmission
Is? It is not bad, but good;
It is the Transmission of Dorje-Chang.
May it bring good fortune and success!
May my son Rechungpa be blessed with [good] luck.

Do you know who my Patron Buddha
Is? She is not bad, but good;
She is the holy Dorje Paumo.
May she bring good fortune and success!
May my son Rechungpa be blessed with [good] luck.

Do you know who are my Guards?

They are not bad, but good. They are
The Ma Goun Brothers and Sisters.
May they bring good fortune and success!
May my son Rechungpa be blessed with [good] luck.

May the View, the Practice, and the Action
All bless you, my son Rechungpa!
May the Principle, the Path, and the Accomplishment
All bless you, my son Rechungpa!
May the Tsa, the Lun, and the Tig Le[4]
All bless you, my son Rechungpa!
May the Bliss, the Illumination, and Non-thought
All bless you, my son Rechungpa!

Most true is the Buddha, most true
The Dharma and the Saṅgha.
May these three Gems bless you
Forever, my son Rechungpa!

Do you know who I am?
I am called Milarepa.
May all Mila's blessings fall upon his son,
May Rechungpa soon exceed his father.

The Jetsun continued, "In Central Tibet [Weu] a bitch will 'catch'
your feet. At that time do not forget your Guru and your meditation."

Rechungpa circled and prostrated before the Jetsun many times,
and then set out on his journey. In the meantime, Milarepa thought,
"Rechungpa will probably look back at me. If I do not stay here, he
will be very disappointed when he finds me gone. I had better remain
for a while." So he sat down, but Rechungpa never turned his head.
Milarepa wondered, "Why does he not look back? Does he have any
wrong ideas about his Guru and his brothers? At any rate, he is a
man who can keep the Dharma and the Succession secret wherever
he goes." Then, holding his breath, Milarepa [flew ahead] and over-
taking Rechungpa, transformed himself into seven identical Repas
standing before a huge rock shaped like a rearing lion. In order to test
Rechungpa's intention, the seven Repas all sang together:

Listen, Repa traveler! Who
Are you and who is your Guru?
Who are your forebears, what

Instructions do you know?
Which is your Transmission, what
Meditation do you practice?
Where's your temple, what's this mountain?
Can you name this rock?
Whither are you bound,
By who's order do you travel,
And in what way do you go?

Rechungpa thought, "No other Repa would say things like this to
me; they must be the transformations of the Jetsun." He then prostrated himself before the Repas and sang:

Hear me, my great Jetsun Father!
You ask who I am. My name
Is Rechungpa from Gung Tang;
My Guru is Milarepa,
My forebears, Marpa and Ngopa,[5]
My great-grandfathers, Tilopa and Nāropa,
My Instructions are of the Ḍākinīs' Whispered
      Lineage,
My Transmission was founded by Dorje-Chang,
My hermitage is on Lashi Snow Mountain.
This hill is Biling Zurkha, this rock
Is known as the Great Rearing Lion,
The place to which I go is Weu,
My Jetsun Guru gave me leave.
This is the story of my journey.
I pray you, Jetsun, for instructions.

Milarepa then withdrew all the transformation bodies into the real
one and said, "I did this to find out why you did not even look back
at me after you left. Now I know that you have not violated the
Samaya precepts. Since you have observed them properly, we will
never separate from each other. You may now proceed to Weu."

Overjoyed at these words, Rechungpa bowed down at the Jetsun's
feet and made many good wishes. Then he set out for Weu, and the
Jetsun returned to the Belly Cave.

That day, some patrons came with food and offerings. But as soon
as they learned that Rechungpa had left, they hid all the things they
had brought for him in a brass basin in the recesses of a cave. Then
they came to Milarepa's abode and found that he was already up.

They asked, "Revered Jetsun, usually you do not get up so early. What made you do so today?" Milarepa replied, "Rechungpa left for Weu this morning, and I went down to the plain to see him off. Upon my return I felt a little sad, and I have been sitting here ever since."

"Did you, Revered Jetsun, ever try to stop him from going to Weu?"

"Yes, I did." Whereupon Milarepa sang:

> Rechungpa, my beloved son, has left
> For Weu. He never follows the advice
> Of others but acts as he wishes.
>
> He said that he would visit Marpa
> And Ngopa's temple, see Loro,
> Nyal, and the Samye Chapel,
> And circle the holy Lhasa.
>
> I advised him thus:
> "When you put all your trust in your Guru,
> What is the need for Jowo Shagja?[6]
> When you meditate in a solitary retreat,
> Why go to see Marpa and Ngopa's temple?
> When you have learned the Whispered Lineage's
> Instruction, why visit Loro and Nyal?
> When you can amuse yourself by watching
> The play of your own Dharmakāya Mind,
> What need have you to see Samye Chapel?
> When you have destroyed all your wrong ideas,
> What need have you to circle Lhasa?
> I repeat, Rechungpa
> Our beloved, has gone to Weu.
> Had you, good patrons, then been here
> You might by circling round have stopped him.

"When a Guru grows old," said the patrons, "it is the primary duty of his disciple to attend him. Your Reverence has gone to every length to dissuade him, but still he would not listen. He is indeed shameless, with little consideration for other people." Milarepa replied pretendingly, "Yes, Rechungpa had no shame and no discipline." Then he sang:

> A son fostered, loved, and cherished
> Seldom cares for his old parents.

Out of a hundred men 'tis hard
To find an exception.

An undisciplined disciple seldom
Helps his Guru when he grows old.
Out of a hundred men 'tis hard
To find an exception.

A lion white, he went to Weu; I was left
Behind abandoned like an old dog.
Yes, my son has left me for Weu.
Like a young tiger who forsakes
The fox, he went to Weu.

Yes, he has left his old father and gone to Weu.
Like a great vulture who forsakes
A cock, he went to Weu.

As a superb steed of Dochin
Leaves the asses from Jungron,
My son has left his old father and gone to Weu!

Like a wild and blue-horned yak
Deserting an elephant,
My son has left his old father and gone to Weu.

With body handsomer than a Deva's,
He went to Weu.
With voice mellower than an angel's
He went to Weu.
With words sweeter than all music,
He went to Weu.
With mind brighter than embroidery,
He went to Weu.
Smelling more fragrant than [good] incense,
He went to Weu!

The patrons then said, "Revered Jetsun, you are indeed most compassionate toward him. On such a long, hard journey you must have
provided a companion for him and made all necessary preparations
for his trip. Please tell us all about it." In answer, Milarepa sang:

He was well escorted when he went.

In time friends are always separated,
But Rechungpa's friend will never leave him;
She is self-arising Wisdom. My son
Rechungpa left with a fine friend.

Even good horses sometimes stumble,
But Rechungpa's will ne'er miss a step.
Riding the steed of Prāṇa-Mind,
Riding on it, he set out for Weu.

Clothes at times are warm, at others cold,
But what Rechungpa wears is always warm,
For it is the blazing Dumo. Wearing
This superb dress, he left for Weu.

Food is sometimes good, and sometimes nasty,
But what Rechungpa eats is tasty at all times,
For it is the savory dish of Samādhi.
With this fine food, he has gone to Weu.

Jewels are the aim of thieves,
But Rechungpa's gems can ne'er be stolen,
For they are the wish-fulfilling Instructions of
        the Whispered Lineage.
With these precious jewels, he has left for Weu.

While singing this song, Milarepa appeared a little sad. The patrons said, "Since Rechungpa has left you without showing the slightest affection, you, Jetsun, should also forget about him. Besides, Shiwa Aui, Sevan Repa, and many other disciples are still here. They can attend you just as well." "Yes," replied the Jetsun, "there are many Repas, but one like Rechungpa is hard to find. There may be many patrons, but it is difficult to find one with true faith. Please listen to my song":

The Nyan Chung Repa of Gung Tang,
The Ngan Tson Dewa Shun of Jenlun,
The Sevan Jashi Bar of Dodra,
And the Drigom Linkawa of Dhamo —
These are the four sons
I cherish as my heart.
Of them Rechung, my long-time
Companion is most dear.[7]
I think of him and miss him much now he has gone.

The word-conditioned "View" is nominal.
Though people call it "View,"
'Tis but a word.
It is most hard to find a man who can
Cease to be distracted by Duality;
It is most hard to find a man who can
Absorb himself in the sole Realization!

The "Practice" that cannot widen
The mind is nominal.
Though people call it "Practice,"
'Tis but a form of Dhyāna.[8]
It is most hard to find a man
Who can merge both Dhyāna and "Insight";
It is most hard to find a man who knows
How to work on the vital point of mind.

When the mind's "Action" is now dark,
Now light, it is but nominal.
Though people call it "Action,"
'Tis a deed of involvement.
It is most hard to find a man
Who can conquer worldly desires;
It is very hard to find a man
Who can complete the Dharma practice.

Observance of discipline when feigned
And artificial is but nominal.
Though people call it "Discipline,"
'Tis nought but mockery.
It is most hard to find a man
Who never violates his oath;
It is very hard to find
An honest witness of his mind.

"Accomplishment" when longed for hard
Is a notion [cherished by fools].
Though people call it "Accomplishment,"
'Tis nothing but delusion.
It is most difficult to find a man
Who can plumb the abyss of Reality;
It is most hard to find a man
Who on the real Path can stay.

The Pith-Instructions may seem
Most profound on paper;
They are but written words.
It is difficult to find a man
With diligence and perseverance;
It is most hard to find a man
With direct teachings from a Lineage.

The Gurus who involve themselves
In worldly life are nominal;
They only bring entanglements.
Small are people's faith and veneration.
It is most difficult to find a man
Ever relying on an accomplished Guru.

The merits of ostentatious faith
And veneration are nominal,
For they change and are short-lived.
Where Karma's bad prejudice is strong,
It is hard to find a man
Who fears and cares for nothing.
It is most hard to find a man
With the Three Determinations.[9]

The small temple on the outskirts
Of a town is but nominal.
Though people call it "Temple,"
It is really part of "town."
Always there is great craving for
Amusement and distraction.
It is most hard to find a man
Staying long in hermitages.

The head of a restrained young monk
Is stiff and hard like stone.
Though people call him "disciplined,"
He is but acting in a play.
It is hard to find a man with perseverance,
It is hard to find another
Observing the strict priestly rules.

The handsome belles of Nya Non
As patrons are but nominal,

For they are deceivers and seducers.
Poor and low is woman's comprehension.
Hard indeed is it to find a patron
To serve one and make all the offerings.

The faiths of evil-doers are in their mouths;
The faiths of you patrons are in your private parts.
I, the Yogi, in my heart have faith.

When a rock grows old
Grime encrusts its face;
When a stream grows old
Wrinkles cover its bed.
When a tree grows old
Its leaves soon fall off.
When a hermitage grows old
Water and plantains disappear.
When a yogi ages, his Experience
And his Realization dimmer grow.
When patrons grow old
Their faith soon wears out.

Some patrons are like peacocks
Who pretend and swagger.
Some patrons are like parrots
Gossiping and gabbling.
Some patrons are like cows —
They think you a calf or goat.

My patrons, it is getting late,
It is time for you to go.
Besides, in the cave beneath,
The sack of flour in the bowl
By mice is being nibbled;
The cake of butter has been tossed
And is now rolling on the ground;
The vixen has upset the wine,
The crows have scattered all the meat,
So run fast and hurry [home].
Patrons I will vow to see you soon.
In a happy mood you may leave me now.

The visiting patrons were nonplused. They looked at one another timidly, and nudged each others' elbows. Too filled with shame to say a word, they all went home. As the Jetsun had unmistakably exposed the truth, they felt guilt and deep regret; but also, as a result, their faith in him was firmly established.

One day they came again and brought excessive offerings, saying, "Please sing for us to awaken our insight into the transiency of beings." Milarepa would not accept their offerings, but he sang this for them:

> Hearken, you mean patrons!
> For the sake of fame to do
> Meritorious deeds —
> For this life's sake to seek
> The protection of Buddha —
> To give alms for the sake
> Of returns and dividends —
> To serve and offer for the sake
> Of vanity and pride —
> These four ways will ne'er requite one.
>
> For the sake of gluttony
> To hold a sacramental feast —
> For the sake of egotism
> To strive for Sūtra learning —
> For distraction and amusement
> To indulge in foolish talk and song —
> For vainglory's sake to give
> The Initiations —
> These four ways will never bring one Blessings!
>
> If for love of preaching one expounds
> Without the backing of Scripture;
> If through self-conceit,
> One accepts obeisance;
> If like a bungling, fumbling fool one teaches,
> Not knowing the disciple's capacity;
> If to gather money one behaves
> Like a Dharma practicer —
> These four ways can never help the welfare of
>   sentient beings!
>
> To prefer diversions to solitude,
> To love pleasures and hate hardship,

To crave for talk when urged to meditate,
To wallow arrogantly in the world —
These four ways will ne'er bring one to Liberation!

This is the song of Fourfold Warning.
Dear patrons, bear it in your minds!

Drigom Repa, who was present, besought the Jetsun to preach still more of the Dharma. In response, Milarepa sang:

The long-lived heavenly beings above
Are hostile to Awareness when arising.
They are ever eager for Dhyāna of No-thought.

The hungry ghosts beneath, not knowing
That they are hunted by the mind's projections,
Resent their pillagers with jealousy and avarice.
Because of their evil Karma,
They are pressed by thirst and hunger.

In between are we poor miserable humans.
Not knowing the golden treasure underground,
From our fellow men we steal and cheat.
The more we cheat and deceive,
The more suffering we have to bear.

The foolish and "enterprising" patrons
Of Nya Non acquire no merits through the Jetsun,
But make offerings to young, handsome Repas.
Yet remorse and shame are all their alms will bring.
Enterprises so wrong and meaningless should cease,
So give your services and offerings to the Buddhas!

Their faith confirmed, the patrons all bowed down to the Jetsun many times and shed many tears. "Oh Revered Jetsun!" they cried, "We beg you to remain here permanently. From now on we will give our offerings and services in accordance with the teaching of Dharma." Milarepa replied, "I cannot stay here long, but I will bestow the blessing of long life and good health upon all of you. Also I will make a wish that we meet again under auspicious circumstances conducive to the Dharma." Then he sang:

In the immense blue sky above

Roll on the sun and moon. Their
Courses mark the change of time.
Blue sky, I wish you health and fortune,
For I, the moon-and-sun, am leaving
To visit the Four Continents for pleasure.

On the mountain peak is a great Rock
Round which oft the vulture circles,
The king of birds. Their meeting
And their parting mark the change of time.
Dear rock, be well and healthy, for I,
The vulture, now will fly away
Into the vast space for pleasure.
May lightnings never strike you,
May I not be caught by snares.
Inspired by the Dharma,
May we soon meet again
In prosperity and boon.

Below in the Tsang River,
Swim fish with golden eyes;
Their meeting and their parting
Mark the change of time.
Dear stream, be well and healthy, for I, the fish
Am leaving for the Ganges for diversion.
May irrigators never drain you,
May fishermen ne'er net me.
Inspired by the Dharma,
May we soon meet again
In prosperity and boon.

In the fair garden blooms the flower, Halo;
Circling round it is the Persian bee.
Their meeting and their parting
Mark the change of time.
Dear flower, be well and healthy, for I
Will see the Ganges' blooms for pleasure.
May hail not beat down upon you,
May winds blow me not away.
Inspired by the Dharma,
May we soon meet again
In prosperity and boon.

Circling round the Yogi Milarepa
Are the faithful patrons from Nya Non;
Their meeting and their parting
Mark the change of time.
Be well and healthy, dear patrons, as I
Leave for the far mountains for diversion.
May I, the Yogi, make good progress,
And you, my patrons, all live long.
Inspired by the Dharma,
May we soon meet again
In prosperity and boon!

Moved by this song, some patrons became devoted followers of the Jetsun, and the faith of all was greatly strengthened.

During his journey to Weu, Rechungpa came to the Buddhist Study Center at Sha, and was appointed a Mindrol Professor[10] there. Then he met, and formed an attachment to a certain noblewoman, but through the grace of the Jetsun became ashamed of his conduct and returned to Milarepa to live with him again. The details of this episode are clearly given in the Biography of Rechungpa.

This is the story of Rechungpa's journey to Weu.

NOTES

1 Jo Shag (T.T.: Jo.Çak., an abbreviation of Jo.Wo.Çakya.): the holy images to which many Tibetans make pilgrimages.

2 The Path of Tantra, which is full of ingenious instructions and Mantras or secret words.

3 This is a free translation. The text reads: "dMigs.gTad.Sa.hPhrañ.Dam.Pa. Dañ....." "dMigs.gTad." literally does not mean "constraint," but "[adherently] facing the object," i.e., the constant pursuing of objects in the outside world by the consciousness.

4 Tsa, Lun, Tig Le (T.T.: rTsa.rLuñ.Thig.Le.; Skt.: Nādi, Prāna, [and] Bindu), i.e., the nerves, the breathing, and the semen.

5 Ngopa: Milarepa's other Guru. See W. Y. Evans-Wentz' "Tibet's Great Yogi, Milarepa," Chapters 5 and 6.

6 Jowo Shagja (T.T: Jo.Wo.Çakya.): See Note 1.

7 Rechungpa was Milarepa's closest disciple, who had spent most of his lifetime living with the Jetsun. See Story 10.

8 Dhyāna is an equivalent of Samādhi. According to Buddhist tradition, it is but a state of mental concentration.

9 Presumably these Three Determinations are: (1) to determine to rest one's mind on the Dharma, (2) to rest Dharma on poverty, and (3) to rest poverty on death.

10 Mindrol Professor (T.T.: mKhan.Po.sMin.Grol.): "sMin.Grol." is the name of a monastery.

THE MEETING WITH
DHAMPA SANGJE

Obeisance to all Gurus

E ARLY one morning when the Jetsun Milarepa was staying at the
Belly Cave of Nya Non, he had a clear vision of a Ḍākinī with
a lion face, who came to him and said, "Milarepa, the Dhampa Sangje
of India is coming to Tong Lha. Are you not going to see him?"
Milarepa thought, "There is no doubt or discomfort in my mind that
needs dispelling. However, Dhampa Sangje is an accomplished being,
and it would do no harm for me to see him." With this thought in
mind, Milarepa held his breath for a [short] period and went to
Tong Lha of Nya Non.

In the mountain pass he met a few merchants who had just come
from the plain below. Milarepa asked them, "Has the Dhampa Sangje
of India arrived yet?"

"We don't know who the Dhampa Sangje is," they replied, "but
last night we saw an old Indian with a bluish-black face, who was
sleeping at the inn." The Jetsun thought, "This must be he, but
these merchants do not know." He then proceeded to the top of the
mountain pass, from whence he saw Dhampa Sangje approaching.

While staying overnight in the Guest House of Compassion, Dhampa Sangje, also, had been persuaded by the Ḍākinī with the lion face
to meet the Jetsun. As soon as Milarepa saw him, he thought, "People say that Dhampa Sangje has the Transcendental Miraculous Power. I shall now test him." He then transformed himself into a clump
of flowers growing beside the road. Dhampa Sangje passed by the
flowers with his eyes widely open as if he did not see them at all.
Milarepa thought, "It seems that he does not have the Perfect Miraculous Power!" But just then Dhampa Sangje turned back. Approaching the flowers, he kicked them with his foot and said, "I ought not

606

do this — this is the transformation of Milarepa." Having spoken these words, he picked the flowers and addressed them: "You have been singing all the precious teachings that are cherished by Ḍākinīs as their very lives and hearts, and so they all became angry. The flesh-eating Ḍākinīs have thus taken your heart, breath, and spirit away from you. Last night I met them and saw that they had carried your bleeding heart away [in their hands]. We then ate it during our sacramental feast, so that you can only live until this evening. Now tell me, what confidence do you have in facing death?" In reply, the Jetsun suddenly arose from his transformation, and sang a song called "The Six Assurances on Facing Death":

> The great Liberation from Extremes
> Is like a gallant lion lying
> In the snow at ease, displaying
> Without fear its fangs.
> In this View do I, the Yogi, trust.
> Death leads to the Liberation Path!
> Death brings joy to he who holds this View!
>
> The stag calm and magnanimous
> Has horns of "One Taste" with many points.
> He sleeps in comfort on the plain of Bliss-Light.
> In this practice do I, the Yogi, trust.
> Death leads to the Liberation Path!
> Death brings joy to he who practices!
>
> The fish of Ten Virtues
> With rolling, golden eyes,
> Swims in the River of Perpetual Experience.
> In this action do I, the Yogi, trust.
> Death leads to the Liberation Path!
> Death brings joy to he who acts!
>
> The tigress of Self-mind Realization
> Is adorned with showy stripes.
> She is the glory of Altruism-without-
> Effort, walking firmly in the woods.
> In this discipline do I, the Yogi, trust.
> Death leads to the Liberation Path!
> Death brings joy to those with Discipline!
>
> On the paper of forms Postive-and-Negative

I wrote an essay with my "awaring" mind.
In the state of Non-duality
I watch and contemplate.
In this Dharma do I, the Yogi, trust.
Death leads to the Liberation Path!
Death brings joy to those with Dharma!

The purified quintessence of the Moving
Energy is like a great eagle flying
On wings of Skill and Wisdom
To the castle of Non-being.
In this Accomplishment do I, the Yogi, trust.
Death leads to the Liberation Path!
Death brings joy to the accomplished man!

Dhampa Sangje replied, "What you have said has no reason at all. You cannot use things in the outer world as parables [or parallels] to compare with the true Realization. If you were a real yogi you would know this *immediate Awareness* in a decisive and unmistakable manner." [In answer to his challenge] Milarepa sang a song called "The Six Positive Joys of the Mind."

In the solitary retreat
Where Ḍākinīs always gather,
I contemplate the Dharma
In great ease and joy.

To the ego-killing Bha Wo,
I pay my sincere homage.
Absorbing in the Void my mind,
I reach the Realm of Immortality,
Where death and birth vanish of themselves.
Happy is my mind with a decisive View —
Happy and joyful as I gain supremacy!

Absorbing myself in the Practice-without-Practice,
I reach the Realm of No-distraction,
Where the Main and Ensuing Samādhis vanish of
    themselves.
Happy is my mind with the decisive Practice —
Happy and joyful as I gain supremacy!

Living in full spontaneity and naturalness,

I achieve the state of Unceasing, in which
All forms of discipline vanish of themselves.
Happy is my mind with the Ultimate Action —
Happy and joyful as I attain supremacy!

Absorbing myself in the Realm of No-initiation,
I achieve the state of No-attainment;
All forms of Buddha's Body vanish of themselves.
Happy is my mind with the Ultimate Initiation —
Happy and joyful as I attain supremacy!

Absorbing myself in the Realm of No-discipline,
I attain the state of No-transgression;
All forms of Precept vanish of themselves.
Happy is my mind with the Ultimate Discipline —
Happy and joyful as I gain supremacy!

Without hope for accomplishment
I achieve the state of No-fear;
Hopes and fears vanish of themselves.
Happy is my mind with the Ultimate Accomplishment —
Happy and joyful as I gain supremacy!

Dhampa Sangje commented, "I, also, have gone through all you have just said. A Buddhist who needs no more practice or improvement has now been found in Tibet! It is very difficult, even in India, to find one or two advanced Buddhists comparable to you. I do not need you, and you do not need me."

Having said these words in a pleasant manner, he turned and was about to go away. Milarepa immediately caught hold of his robe, saying, "It is said that you have a teaching called 'Relieving all Sorrows,' [1] and that in practicing it one reverses his mind inwardly, thus instantaneously realizing the Buddha's Mind. Now please explain it to me in a song." Dhampa Sangje replied, "So far, no one has ever heard me sing, and no one will." However, the Jetsun asked him so persistently that finally Dhampa Sangje sang:

This is the Dharma called "Relieving All Sorrows":

When demons come to harm you is the time
To apply your Occult Powers.
When pain and sickness strike you is the time
To merge them with your intrinsic Awareness.

Whenever subtle Nhamdogs rise
It is time to stir the passions
And transcend them.

When lying in a hidden place alone,
Is the time to rest one's naked Awareness.
When mingling with many people,
It is time to bring all to the
View. When comes drowsiness
It is time to use the bīja Pai.[2]
When distracting thoughts arise,
It is time to lead them to the Real.
When the mind runs after worldly things,
'Tis time to observe the truth of Suchness.

In short, this teaching of Relieving Sorrows
Turns all adversities into good fortune.
Whatever wild thoughts rise, you feel but joy.
Whenever illness comes, you use it as your aid;
Whatever you encounter, you feel but happiness.
Whene'er death comes, you utilize it for the Path.
This teaching of Relieving Sorrows is the Dharma
Of all Buddhas in the Three Times —
It is the instruction given by Dorje-Chang,
The life and heart of all Ḍākinīs in the Four
          Divisions;[3]
It is the pith of the Tantras Four,[4]
The quintessential Dharma of the Whispered Lineage,
The key of all Essential Teachings!
Such is the teaching of "Relieving All Sorrows"!

Milarepa listened to this song with great delight as he sat to one side with his penis freely exposed. Dhampa Sangje remarked, "You are like a lunatic who neglects to cover up the place that should be covered." In reply, the Jetsun sang "The Song of a Lunatic":

To all Gurus I pay my homage.
I take refuge in the Gracious One,
I pray you, dispel my hindrances;
Bring me to the right Path, I pray.

Men say, "Is not Milarepa mad?"

I also think it may be so.
Now listen to my madness.

The father and the son are mad,
And so are the Transmission
And Dorje-Chang's Succession.
Mad too were my Great-grandfather, the Fair Sage,
    Tilopa,[5]
And my Grandfather, Nāropa the great scholar.
Mad, too, was my Father, Marpa the Translator;
So too is Milarepa.

The demon of the intrinsic Bodies Four
Makes Dorje-Chang's Succession crazy;
The devil of the Mahāmudrā made
My Great-grandfather Tilopa crazy;
The demon of the secret Awareness
Made my Grandfather Nāropa crazy;
The devil of the Tantras Four
Made my Father Marpa mad;
The demons of Mind and Prāṇa
Have driven me, Milarepa, mad.

The impartial Understanding itself is crazy;
So are the free, self-liberating Actions,
The self-illuminating Practice of No-perception,
The Accomplishment-without-Hope-and-Fear,
And Discipline-without-Pretension.

Not only am I mad myself,
I madly afflict the demons.
With the Gurus' Pith-Instruction
I punish all male demons;
With the blessing of Ḍākinīs
I harrow female demons;
With the he-devil of Happy Mind
I enter the Ultimate;
With the she-devil of Instantaneous
Realization I perform all acts.

Not only do I punish demons,
I also suffer pains and sickness —
The Great Symbol hurts my back,

The Great Perfection afflicts my chest.
In practicing the Vase-breathing,
I catch all kinds of sickness —
The fever of Wisdom attacks me from above,
The cold of Samādhi invades me from below,
The cold-fever of the Bliss-Void assails me in
      the middle.
From my mouth I vomit the blood of Pith-Instructions;
Lazily I stretch, thrilled by the Dharma-Essence.

I have many sicknesses,
And many times have died.
Dead are my prejudices
In the [vast] sphere of the View.
All my distractions and drowsiness
Have died in the sphere of Practice.
My pretensions and hypocrisy
Have died in the sphere of Action.
Dead are all my fears and hopes
In the sphere of Accomplishment,
And my affectations and pretenses
In the sphere of Precepts. I, the Yogi,
Will die in Trikāya's Realm.

Tomorrow when this yogi dies
No fair shroud will he see,
But the subtle, divine Revelations.
His corpse will not be bound by hempen rope,
But by the cord of the Central Channel.
His corpse-bearers to the cemetery
Will not be nose-wiping sons,
But his blessed Son-of-Awareness.
Not by the gray, earthy road,
But along the Bodhi-Path
The [funeral parade] will go.

The Gurus of the Whispered Lineage will lead
      the way;
The Ḍākinīs of the Four Divisions will be the
      guides;
The corpse will not be brought
To the red and massive hill,
But to the Hill of Ādi Buddha;

The corpse will not be carried
To the cemetery where foxes play,
But to the Park of Skill and Wisdom;
It will be buried only
In the Grave of Dorje-Chang.

Dhampa Sangje was greatly pleased by this song. He said, "Your kind of craziness is very good." The Jetsun replied, "Since we two yogis have now met, it would be appropriate for us to have a sacramental feast together."

"Well, since you are a Tibetan, you should play the part of host," commented Dhampa Sangje, "you be the first to prepare the feast." Milarepa then removed his skull with the brain inside, and, cutting off his forearms and neck, used them to build a hearth. Then he put the skull upon the hearth. From his navel he ejected the Dumo Fire to heat the skull, and then the brain began to emit five-colored rays in all directions. Dhampa Sangje transformed himself into seven bodies standing upon seven stalks of grass, and Milarepa also transformed his body into seven [Maṇḍalas] of Dem Chog, complete with the Eight Gates, etc., upon the tips of seven stalks of grass. In each of the Maṇḍalas Buddha Dem Chog was offered the sacramental feast with six wondrous enjoyments.[6]

The grasses upon which Milarepa's transformed bodies stood were slightly bent [as if by the weight of the load]. The Jetsun then said to Dhampa Sangje, "As to proficiency in the Vase-breathing Practice, there is no difference between you and me. Why, then, is the grass [upon which I stand] slightly bent?" Dhampa Sangje replied, "There is no difference between my Realization[7] and yours. This is simply due to the fact that you were born a Tibetan. Your Views and Actions are identical with mine, therefore both the disciples in your Lineage and in mine will see eye to eye in their practices and understandings."

By their magic powers Milarepa and Dhampa Sangje then returned to their own abodes.

This is the story of Tong Lha.

NOTES

1 The Instruction, or Dharma of Relieving All Sorrows (T.T.: Dam.Chos.sDug. bsÑal.Shi.Byed.).

2 Bija Pai: Bija is the seed-word of a Mantra. For Pai, see Story 14, Note 4.

3 These four divisions are probably the East, South, West, and North of the Maṇḍala.

4 The Four Tantras are: Kriya-tantra, Carya-tantra, Yoga-tantra and Anut-tara-tantra.

5 The text reads: "Yañ.Mes.Te.Lo.Çer.bZañ.sMyo." "Çer.bZañ" is perhaps the abbreviation of dGe.Wahi.bÇes.gÑen.bZañ.Po., meaning the good sage or good teacher.

6 This probably refers to the six different tastes: sour, sweet, bitter, pungent, salty, and aromatic; it can also refer to the six sexual attractions arising from color, form, carriage, voice, smoothness, and features.

7 Lit.: "There is no difference between your accomplishments in Realization and Purification, and mine."

༄༈

54

THE SALVATION
OF THE DEAD

Obeisance to all Gurus

WHEN the Jetsun Milarepa was dwelling at the Belly Cave of Nya Non, many followers of Bon were living nearby in a place called La Shin. In the vicinity of La Shin there also dwelt a very rich man who, [although born a Bon] was a devoted Buddhist and, being a patron of the Jetsun, never patronized any Bon monk. He had been initiated with the Pith-Instructions by Milarepa, and also practiced them.

One day this man caught a fatal illness, which brought him to the point of death. Planning to make his last will and testament, he summoned all his relatives and said to them, "For my salvation's sake, please offer all my properties and belongings to the Jetsun Milarepa and his disciples. You have all been followers of Bon, but I hope you will become Buddhists and practice the beneficial Dharma in your next lives."

But his relatives would not follow his instructions. Fearing that they would never invite the Jetsun to visit him, the man said to his daughter, "Why do you people stab a dying man in the heart? If you do not follow my wishes and instructions, I will kill myself. Then you will be condemned by all!"

Hearing these words, they gave in, and consented to do what he wished. The man then requested, "Do not perform any Bon rite-for-the-dead for me — it is nominal and useless. But please invite the Jetsun to come for my sake!" Thus saying, he died.

In accordance with the deceased's wish, the Jetsun and his disciples were invited to the house. They all stayed on the top floor,[1] while the Bon monks, who were also invited for the occasion, remained on the lower floor to perform their rites.

615

[While these rites were in progress, suddenly], on the base of the Bon Maṇḍala, there appeared the [unmistakable] form of the dead man. Greenish in color, with long hair, it stood there cheerfully drinking beer. Bedha [Milarepa's sister] passed by and saw it. The Bon monks said to her, "Milarepa and his followers always fight against us. But look, everyone here can witness that we Bonists have actually brought the deceased one back — Milarepa and his men could never do this!" Saying which, they jeered and laughed at the Jetsun.

Bedha then reported this incident to Milarepa, who replied, "This is not the apparition of the dead man. It is only a trick the Bonists have played to beguile people. Now, Shiwa Aui, go and grasp the apparition's ring-finger, and ask him for the name that was given him by the Jetsun Milarepa in the Belly Cave during his Initiation."

After a while Shiwa Aui returned and said, "The apparition could not withstand the Jetsun's glowing light-of-mercy. When I was just about to speak, it said, 'I am leaving now. I am the one who leads dead men's spirits for the Bonists — a ghost who comes to this world-of-appearance to make a big noise and eat human flesh. Since not the slightest benefit can be gained from the Bon teaching, I have just come here to get my wages from the Bon priests.'

"Then I chased it out," continued Shiwa Aui, "and, with its greenish face and long hair, it dashed away through the streets of the village and to the other side of the mountain, where it became a wolf."

Having witnessed this occurrence, all the people there were convinced that the apparition was not the real spirit of the dead man.

The Jetsun then said to the Bonists, "You are showing the way for a murderer, but I am showing the way for the dead man." The Bon relatives asked, "Then you, Jetsun, must be able to see him; otherwise, how could you show him the way?" Milarepa replied, "Yes, I see him. Because of some slight [bad] Karma in his former lives he was unable to complete his meritorious deeds, and has now been born as an insect. Under a lump of brownish yak dung you will find a long, slender insect — that is he. I am now going to send him to the Land of Liberation."

"To convince us, please show us how you liberate him," said the patrons.

"Very well, let us go there, and [you will] see."

All the people then went with the Jetsun [to the upper valley] where they soon came to a lump of brownish, dry dung. The Jetsun first called the man by his secret names a few times, and then said, "I am your Guru, Milarepa. Now, come out, and come here!"

From somewhere under the dung a small insect appeared, flew directly toward the Jetsun, and alighted on him. Milarepa then preached the Dharma and performed the Transformation Yoga and the Rite of Deliverance for it. [At once the insect died] and its corpse began to give out a thin, bright light, which entered and dissolved into the Jetsun's heart. Milarepa meditated for a short while, and then from his heart the dead man's consciousness emerged, embodied in a white "Ah" word glowing with brilliant light; and it ascended higher and higher to the sky. Meanwhile the people all heard its voice saying, "The precious Jetsun has now delivered me to the joy of Liberation. Oh great is his blessing! Great is his bounty!"

Having witnessed these things, all the spectators were convinced [and confirmed with] great faith. They bowed down to the Jetsun and cried, "This is marvelous! This is wonderful!"

"I have many other things even more marvelous than this," replied Milarepa. Whereupon he sang:

> I pray to my wondrous Guru, Marpa;
> I cherish his grace in my mind.
> Pray bless my disciples with your mercy.
>
> Of all marvels, the greatest is
> The first meeting with my Guru.
>
> Of all marvels, the greatest is to earn
> Instructions from the Whispered Lineage.
>
> Of all marvels, the greatest is
> To renounce all worldly things.
>
> Of all marvels the greatest is
> To stay in the hermitage.
>
> Of all marvels the greatest is the birth
> Of inner Experience and Realization.
>
> Of all marvels the greatest is
> To endure hardship in solitude.
>
> Of all marvels the greatest is
> Indifference to the Eight Worldly Gains.
>
> Of all marvels the greatest is
> To please my Guru through devotion.

Of all marvels the greatest is
The will left by the dead Bonist.

Of all marvels the greatest is
Observance of the dead man's will.

Of all marvels the greatest is
The liberation of the dead.

Of all marvels the greatest is
The growing faith in this assembly.

The relatives of the dead man all said, "Surely he did not make any mistake in choosing his faith. In order to attain Buddhahood at the time of death one should certainly do what he has done.'"

"We all need a savior like the Jetsun," said Shiwa Aui, "But it is most difficult to meet such a one and to have faith in him."

Milarepa then replied, "If you, my disciples, want to guide dead men's consciousnesses to the Path, you need these qualifications." Whereupon he sang:

Good and sure is the grace of the Whispered Lineage,
Through which one may attain the Accomplishment
    of Ḍākinīs.
My son disciples, ne'er mistake
Your Dharmic Transmission.

To cleanse the Karma of ill-fated ones,
You yourself must keep pure discipline.
To receive offerings and worship from the patrons,
You must have compassion and the Bodhi-Mind.
To be honored as the Chief Lama in the group,
You require Realization and merits.

To please the accomplished Guru, you need
Unshakable faith and perseverance.
To take the oblation for the dead, you must
Have the merit of superb Enlightenment.[2]
To emancipate the dead,
You need miraculous Power
And genuine Accomplishment.
To convert faithless men you must
Be able to work miracles.

To perform the Maṇḍala Ritual on the seventh day,
You must truly deliver
The dead man to the Path.

My disciples and patrons of the Bon,
Hold doubt in your minds no more.

The Jetsun's sister Bedha said, "Brother, you have redeemed other people's 'souls' like this, but you have done nothing to save the 'souls' of our own parents! Why?" Saying this, she sobbed bitterly. Milarepa took her hand and said, "Bedha, do not feel sad like this. To repay the bounty of our parents I have done these things for them." Then he sang:

I pray to the Jetsun Gurus — pray
Help me to repay my parents' bounties.

In guiding my parents' "souls"
Out of their phantom bodies,
I merged them with my own mind,
And dissolved them in the Mind-Essence
Of the Victorious One.
By His mercy a rainbow light
Shone forth from the Pure Land;
And into the "appearing" yet void
Buddha Kāya their bodies vanished.
How wondrous is it thus to merge
In Immanent Buddhahood.

Their voices, unreal echoes,
Were merged with Buddha's speech.
How wondrous is it thus
To merge with the Self-sound.

Their minds, in Bardo wandering,
Were caught by my Samādhi's power.
Thus thy beheld the Self-face of
The Illuminating-void Awareness.

Holding the mind in its natural state
All confusions are dispelled.
How wondrous is this state immutable.

In my life-long devotion,
With love and with good will
I recite the Mantra day and night.
By this merit my parents' sins are cleansed;
In the Six Realms they will ne'er be born again.

With holy companions, they are living now in joy;
With pleasures and enjoyment, they now live happily.
In the Pure Land of Happiness they are
Surrounded by Bha Wos and Ḍākinīs.
Dear sister Bedha, worry not nor grieve for them!

Bedha said, "This is indeed wonderful. But please tell me, what ritual did you perform for them?" In answer, Milarepa sang:

I pray to the Refuge of all beings —
Pray help me to repay my parents' bounties.

In the Maṇḍala of Non-dual Bliss
I placed the Buddha images
Of illuminating Self-awareness.

In the vase of Holy Scriptures and Instructions
I placed for rinsing, water of the Six Pāramitās.
With it I cleansed the filth of the Five Poisons.

With the Ghagyu Guru's nectar
I conferred the Four Initiations
On their bodies, mouths, and minds.
I showed them the non-distinction of Great Bliss,
And the successive Realizations of the Path.

The unity of the Trikāya
Was the oblation I made for them;
The Emancipation-from-Desires
Was the ritual I performed for their deaths.
With perfect knowledge of timing I brought
For them the offering of spiritual assistance.
For them I dedicated the Mahāmudrā,
For them I vowed to serve all [sentient beings].

My wishes, and those of parent-like beings
Are all fulfilled and merged in one.

By thinking of my Guru's grace
I repaid their bounties.

Having heard this song, Bedha was firmly convinced. To persuade his
sister to practice the Dharma with determination, Milarepa sang again:

I bow down at the feet of Marpa.
Pray quench the passions of my kinsmen,
And with the Dharma fuse their minds.

Awake and listen, sister Bedha!
If when young you do not practice,
Why practice then when you grow old?
If you depend not on the Jetsun Guru,
Why rely on pleasant Gurus?
Without the Instruction of the Whispered Lineage,
What's the use of vain talk and arid words?

If you do not know your mind,
What's the use of learning?
If in the Void you cannot rest at ease,
Vain remarks will but increase your sins.

Self-conceited people
Who always make a show
Have no experience within.
Overweening and suspicious people
See not that appearances
Are but amusing plays.

The pretentious and over-critical
Are men without compassion, faith, or Bodhi-Mind.

He who never thinks of
Buddhahood, is angry,
And anxious over money,
Cannot a real Buddhist be.

Lacking compassion for all beings,
Filial piety causes Samsāra.
If one acts against the Dharma
Friends soon turn to enemies.
Those who only harm their friends

Are of the devil's kin,
However charming they may be!

He who claims to be a yogi
But cannot practice Immanence in depth,
Is only a bewildered man.
To those who cannot patiently help others
Friendship brings only quarrels and regret.

Dear sister Bedha, your sorrow for our mother's grief
Shows that you have yet to clear
Your obstacles and sins.

The Jetsun then sent her to meditate, and as a result, she attained extraordinary Experiences and Realizations. The Jetsun was very much pleased. To inspire and encourage her, he sang again:

Listen once more, sister Bedha!
If one ne'er loses faith in Dharma,
The ending of all pain will come.
If one ne'er accuses others,
People see one as an angel.
If one has no harmful thoughts,
Then one's merits will increase.

He who clings not now to things,
Will in his next life be joyful.
One who has little arrogance,
Will be loved by all.

Whoe'er intrinsic mind retains
Will soon win through to Buddhahood.
Whoe'er retreats in strict seclusion
And refrains from talking,
By Ḍākinīs will be blessed.

If you have no desire for pleasure,
Your Ripening Karma will be killed.
If till death you meditate,
You are the King of kings!

If mind be free of fraud and tangles,
Ḍākinīs and Bha Wos receive you.

If you pray [now and always] to your Jetsun Guru
Accomplishment and blessing will be yours.

Bear these words in mind, and meditate!
May joy and good fortune e'er be with you!

[Later], Bedha was able to meditate in solitude with great perseverance. As a result she gained exceptional Experiences and Realizations, and eventually she could match the merits of the four [foremost] spiritual daughters of the Jetsun.

The Bonists who attended the ceremony on this occasion were all confirmed with irrevocable faith toward Milarepa.

This is the story of the salvation of the dead man, and of Milarepa's guiding his sister to the Bodhi [Path].

NOTES

1 Tibetan houses are usually constructed with three floors, the stable and storeroom being located on the ground floor, and the living room, kitchen, etc., on the middle floor. The prayer room, altar, and guest room usually occupy the top floor.

2 The merit of superb Enlightenment: This is a free translation. Literally it should read: "The merit of the [initial stage] of the Enlightment in the Path" (mThon.Lam.Gyi.Yon.Tan.). The initial stage, or the First Bhūmi, is considered the most important and critical stage in the Bodhisattva's Path. True Enlightenment is realized when one reaches this stage. See Story 44, Note 3.

FULFILLMENT OF THE
DĀKINĪS' PROPHECY

Obeisance to all Gurus

ONCE when the Jetsun Milarepa was dwelling in the upper valley of Tsar Ma at Nya Non, some of his patrons fought one another over the dowry of a new bride. When they came to the Jetsun for meditation he summoned all the participants, reconciled them with good advice, and preached much Dharma for them. Then he sang:

> Listen, you conceited men
> With rocks upon your heads!
> This is the sort of trouble that is caused by women
> Who for a long time have not had a man.
> Man-craving women are all trouble-makers
> Who foster only evil thoughts within.
> Wicked are the spreaders
> Of discord everywhere.
> This bride of an evil valley at an evil
> Time has become invaluable to the "blind";
> This filthy baggage has been the cause
> Of dispute among the men.
> Alas, these are unworthy, worldly acts;
> Elders, do not instigate them,
> Young men, be sane and sober.
> According to the Dharma's teaching
> Everyone here assembled
> Should try to change his mind!

Moved by this song, the disputants were all pacified. Then the lady patron Jham Mei, a very faithful follower of the Jetsun, made sumptuous offerings to him. Standing up from a row in the assembly, she asked, "Revered Jetsun, Precious One, please tell us, how have you accomplished your altruistic deeds? How many disciples do you have? And among them, how many have attained Enlightenment?" Milarepa replied, "It is very wonderful that these questions have arisen in your mind. As prophesied by the Dākinīs, I have done these things to benefit sentient beings":

> I pray to the Gurus and Dākinīs — pray
> Help me without effort to benefit all men.

> As Dākinīs foretold, like the sun
> Is the Nirmāṇakāya Dhagpo,
> Whose light will brighten all; like the moon
> Is Nirmāṇakāya Rechungpa;
> And Shiwa Aui, the elder brother,
> Is a tiger-like meditator.
> With Drigom and other Repas I have five-
> And-twenty leading disciples as foretold.

> Among my disciples, five-and-twenty are accomplished
>   beings;
> One hundred the Realization have attained;
> One hundred and eight, the Spontaneous Experience;
> Near one thousand, union with the Dharma; and more
> Than a hundred thousand have won Dharmic affiliations.
> A few disciples have
> Learned other arts from me.
> Your questions are most good,
> You are indeed well-endowed!

Hearing this, the disciples at the meeting all exclaimed, "Oh, many accomplished beings will come! How wonderful is this!" All were overwhelmed with joy and exaltation. Then they besought Milarepa to make good wishes for them. The Jetsun said, "Since this time both the receiver and the patrons are sincere, good wishes are automatically made. Nonetheless, I shall follow Buddha's example and say the dedication-wishes for you. You should now follow, and repeat this song after me":

> I pray to my Guru, Patron Buddha,
> And all gods — pray fulfill all my good wishes.
> Let all here now recite with me,

For I know the way to Buddhahood.
Pray remember me, ye Buddhas, Bodhisattvas, and
    Sanghas!

Since beginningless time in this great Saṃsāra,
I and all sentient beings have practiced
Charity, discipline, and other merits.
Thinking of them, my mind is full of joy!
To my parents and teachers I dedicate
All the merits that in this life I may have earned
In giving alms and service
To Buddhahood's attainment.
Before the [last] day comes, may I,
By the power of my merits,
Meet a Mahāyāna teacher
And observe the Precepts Three.
May all my good wishes be fulfilled,
And may I never commit sinful deeds.

By the power of my merits may I
Gain long life and prosperity.
Meeting good companions and favorable conditions,
May all hindrances to Liberation pass away from me.

While Milarepa was singing this song, an echo from Heaven was
heard by all.

After some time, the people of Nya Non heard that the Jetsun was
about to leave for other hermitages. They all came with good offerings,
and besought him not to go. The Jetsun replied, "I have been staying here for quite a long time. My patrons may now have become
wearied [of me]. I am going to another place to await the coming
of my death. If I do not die soon, there will always be a chance for
us to meet again. In the meantime, you should all try to practice
these things":

Obeisance to my perfect Guru!

Property and possessions
Are like dew on the grass —
Give them without avarice away.

A human body that can practice Dharma is most
    precious —

[To attain it again] you should keep the Precepts
   well
As if protecting your own eyes!

Anger brings one to the Lower
Realms, so never lose your temper,
Even though your life be forfeit.

Inertia and slackness never bring Accomplishment —
Exert yourself therefore in devotion.

Through distractions Mahāyāna can'ne'er be understood —
Practice therefore concentration.

Since Buddhahood cannot be won without,
Watch the nature of your mind within.

Like fog is faith unstable —
When it starts to fade, you should
Strengthen it more than ever.

The patrons all cried, "Whatever you say, we won't let you go! By
all means, please remain here!" Thus they besought him with the
utmost earnestness. The Jetsun replied, "If I do not die, I shall try
to come back to your village. If for some time we cannot see each
other, try at times to remember and practice these things." Whereupon
he sang:

Alas, how pitiful are worldly beings!
Like precious jade they cherish
Their bodies, yet like ancient trees
They are doomed in the end to fall.
Sometimes bridle your wild thoughts,
And pay heed to the Dharma.

Though you gather wealth as hard
As bees collect their honey,
The ills that on you may fall
Can never be foretold.
Sometimes bridle your wild thoughts
And pay heed to the Dharma.

One may offer to a Lama
Loads of silk for many years;
But when an ill-fortune descends,
Like a fading rainbow
One's faith at once dissolves.
Sometimes bridle your wild thoughts
And pay heed to the Dharma.

Like a pair of mated beasts,
Lovers live together,
But calamity by the wolf's attack
May fall on you at any time.
Sometimes bridle your wild thoughts,
And pay heed to the Dharma.

You may cherish your dear son,
Like a hen hatching her egg;
But a falling rock may crush it at any time.
Sometimes bridle your wild thoughts
And pay heed to the Dharma!

A face may be pretty as a flower,
Yet at any time it can be spoiled by violent hail.
Think at times of how this world
Is sorry, transient, and futile.

Though son and mother have affection
For each other, when discords arise,
Like foes they clash and quarrel.
Sometimes toward all sentient beings
You should feel compassion.

Basking in the warm sunlight
May be pleasant and a comfort,
But a storm of woe may rise
And choke you at any time.
Remember sometimes the deprived,
And give alms to those in need.

Oh, dear men and women patrons,
For he who cannot practice Dharma,
All his life will be meaningless,
All his acts wrongdoings!

"Yes, Revered Jetsun, we shall follow your instructions," said the patrons, "But we cannot bear to see you go away. Please, remain for our sake!" [But] Milarepa stayed in the Belly Cave for [only] a short time, and then went to the lower part of the valley. Standing on a rock, he left a pair of indented footprints on it as a token of memory to which the people of Nya Non might pay their homage and respect. Then, without the knowledge of the patrons, he went away.

This is the story of Milarepa giving his final admonishment to the patrons of Nya Non.

ADMONISHMENTS TO PHYSICIAN YANG NGE

Obeisance to all Gurus

THE Jetsun Milarepa and his five disciples now set out for Tong Lha. On the way they encountered five robbers, who searched them and found only some bowls and skulls. Then they asked, "Are you people called 'Milarepas'?" The Jetsun answered, "I am Milarepa." The robbers all bowed down to him and said, "We are indeed fortunate to meet you! Now please grant us some instructions." The Jetsun then preached for them the teaching of Karma, including such topics as the joy and merit of the higher realms, the miseries and vices of the three lower realms, and how good and bad deeds, respectively, would bring forth happiness and suffering. Then he added, "This is my advice: take it or not, it is entirely up to you. Listen to this song":

> I bow down to the perfect Gurus.
>
> High above, in the Heaven of Pleasures,
> The Devas sow their rice,
> And the crop is ripe
> As the seeds are sown.
> It is not that their method
> Of farming is superior,
> It is simply the Karmic reward
> For their good deeds in former lives.
> Men of endowment, give your alms!
>
> Down below are wretched beings
> In the great Eighteen Hells. When
> Their bodies by the saw are cut

630

The wounds are healed at once;
'Tis not because their skin is healthy,
But is Karmic retribution
For those they killed in former lives.
Men of endowment, never kill!

In the dark realm yonder
Wander hungry ghosts.
As they finish eating
They feel hungry again;
The reason is not their stomachs' size,
It is Karmic retribution
For stinginess in former lives.
Men of endowment, never be parsimonious!

Near the Cleansing Pond
Is Duinjo's wondrous cow,
Ever ready to give milk.
But it is up to you
Whether or no you catch her.

Under the root of the Wish-fulfilling Tree
Is the drug that cures all five diseases.
Yet it is entirely up to you
Whether or no you dig for it.

In front of a good Guru
Is the Key of Pith-Instructions
To the door of the Two [Perfections],[1]
But it is entirely up to you
Whether or no you open it.

Hearing this song, great faith was aroused in all five robbers. Four
of them swore that they would never kill or rob again. One decided
to follow the Jetsun, and was accepted as a servant-disciple. Later he
gained the Realization and became an advanced yogi.

After this incident, Milarepa and his disciples went down to Din Ri
Namar. Meeting a shepherd on the way, Milarepa asked him, "Tell
me, who is the outstanding patron in this place?" The shepherd answered, "There is a physician called Yang Nge — he is a rich and devoted Buddhist." They proceeded to the physician's house, and saw
him standing among many people who were gathering there. Mila-

repa said, "Dear patron, we were told that you are the richest man here. We ask you to give us some food this morning." The physician replied, "On the other side of the mountain there is Milarepa, on this side, Dhampa Sangje. The stream of yogi pilgrims never stops flowing. How can I afford to give charity to every one of them? Now, I shall only give alms to Milarepa if he comes here himself. Of course, I know that I may not have the good Karma to see him at all." The Jetsun replied, "I can say that I am Milarepa himself. Now bring us the food."

"It is said that the Jetsun Milarepa can use anything at hand as a metaphor to preach. Now please use the bubbles of water in this ditch before us as a metaphor and give us a discourse," said the physician. In response, the Jetsun sang a song, "The Fleeting Bubbles":

> I pay homage to my gracious Guru —
> The Essence of all Buddhas at all times.
> Pray make everyone here think of the Dharma!
>
> As he said once, "Like bubbles is
> This life, transient and fleeting —
> In it no assurance can be found."
> A layman's life is like a thief
> Who sneaks into an empty house.
> Know you not the folly of it?
>
> Youth is like a summer flower —
> Suddenly it fades away.
> Old age is like a fire spreading through
> The fields — suddenly 'tis at your heels.
> The Buddha once said, "Birth and death are like
> Sunrise and sunset — now come, now go."
> Sickness is like a little bird
> Wounded by a sling.
> Know you not, health and strength
> Will in time desert you?
> Death is like an oil-dry lamp
> [After its last flicker].
> Nothing, I assure you,
> In this world is permanent.
> Evil Karma is like a waterfall,
> Which I have never seen flow upward.
> A sinful man is like a poisonous tree —
> If on it you lean you will be injured.

Transgressors are like frost-bitten peas —
Like spoiled fat, they ruin everything.
Dharma practicers are like peasants in the field —
With caution and vigor they will be successful.
The Guru is like medicine and nectar —
Relying on him, one will win success.
Discipline is like a watchman's tower —
Observing it, one will attain Accomplishment.

The Law of Karma is like Saṃsāra's wheel —
Whoever breaks it will suffer a great loss.
Saṃsāra is like a poisonous thorn
In the flesh — if not pulled out,
The poison will increase and spread.
The coming of death is like the shadow
Of a tree at sunset — it runs
Fast and none can halt it.
When that time arrives, what else
Can help but the holy Dharma?
Though Dharma is the fount of victory,
Those who aspire to it are rare.

Scores of men are tangled in
The miseries of Saṃsāra;
Into this misfortune born, they strive
By plunder and theft for gain.

He who talks on Dharma
With elation is inspired,
But when a task is set him,
He is wrecked and lost.

Dear patrons, do not talk too much,
But practice the holy Dharma.

"This is indeed very helpful to my mind," commented the physician, "but please preach still further for me on the truth of Karma and the suffering of birth, old age, illness, and death, thus enabling me to gain a deeper conviction on Buddhism." In response, the Jetsun sang:

In the realm of the Great Unborn
He shines with the Four Infinities —

To my wish-granting Jetsun Guru,
The Guide to the Path of Greatest Joy,
I pay my heart-felt praise.

Please listen to these words,
Dear friends here assembled.
When you are young and vigorous
You ne'er think of old age coming,
But it approaches slow and sure
Like a seed growing underground.

When you are strong and healthy
You ne'er think of sickness coming,
But it descends with sudden force
Like a stroke of lightning.

When involved in worldly things
You ne'er think of death's approach.
Quick it comes like thunder
Crashing round your head.

Sickness, old age, and death
Ever meet each other
As do hands and mouth.

Waiting for his prey in ambush,
Yama is ready for his victim
When disaster catches him.

Sparrows fly in single file. Like them, life
Death, and Bardo follow one another.
Never apart from you
Are these three "visitors."
Thus thinking, fear you
Not your sinful deeds?

Like strong arrows in ambush waiting,
Rebirth in Hell, as hungry ghost, or beast
Is [the destiny] waiting to catch you.
If once into their traps you fall,
Hard will you find it to escape.

Do you not fear the miseries

You experienced in the past?
Surely you will feel much pain
If misfortunes attack you?
The woes of life succeed one another
Like the sea's incessant waves —
One has barely passed, before
The next one takes its place.
Until you are liberated, pain
And pleasure come and go at random
Like passers-by encountered in the street.

Pleasures are precarious,
Like bathing in the sun;
Transient, too, as snow storms
Which come without warning.
Remembering these things,
Why practice not the Dharma?

Hearing this song, great faith in the Jetsun was aroused in all. They presented him with many good offerings, and asked him to stay there permanently. Milarepa did not accept their invitation, but only consented to remain overnight.

The physician besought the Jetsun to give them some instructions before he left. Then he summoned all the villagers, and added, "If, Revered Jetsun, you cannot stay here even for a few days, then please grant us some Dharma to practice." In response, Milarepa sang:

Listen with care, all you assembled here;
Do you truly want to practice Dharma?
If you do, you should try these things:
When lying down in bed, let not
Yourself go with ignorance;
At evening, recite the Patron Buddha
Mantra; at night, pray to the Holy Ones;
At midnight, meditate on Non-distinction. When
The day breaks, practice the Life-Prāṇa; in the morn,
Repent of your wrongdoings; when the sun
Rises, identify your mind with forms.

In practice, the main thing
Is the Self-mind to watch;
The pith of all instructions
Is received from your Guru.

You should, then, always pray
To your Patron Buddha;
Keep the Samaya Rules
With your Vajra brothers;
To the Three Precious Ones
Always offer service.

E'er on your head visualize Him who is All Merciful,
Reciting the holy Mantra of the Jewel Lotus.[2]
Always to the poor give charity, and help
Those in need; ever serve and give alms
To priests of learning and discipline;
At all times take care of your parents.
Were a hundred scholars and Gurus gathered
Here, they could not give you better instruction.
May prosperity and joy
Follow you through all your lives!
May good health and long life
Be with you at all times!

Moved by this song, the audience were all confirmed with an un-shakable faith toward the Jetsun. Later, the physician entered the Path at the time of his death.

After this incident, Milarepa and his disciples set out for Chu Bar.

This is the story of the Physician, Yang Nge.

NOTES

1 Two Perfections: the Perfection of Merit, and the Perfection of Wisdom.

2 That is, the Mantra of Avalokiteśvara: Om.Ma.Ne.Padme.Hum.

RECHUNGPA'S DEPARTURE

Obeisance to all Gurus

R ECHUNGPA, the heart-son disciple of the Jetsun Milarepa, had difficulty because of his affiliation with the [noblewoman], Lady
Dembu. In order to free him from this hindrance, Milarepa transformed himself into a beggar and came to Rechungpa for alms. Now
Rechungpa possessed [at that time] a very large piece of jade, obtained from a ravine in the valley of Yagder. This he gave to the
"beggar," saying, "Use this jade to buy your food." Milarepa thought,
"My son has no attachment to material wealth, but has great compassion."

As a consequence of this almsgiving, Rechungpa separated from the
Lady Dembu; disheartened and wearied of her, he left, and returned
to the Jetsun.

On his way back he came to the house of a rich man and was
given two portions of dried meat, which he preserved with great care
in order to bring them back to the Jetsun as a present. At that time
Milarepa was staying at Chu Bar with some of his disciples. He said
to them, "Rechungpa is coming, and is bringing us something so extremely large that a whole valley is not big enough to contain it."

Before long Rechungpa arrived. He offered a bag of the dried meat
to the Jetsun and asked after his health. In answer, Milarepa sang:

> A yogi, I roam the mountains;
> Like a great Maṇḍala,
> My body is full of bliss.
> Cleansed of desires and pride,
> I feel well and happy.
> With longing for diversions killed
> I feel joy in solitude.
> Since I have renounced all things,

Happy am I in no-man's land.
Since I have cut off ties of kinsfolk
Getting and saving are not worries —
Happy and joyous do I live.
Without desire for scholarship or study
Of more books, I have no inferior feelings —
With Mind-Essence I feel only happiness.

I am well and happy
Without "gab" and "babble,"
For I do not want proud talk.
I am well and happy
Without plans or schemes.
For my mind is free from fraud.
I am well and happy, for I never
Involve myself in slanderous gossip
And I desire no fame or glory.
Where'er I stay, whate'er I wear
Or eat, I feel truly happy.
At all times am I happy and well. Son
Rechungpa, you are in health on your return?

Whereupon Rechungpa offered the dried meat to all the Repas without discrimination or stinginess. One of them asked Milarepa, "Revered Jetsun, you have just told us that Rechungpa would bring us a big present, larger than the whole valley can contain; but where is it?" With a smile Milarepa replied, "The valley is your stomach, and the meat is that big present — too big to be stuffed into it." Hearing this, the Repas all burst into hearty laughter.

The Jetsun then said, "I am going to give you all an Initiation, but according to the Dharma an offering to the Guru is necessary; you may bring anything you have, but Rechungpa is a special case — he can do without one." Hearing this, Rechungpa unhappily joined in the ceremony.

When he approached the Maṇḍala he saw the big jade which he had given to the beggar standing right in its center. He was dumfounded; then suddenly he realized that the beggar was his Guru's transformation, used to sever the bonds between himself and Lady Dembu. [Reviewing the whole event in retrospect], Rechungpa now felt deeply grateful to the Jetsun.

"Rechungpa," said the Jetsun, "Had it not been for me, this jade would have carried you to destruction. It is only because of your unceasing faith and veneration toward me, and your great compassion for all sentient beings, that you are freed from this hindrance. Now you should be grateful and happy. Listen to my song":

> Great was the blessing of the Father Guru,
> Important was Milarepa's miracle,
> Vital were Rechungpa's charity and love!
> The jade you gave the beggar
> Is with us here; this evening
> We may offer it to Dem Chog
> At our Initiation rite.

> To give alms to the needy with compassion
> Is equal to serving Buddhas in the Three Times.
> To give with sympathy to beggars is
> To make offerings to Milarepa.
> Sentient beings are one's parents; to
> Discriminate between them is harmful and
> Ignorant. True sages and
> Scholars are always in accord;
> Clinging to one's School and condemning others
> Is the certain way to waste one's learning.
> Since all Dharmas equally are good,
> Those who cling to sectarianism
> Degrade Buddhism and sever
> Themselves from Liberation.
> All the happiness one has
> Is derived from others;
> All the help one gives to them
> In return brings happiness.
> One's pernicious deeds
> Only harm oneself.

> Enter this Maṇḍala with benevolent
> Mind; confess, repent you of your sins, observe
> All precepts with determination.

Rechungpa was deeply moved. In remorse, he confessed all his transgressions before his Guru and his brothers-in-the-Dharma in this song:

> Yearning for physical enjoyments,

In pursuit of pleasure I indulged.
Falling for tempations, I committed
Debasing deeds that lead to misery.
Before the *body* of my Father Guru
I now confess them fully.

Craving for talk leads to deceit
And lies, a glib tongue and clever
Words drag one right down to Hell.
Wine and meat that please the mouth
Turn one into a hungry ghost.
All my untrue and shameless talk,
I now confess in full before my Father Guru's *mouth*.

To crave for pleasure causes evil thoughts,
To yearn for fame creates most filthy acts.
All my sinful deeds, caused by desire and greed,
I now confess in full before
My Father Guru's *mind*.

Wandering in towns and hamlets,
My practices were interrupted;
Performing many exorcisms,
My Mantra power grew feeble;
Becoming far too active, my good
Samādhi experience faded.
To the Maṇḍala's Gods
I now confess these wrongs.

In a house where many people live
I distinguished between "mine" and "yours."
All my smallness and degradation
I confess to my Dharma-brothers.

Thereupon the Jetsun initiated the Repas with the "Pointing-out" exercise in an elaborate manner. After the ceremony, Repa Shiwa Aui arose from the assembly and asked, "Rechungpa is a yogi who has completely mastered the Prāṇa-Mind. Why should a man such as he still need the Jetsun's protection and care when he takes a lady for Tantric practice? And why should such a man still repent before you for this act?" The Jetsun replied, "This is because [in order to practice the secret action], one must know the right time and the right conditions." Whereupon he sang:

I bow down to my gracious Guru Marpa —
Pray lead me with your blessing to the Path,
Help me to understand the mind-state of my disciples!

Knowing not the right time to
Practice, one's Yoga will stray;
Knowing not the right time to
Speak, the elders will go astray;
Knowing not the right time to give
Food, the good housewife will go astray;
Knowing not the right time to perform
Their duties, the servants will go astray;
Knowing not the right time to meet
The foe, the fighters will go astray;
Knowing not the right time to meet
Conditions, noble monks will stray;
Knowing not the right time to help others,
Altruistic deeds will go astray.

Without perseverence and determination,
To stay in the mountains will be a waste of time.
If men consider not nor help each other,
Companionship and brotherhood are lost.
If a disciple does not keep his Guru's rules,
The relationship with him will soon be broken.
Boundless, alas, are errors and deviations,
How can one list them all?
Dear sons, you should practice
In accordance with my words!

Hearing this song, all the disciples gained a decisive understanding. Rechungpa then made a solemn vow before the Jetsun that he would observe and obey all his instructions. Thereafter he served Milarepa [even more] earnestly than before.

One night Rechungpa dreamt that he put a load of wool on [the back of] a dog, and shouted, "Write the words! Write the words!" Then they set out, and reached a mountain pass. From one side of the mountain came eighty-eight people to escort them, and from the other came another eighty-eight people to welcome them. Rechungpa asked the Jetsun to interpret this dream for him. In answer, Milarepa sang:

THE HUNDRED THOUSAND SONGS OF MILAREPA

The dog shows that you will have
A friend, the wool that your mind
Will be benign and gentle.
"Write the words" means that
You will be well-learned.
The shouting shows you will sing
From wonderful Experience.
The two groups of eighty-eight
Means that so many people
Will escort and welcome you.

Another night Rechungpa dreamt that he threw off his clothes and washed his body with water, then became a bird that flew away and alighted on a tree. Then he saw a mirror and looked into it. In explaining this dream, Milarepa sang:

Throwing off your clothes implies
Relinquishment of all desires.
Washing your body with clean water means
Purification through the Instructions.
[Transforming into] a bird implies
Kindness and compassion. The bird's
Two wings are the Two Provisions.
Alighting on the branch reveals
That in the Bodhi Tree you'll sit.
The mirror you saw implies
Revelations by Ḍākinīs.

Again one night Rechungpa dreamt that he rode backward on a donkey, and wore a robe called "Hope!" The Jetsun explained the dream in this song:

Turning your back toward Saṃsāra
You ride the Mahāyāna's ass.
When Nirvāṇa's welcome comes
You will fulfill the hopes of all.

Another night Rechungpa dreamt that he put a jewel upon his head and donned an immaculate robe. Then he looked into a bright mirror having no stain upon it. In the right hand he held a Vajra, in the left a human skull full of blood. He also dreamt that he sat cross-legged on a lotus seat; his back radiated beams of light and his body was ablaze with a great fire. He saw a fountain springing up before him, and the sun and moon shone from his heart. On his left stood men and women in even number; on his right, a child was herding a kid, which then multiplied into many goats. Rechungpa went to the Jetsun and asked him to interpret the dream. The Jetsun replied, "The meaning of the dream is this":

> The jewel means that you should always
> Think of your Guru upon your head;
> The pure white robe implies the Whispered
> Lineage; looking into the mirror means
> The "Pointing-out" Performance; holding
> The Vajra in the right hand indicates
> The destruction of all wandering thoughts.
> The skull in your left hand is a symbol
> Of your Bliss-Void Experience; the lotus
> Seat implies your freedom from all faults;
> Your sitting cross-legged indicates
> You will be in Samādhi long;
> The light radiating from your back
> Means that you will realize aright.
> The fountain that gushes forth before you means
> That you will have Signs and Experiences;
> The fire that from your body flames
> Is the burning of Dumo heat;
> The sun and moon are proof
> Of your Illumination.
> The men and women standing on your left
> Means that Bha Wos and Mos will welcome you;
> On your right the kid and goats are proof
> That you will protect your disciples;
> The multiplying of the kids foretells·
> The spreading of the Whispered Lineage.

The Jetsun continued, "Since you have reached this state, it will not be necessary for you to stay with me any longer. You should leave, now that the right time has come for you to benefit sentient beings on a grand scale." Then he· sang:

> Hearken, my son Rechungpa! Knowing
> The dependent origination
> Of Samsāra and Nirvāna, if
> You can rely on a holy Guru,

To you will come the Pith-Instructions
Without effort and search.

Listen, my son Rechungpa! If you
Can conquer the desire for city
Life and remain in the hermitage,
The Accomplishment will come of itself
Without effort and striving.
If you can forego evil deeds and clinging
And can renounce all your wants and cravings,
Quietly will you tread the Path of Joy
Without attachment or desires.

Listen, oh my son, the root
Of Saṃsāra is *to bear*;
If you can cut off the clinging-love
For sons and live in solitude,
Quietly will you enter Buddha's Land.

Listen, my son, though through
Tibet the Dharma spreads, many
Adulterate it. People call
Themselves Gurus and disciples,
But with their clever tongues
They indulge in obscene talk.
Go, my son, go and teach them,
Show them the right teachings
Of the pure Lineage!

Listen, my son Rechungpa,
If from your heart you want
To practice holy Dharma,
Remember that Buddhism should
Make one conquer one's desires.
Try to renounce all greed,
Refrain from talking much.

Listen, son Rechungpa,
If you want Buddhahood
Forget all pleasures of this life, strive
For Realization stabilized within,
And never from the *base* of your Self-mind depart.

The Jetsun then said, "Rechungpa, in the past when you should have remained in one place, you wanted to go away. But now you should go to the Doh of Loro [near] Shar Bo forest [which is close to] Shambo Snow Mountain on the Tibetan border. There you can benefit sentient beings."

> Rechungpa, my elder son,
> You are going now to Weu.
> Of my four sons you are
> The most manly one.
> Dear son of various Successions,
> Think of your Guru on your head, and go.
>
> Keep the Samaya Rules with care, and go!
> Torch-bearer of the Whispered Lineage,
> Go and dispel the mists of ignorance!
> Go and ripen gifted disciples,
> Reveal nothing to the incapable.
>
> Go and plant the life-tree of Dharma,
> Looking with love after the gifted.
> Go south to the border regions,
> And meditate on Shambo Mountain.
>
> Son Rechungpa, you will have your temple
> On the border between Tibet and Doh.

Having made all preparations for the journey, Rechungpa came to the Jetsun, bowed down to him, and sang this song:

> Following your order, Father Guru,
> Your elder son is going now to Weu.
> Pray bless him with your Vajra Body,
> On his journey; pray, with your
> Immaculate Words, protect
> Him from all hindrances;
> With your mindless thought
> Lead him to the Path.
> Dear Father Jetsun, of yourself
> Take care and preserve your health.
>
> Your son is going now to Weu;
> Pray escort him on his journey.

Pray, Precious One — the shelter
Of all beings, who embodies
All Buddhas of all times —
Take care and keep in health.

Pray, Omniscient One, who works
Wonders with the Eyes of Dharma,
Pray keep well and of yourself take care.

Pray, Precious One, whose bounty
[I] hardly can repay —
Pray dispel all darkness,
And in good health remain.
Pray, mighty Guru, the Bodhi-
Path's benevolent guide,
Pray of yourself take care.

In sending Rechungpa upon his journey, the Jetsun sang a song
of the View, Practice, and Action:

Son, the View is to rid oneself of sectarianism,
The Practice is to remain in the hermitage,
The Action is to eschew bad companionship,
The Discipline is to harmonize all forms,
The Accomplishment is gained by thinking [e'er]
      of death.

The Jetsun continued, "In the year of the Hare, the month of the
Horse, and on the fourteenth day, you should return. This is very important." Then he gave Rechungpa a piece of gold and bestowed upon
him many of his most cherished Instructions. Rechungpa said, "Though
I cannot bear to depart from you, I have to obey your order. I must
now leave for Weu." As Rechungpa said this, tears rolled down his
face. To make the wish of seeing the Jetsun again, he sang:

The rivers of India and Nepal,
Divided by different valleys,
Flow in different directions.
Yet, as rivers, they are all alike —
In the great ocean they will meet again.

Divided by the Four Continents,
The sun rises in the East, the moon

Sets in the West; as light-bearers
They are both alike: on a cloudless
Autumn evening they sometimes see each other.

Veiled by ignorance,
The minds of man and Buddha
Appear to be different;
Yet in the realm of Mind-Essence
They both are of one taste. Some-
Time they will meet each other
In the great Dharmadhātu.

Because of Māyā's working,
The father Jetsun remains
On the hill, while Rechungpa,
The son, travels to far places;
Yet in the Dharmakāya
Never do they separate.
In the Og-Men Heaven
They will meet again.

Dear Father Jetsun, please keep well.
I, Rechungpa, am leaving now for Weu!

Rechungpa bowed down to the Jetsun, touching his feet with his head, and once more made many wishes. Then he set out for Weu.

While Rechungpa was living at the Forest Temple of Shar Mo, his lady came to him for forgiveness. At first he would not see her, but later, because of his compassion and the earnest entreaties of Rin Chin Drags, he relented and granted her an interview. She was destitute and appeared to have undergone many physical and mental trials. Seeing her in such a pitiful state, Rechungpa was deeply moved. He shed many tears, gave her a nugget of gold, and sang this song:

I bow at the feet of Mila
The supreme. Pray in your pity
Make me remember your bounties.

You, the zealous talker,
Look not as you did before.
On my return to my Guru
I saw in the Maṇḍala that great lump

Of jade about which our dispute arose.
When I saw it, all the hairs
Of my body stood on end.

Formerly, my Guru said,
"Do not, do not go to Weu."
But later he said,
"Go now to Weu!"
Thinking of this, I can but feel amazed.

In the life of my Father Jetsun,
One finds that he treats gold like stones;
Giving me this gold, he said,
"Take it, take it with you now."
Thinking of this, I can but feel amazed.

With this piece of gold you can
Guild images of Buddha,
And cleanse your bodily sins.
With this piece of gold you can
Practice rituals and Mantras,
Cleansing thus your sins of speech.
With it you can also build
Many stūpas and Tsa Tsas,
Cleansing thus your sins of mind.

Referring all things to your Self-mind within,
Practice the teachings of the Whispered Lineage;
Pray and pray again to your Jetsun Guru,
Often rouse the thought of renunciation.
If you can do this you will
Attain great Accomplishment!

Feeling deep pity for her and her uncle, Rechungpa took them both under his care. He then imparted the Instructions to them and set them to meditating. The uncle was thus cured of leprosy, and the lady also gained good Experiences and Realizations. Later, it was said, she became a very good yoginī and benefited many sentient beings.

This is the latter part of the story of Rechungpa's journey to Weu.

THE STORY OF DRASHI TSE

Obeisance to all Gurus

O NE time at Lha Dro of Drin, the Jetsun Milarepa was patronized by Drashi Tse, who, in an assembly attended by many patrons, stood up and said, "Revered Jetsun, when I hear people preaching the Dharma I always feel very happy. But I know that I cannot be a great yogi and a well-learned priest at the same time. Witnessing the fact that you, the Jetsun, have devoted yourself solely to the practice, I was confirmed with great faith. Do you think I should concentrate my effort on meditation alone, or not?" The Jetsun replied, "It is for the very sake of practice that the Dharma is preached and studied. If one does not practice or meditate, both studying and preaching will be meaningless. Now listen to my song":

> Without practice, the Dharma of preaching
> Leads only to pride. Without fostering,
> An adopted son always becomes a foe.
> Without instruction, a load
> Of books is but a burden;
> Except for lies and boasting
> What good can they ever do?
> Hearing the wily *Expedient*
> *Teachings*, people feel delighted,
> But very few would follow
> The Guru's *Final Teachings*.
>
> With faith practice holy Dharma,
> Dear patrons and disciples!
> Without deceit or boasting,
> Humble, honest, and straightforward,
> I now tell you the truth!

The Jetsun continued: "If one decides to practice the Dharma, he will learn a great deal; but if he could contemplate the Essential Truth for just a short time, it would help him more. If one talks much, the higher teaching will be overshadowed by his lower realizations. If one cannot stabilize his mind, all his seemingly good deeds will become self-deceiving. If one has a great attachment and desire for this world, any form of Dharma he may practice will be no more than a Dharma-of-the-mouth. Certain people study Buddhism for pleasure, then with great pride in their learning they begin to lose faith in the great teachers of the past. As a result, they will lose the blessings.

"Many people think they will have ample time to practice the Dharma, but without their notice or expectation, death suddenly descends upon them and they lose forever the chance to practice. What then can they do? One should turn all his Buddhist knowledge inside his mouth, and meditate. If one does not further his studies and meditation at the same time, but thinks that he should first learn a great deal before starting the actual practice [he will be completely lost], because knowledge is infinite, and there is no possibility of mastering it all.

"Again, if one talks to a revered priest who is rich in Buddhist learning he will be told that there is not a single thing in Buddhism that is not needed. He may then acquire many, many profound teachings; but he does not know which one to practice. He may choose one and practice it, but gain no Experience at all. Then doubts and skepticism creep into his mind and he begins to think, 'Should I try some *other* practice? Would not another Yoga suit me better than this one?' Thus he will never accomplish anything. This is comparable to a man who studies the Soma plant[1] but forgets the basic principles and his original intention, like a child holding a wild flower in its hand." Milarepa then continued his admonishment in this song:

> Hearken, my faithful patrons! Even sinful
> Persons, not knowing the great power of Karma,
> Dream of achieving Liberation.
> Life wears out as days and years go by,
> Yet in pursuing pleasures
> People spend their lives. They ask,
> "Will this month or year be good?"
> Blind to life's speedy passing,
> Fools cherish foolish questions.

He who truly wants to practice Dharma
Should make offerings to the Holy Ones,
Take refuge in the Triple Gem,
Give service to the Jetsun Guru,
Pay respect to his parents, give
Alms without hoping for reward.
He should offer help to those in need;
He should live and act up to
The Dharma's principles.
Not much is needed for Buddhist practice;
Too many vows lead to self-cheating.
Dear patrons, try to practice what I say.

"Your instructions are very helpful, and easy to understand," said the patrons. "We shall try to follow them without fail. Now please give us still more advice appropriate to our needs."

Milarepa replied, "I have many good teachings to give if you can practice and follow them. Otherwise I see no point in doing so."

"We will practice them. Pray by all means teach us!"

"Well, then, these are the things you should do":

My dear patrons, if you decide to follow
My words and cultivate the Ultimate,
Remember that all will die,
And that to practice Dharma
Is the only good way of life.
Worldly wealth is a delusion —
Though much you may accumulate,
In the end you must abandon
All, so 'tis better to give alms.

Affection for one's loved ones may
Be very deep, yet one must
Eventually leave them.
Better 'tis to practice the Non-dual Truth.

However strong a house is built
Eventually it will fall.
'Tis better far to live in no-man's land.
Whatever food one may preserve,
In time will be consumed. Better far
Is it to store the food of Dharma.

Worldly affairs cannot be trusted;
It is better to renounce them all.

Since foolish talk is endless
'Tis better to shut one's mouth.

Instructions are like the art of oiling another's
      skin;
Better is it to rely on a proficient Guru.
[Spiritual] Experiences resemble
The moon's [brief] emergence from the clouds. 'Tis better
Unceasingly to practice,
Like an ever-flowing stream.

These are the ten essentials
That have risen in my mind.
May you, Drin's men and women patrons,
All gain good progress in the Dharma!

Then Milarepa taught them how to take the Three Refuges, how
to rouse the Bodhi-Mind, to dedicate [themselves], and to take the
[Bodhisattva's] Vow. These instructions greatly inspired them with
good spiritual thoughts. Among those attending, many learned to practice meditation, and a few even gained good Experiences.

This is the story of Drashi Tse.

NOTES

1 Soma plant: "A climbing plant the juice of which was offered in libations
to the gods; the Hindus also worshiped it on account of its intoxicating qualities."
(Quoted from Sarat Chandra Dass' Dictionary, p. 1282.)

THE SONG OF
GOOD COMPANIONS

Obeisance to all Gurus

WHEN the Jetsun Milarepa was staying in the Stone House of Drin, Tsese, Ku Ju, and many other patrons came to him for the Dharma. Tsese said, "Please give us some Buddhist teaching that is easy to understand." Milarepa replied, "Very well, lend your ears and listen carefully to this song:"

> Pray, Father Guru, supreme Marpa,
> Pray bless us and bring the Dharma to our minds.
>
> Dear patrons, with care listen
> For a moment to my words.
>
> Superior men have need of Dharma;
> Without it, they are like eagles —
> Even though perched on high,
> They have but little meaning.
>
> Average men have need of Dharma;
> Without it, they are like tigers —
> Though possessing greatest strength,
> They are of little value.
>
> Inferior men have need of Dharma;
> Without it they are like a peddler's asses —
> Though they carry a big load,
> It does them but little good.

Superior women need the Dharma;
Without it, they are like pictures on a wall —
Though they look very pretty,
They have no use or meaning.

Average women need the Dharma;
Without it they are like little rats;
Though they are clever at getting food,
Their lives have but little meaning.

Inferior women need the Dhama;
Without it, they are just like vixens —
Though they be deft and cunning,
Their deeds have little value.

Old men need the Dharma; without
It, they are like decaying trees.
Growing youths the Dharma need;
Without it, they are like yoked bulls.
Young maidens need the Dharma; without
It, they are but decorated cows.
All young people need the Dharma; without it
They are like blossoms shut within a shell.
All children need the Dharma; without it
They are like robbers possessed by demons.

Without the Dharma, all one
Does lacks meaning and purpose.
Those who want to live with meaning
Should practice the Buddha's teaching.

The lady patron, Ku Ju, then said, "Revered Jetsun, you now have
many sons and disciples, yet you still like to live as a recluse. You
must find it a very happy life. Do you have good companions [un-
known to us] living with you?"

"Yes, I do. Now listen to this song":

I bow down to my Father Gurus.

Living as a yogi recluse,
I have one-and-twenty good companions:
The Gurus, Patron Buddhas, and Dākinīs
Are the three for prayer; the Buddhas, Dharmas,

And Saṅghas are the three for refuge;
The Sūtras, Tantras, and Śāstras are
The three for learning; the Nerves, the Drops,
And Breathings are the three for practice
Of the Skillful Path; Bliss, No-thought,
And Illumination are the three
For meditation; piety, pure
Thought, and compassion are the three
For the Bodhi-Path; Bha Wo, Bha Mo,
And the Guards are the three escorts
Through whom to conquer hindrances.

"These things are wonderful," said Ku Ju, "but would you mind telling us more about them in similes?" In response, Milarepa sang:

Pray bless me, all Gurus in the Lineage.

Sitting upon the sun-moon seat[1] the Gurus
Of the Succession are on my head.
To describe them with a parable,
They are like a string of jewels —
Blessed and joyful is my mind.

The Three Precious Gems are my reliance —
Ever protected am I in their love.
To describe this feeling with a simile,
'Tis like a cherished baby
Fed on his mother's lap
Without fear or sorrow —
Blessed and joyful is my mind.

On my right are many Bha Wos
Whose blessing dispels all my hindrances.
To describe them with a parable,
They are like blades revolving o'er my head
Protecting me from all injuries —
Blessed and joyful is my mind.

On my left are many Ḍākinīs,
Blessing me with the gift of Two Accomplishments.
To describe them with a simile,
They are like kind mothers and sisters

Circling round me to fulfil my wishes —
Blessed and joyful is my mind.

Before me are the Guards of the Doctrine
Who carry out my orders.
To describe them with a parable,
They are like obedient servants
Fulfilling all my wishes —
Blessed and joyful is my mind.

My View on Reality is perfected in three aspects,[2]
With it I overwhelm the Hīnayāna teaching.
To describe this with a simile,
'Tis like a fearless lion strutting in the snow —
Blessed and joyful is my mind.

My Practice of Skill and Wisdom
Is like an eagle's mighty wings
With which I soar into the firmament.
I fly through the sky without fear of falling —
Blessed and joyful is my mind.

My Action is full of strength and valor,
Both distractions and drowsiness are destroyed.
To describe this with a parable,
'Tis like a tiger stalking through
The woods without fear or dread —
Blessed and joyful is my mind!

Having actualized the Trikāya,
With ease I benefit all beings
Through Bodies transformed.
To describe this with a simile,
'Tis like a golden fish that plays
With glee in water without effort —
Blessed and joyful is my mind.

Having mastered all manifestations,
I sing little songs
Opportune to the occasion.
To describe this with a simile,
'Tis like a dragon roaring in

The sky without fear or dread —
Blessed and joyful is my mind.

I am the Yogi Milarepa
Who wanders from one retreat to another.
To describe this with a simile,
'Tis like the wild beasts who live
In the mountains without fear —
Blessed and joyful is my mind.

I have sung for you, in cheerful mood,
A song with five parables and six meanings —
Listen carefully, men and Devas here assembled!
Do not be misled,
But observe your minds;
Try to reach the state
Of dying without regret.
In the light of Dharma
I wish you all good fortune!

All those attending were satisfied and pleased. Thereafter, they made good efforts in virtuous deeds. Several of the young men present were accepted as servant-disciples by the Jetsun, who initiated them with the Pith-Instructions and then sent them to meditate. A few of them later became enlightened yogis.

This is the story of Tsese, Ku Ju, and the patrons of Drin.

NOTES

1 Sun-moon seat (T.T.: Ñi.Zlahi.gDan.): The Tantric deities are usually pictured as sitting upon a seat containg three layers: the first layer is a lotus, the second a sun, the third a moon symbolizing, respectively, the purity, the positive force, and the negative force.

2 The translator is not certain about these three aspects, or three functions (T.T.: rTsal.gSum.). They probably denote the Foundation, the Path, and the Accomplishment.

THE EVIDENCE OF ACCOMPLISHMENT

Obeisance to all Gurus

A T ONE time when the Jetsun Milarepa was staying at the Sky Castle on Red Rock Mountain Peak, some sheep-owners came from
Drin to visit him. They said, "Please give us some instructions that
will help our minds." The Jetsun replied, "If you want to receive
the Dharma you had better follow my example and first renounce
the things that are against it."

"But what are they?" they asked.

In answer, Milarepa sang:

> Hearken to me, friends and patrons!
> An act that has no meaning,
> Unnatural pretense, and fearless empty talk,
> Are three things against the Dharma
> Which I have renounced. 'Tis good
> For you to do the same.
>
> The place that inflates one, the group
> That stirs up quarrels, the status
> By hypocrisy maintained,
> Are three things against the Dharma
> Which I have renounced. 'Tis good
> For you to do the same.
>
> The Guru with little knowledge,
> The disciple with small faith,
> The brother who keeps little discipline,
> Are three things against the Dharma

Which I have renounced. 'Tis good
For you to do the same.

The wife who always complains,
The sons who e'er need punishment,
The servant who ever swaggers,
Are three things against the Dharma
Which I have renounced. 'Tis good
For you to do the same.

After hearing this song, the patrons all went home filled with inspiration and faith.

At another time Milarepa was blown off a high cliff by a strong gale of wind. His body hit a tree in falling. Just as the disciples, filled with apprehension, were wondering [if he were badly hurt], Milarepa appeared and showed them that no injury had been done. Then he sang:

Blown off a cliff by a strong gale,
I was hit by a cruel tree
And gripped by pain unbearable,
But the Ḍākinīs healed me.

. . .   .

Again one day, Milarepa appeared to fall from the top of a cliff. [From below] the disciples saw this happen and immediately dashed to the spot to receive his falling body. But when they reached it, Milarepa was already seated there, bursting with laughter. They asked him what had happened. In answer, he sang:

Stretching eagle-wings of the Non-dual,
I flew to the top of Red Rock Cliff.
To fall, is to fall to the bottom of an abyss;
To play, is to play jokes on my disciples;
To liberate, is to liberate from Saṃsāra and Nirvāṇa;
To receive, is to receive the Bliss-Void of self.

. . .   .

Again one day, as Milarepa was sitting on the edge of a high cliff, a girl came by. Seeing him, she cried out, "Do not sit there, do not sit there! That is too dangerous!" Ignoring her warning, he remained where he was. Then the earth beneath him began to slip and trickle down [the cliff]. As a huge lump of earth was about to fall, Milarepa made a Mudrā-of-Threat, and flew away. In the meantime the disciples thought that he must have been seriously injured and rushed to the scene. But [when they arrived] they found him sitting there at his ease, singing this song:

> This body is like a flower.
> From the dangerous Red Rock
> The devils tried to grab it,
> But the Ḍākinīs bore it safely.
> No devil again will try.

The disciples then asked, "How, Revered Jetsun, can you fall from a high cliff and hit a tree without being injured?" Milarepa replied, "My body has become the Rainbow Body, and my Kleśas, Wisdom; having realized the truth of Non-being I shall never die. Since I have conquered the Eight Worldly Desires, all the Four Demons have been disgraced and frustrated by me." "Do you consider that you have now completely conquered the Four Demons?" they asked. "Yes," he replied, "You may say so. Hereafter, for the next thirteen generations, followers of my Lineage will be immune from the intrusions of the Four Demons."

. . .   .

One day a Tantric yogi from Weu came to visit the Jetsun. Sevan Repa asked him, "What kind of accomplished beings are to be found in Weu?" The yogi answered, "We have accomplished yogis whom the Non-men serve and provide with food." "According to my standards," replied the Jetsun, "These cannot be considered as accomplished beings." Sevan Repa then asked, "Do you, Revered Jetsun, also receive offerings from the Non-men?" "Yes, I receive them in this way":

> Inexhaustible as the Treasury
> Of Heaven, Samādhi is my servant;
> Ḍākinīs prepare my food and drink;
> But this is not evidence
> Of an accomplished being.

The yogi retorted, "But in Weu we do have yogis who can see the Patron Buddhas." In reply, Milarepa sang:

To him who sees the mind's nature
And dispels the mists of ignorance,
The Ḍākinīs show their faces;
Yet, in the Real Realm,
There is nothing to be seen.
Without deliberate "non-observation" in one's mind,
All Dharmas rise and are illuminated by themselves.
This is preached by all Ḍākinīs.

The profoundest teaching can be had
Only from one's Guru, with whom all
Supreme and Worldly Accomplishments
Will be obtained and all good wishes
Fulfilled in this very life;
This is assured by all Ḍākinīs.
But even all this is not evidence
Of an accomplished being.

The yogi asked again, "With what simile would you describe the mind's nature?" In answer, Milarepa sang:

This non-arising Mind-Essence cannot
Be described by metaphors or signs;
This Mind-Essence that cannot
Be extinguished is oft described
By fools, but those who realize
It, explain it by itself.
Devoid of "symbolized" and "symbolizer,"
It is a realm beyond all words and thought.
How wondrous is the blessing of my Lineage!

Hearing this song, the yogi was awakened from his previous misconceptions, and was confirmed with an irrevocable faith toward the Jetsun, who accepted him as a servant-disciple and initiated him with the Instructions. Through practice he eventually became an outstanding and enlightened yogi.

This is the story of conquering the Four Demons, and of Milarepa's interview with the Tantric yogi.

THE MIRACLES AND THE
LAST ADMONISHMENT

Obeisance to all Gurus

Once when the Jetsun Milarepa was staying at Chu Bar, his body became invisible to certain people. Others saw him [sitting still and] neither eating food nor engaging in any activity. But everyone noticed that at times he laughed, and at others he cried. Shiwa Aui then said to him, "Yesterday I could not see you. Some people could, but they saw you sitting still [as if] in Samādhi. What were you doing then, and why did you first laugh, and then cry, without any apparent reason?" The Jetsun replied, "Since yesterday many people have been attending my discourses. When I saw their happiness I laughed, when I saw their sufferings, I wept."

"Please tell us all about it."

"If you want to hear this story, you should now prepare a Maṇḍala offering."

This was done, and after the ceremony the Jetsun said, "Yesterday I went out to preach the Dharma to all sentient beings in the Six Realms. Seeing the joys of Devas and human beings and those who do good deeds, I laughed; but when I saw the miseries in the three lower Realms, and those who indulged in evil deeds, I wept." Shiwa Aui then asked, "Please tell us what are the joys and miseries that sentient beings in the Six Realms experience? Especially, please tell us, what are the pleasures that the Devas enjoy?" The Jetsun replied, "Do not be fascinated by the pleasures of heavenly beings; they also have miseries like these":

I pray to the Gracious Ones. Pray embrace
All sentient beings in your blessing!

The pleasures enjoyed by men and Devas
Are like the amusements of the Heavenly Yak[1]
It may low like thunder,
But what good can it do?

[Swooning in a state of trance],
The Devas in the Four Formless Heavens[2]
Cannot distinguish good from evil.
Because their minds are dull and callous,
Insensible, they have no feeling.
In unconscious stupefaction,
They live many kalpas in a second.
What a pity that know it not!

Alas, these Heavenly births
Have neither sense nor value.
When they think vicious thoughts
They start to fall again.
As to the reason for their fall
[Scholars], with empty words, have dried
Their mouths in explanations.

In the Heavens of Form,[3] the Devas of
The five higher and twelve lower Realms can
Only live until their merits are exhausted.
Their virtues are essentially conditional,
And their Karmas basically Saṃsāric.

Those Dharma practicers subject to worldly
Desires, and those "great yogis" wrapped in stillness,
Have yet to purify their minds;
Huge may be their claims and boasts,
But seeds of habitual thoughts
In their minds are deeply rooted.
After a long-dormant time,
Evil thoughts will rise again.
When their merits and fortunes are consumed,
They to the lower Realms will go once more!
If I explain the horrors of a Deva's
Death, you will be disheartened and perplexed.
Bear this in your mind and ever meditate!

In a sad mood, the disciples asked the Jetsun to preach for them the sufferings of the Asuras. In response, he sang:

I pray to the Gurus and Ḍākinīs —
Pray bless and enable all
To rouse the Bodhi-Mind.

Great are Asuras' sufferings.
Misled by malignant thoughts,
To all they bring misfortunes.
Knowing not their true Self-mind,
Their deeds are self-deceiving,
Their feelings coarse, their senses crude.
Deeming all to be their foes,
Not even for moment
Can they know the truth. Evil
By nature, they can hardly bear a loss; harder
Is benevolence for them to cherish. Blinded
By the Karma-of-Belligerence,
They can never take good counsel.

Ill nature such as this is caused
By seeking pleasures for oneself
And bearing harmful thoughts toward others.
Pride, favoritism, vanity, and hatred
Are the evil Karmic forces
That drag one to a lower birth,
Making sinful deeds more easy.

Ripening Karma brings
An instinctive hatred;
Failing to distinguish right from wrong,
They hardly can be helped by any means.
Bear this my disciples, in your minds,
And meditate with perseverance all your lives!

Shiwa Aui said, "Now please tell us about the sufferings of human beings." In answer, Milarepa sang:

I bow down at the feet of Jetsun Marpa —
The Buddha as a man disguised.

We human beings are endowed with power

To do good or evil deeds;
This is because our body
Is made of all Six Elements.[4]

You junior Repas who desire to be great scholars
Should know the "kernel and shell" of Buddhism,
Lest learning lead you only to confusion.

Knowing not the *root of mind*, useless
Is it to meditate for years.
Without sincerity and willingness,
Rich offerings have no real meaning.
Without giving impartial aid to all,
Patronage of one's favorite is wrong.
Knowing not the right counsel for each man,
Blunt talk will only bring trouble and discord.

He who knows the appropriate way
To help men of diverse dispositions,
Can use expedient words for kind and fruitful
Purposes. He who knows little about himself
Can harm many by his ignorance.
When good will arises in one's mind, stones,
Trees, and earth all become seeds of virtue.

Again, an over-punctilious person knows not how to
     relax;
A gluttonous dog knows not what is hunger;
A brazen Guru knows not what is fear.
Rich men are wretched creatures with money,
Poor men are wretched creatures without money.
Alas, with or without money, both are miserable!
Happiness will come, dear children,
If you can practice the Dharma. Remember,
Then, my words and practice with perseverance.

"It is very true that human beings suffer like this," agreed the disciples. "Now please tell us about the sufferings in the Three Miserable Realms, even though just to mention them may be distressing. Also, to spur our spiritual efforts, please preach for us the causes of Hell and its woe." In response, the Jetsun sang:

I pray to my Guru-protectors, pray

Dispel fear of the Miserable Realms.

Those who for meat and blood
Slaughter living beings,
Will in the Eight Hot Hells be burned.
But if they can remember the good Teachings,
They soon will be emancipated.

Ruthless robbers who strike and kill,
Wrongly eating others' food
While clinging to their own with greed,
Will fall into the Eight Cold Hells.
Yet, if they hold no wrong views against the Dharma
It is said that the time for deliverance will come.
[The Holy Scriptures] also say
Whene'er the denizens of Hell
Recall the name of Buddha,
At once they will be delivered.

Ever repeating sinful deeds means
Dominance by vice and evil Karma.
Fiends filled with the craving for pleasures,
Murder even their parents and Gurus,
Rob the Three Gems of their treasure,
Revile and accuse falsely the Precious
Ones, and condemn the Dharma as untrue;
In the Hell-that-Never-Ceases[5]
These evildoers will be burned;
Far from them, alas, is Liberation.
This, my sons, will certainly distress you,
So into the Dharma throw your hearts
And devote yourselves to meditation!

The Repas said, "Merely to hear these horrible things so frightens
and distresses us that we wonder how anyone can actually undergo
them! Nevertheless, for the benefit of sentient beings, please tell us
now about the sufferings of the Hungry Ghosts." In reply, Milarepa
sang:

I bow down to all Gurus. Pray
Protect the denizens of Hell
From fears with your compassion!

Filled with the urge to kill themselves
Those in Hell cannot escape from fear.

Hungry Ghosts, seeing all forms as foes,
Run from each successive terror. Wild beasts
Fight and eat each other.
Who of them is to blame?
The sufferings of Hungry
Ghosts grow from their stinginess.
Like a rat is he who fails
To give alms when he is rich,
Begrudges food when he has plenty,
Gives no goods to others, but checks
Them over, counts, and stores them —
Discontented day and night.
At the time of death he sees
That his hard-earned wealth will be
Enjoyed by others. Caught in
Bardo by the agony of loss,
He lives the life of a Hungry Ghost.
Due to his delusive thoughts
He suffers thirst and hunger.
When he sees his goods enjoyed by others
He is tormentated by avarice and hate.
Again and again will he thus fall down [to Hell].

I, the great Yogi of Strength,
Now sing for you the woes
Of Hungry Ghosts. Dear sons
And disciples here assembled, think on
My words and meditate with perseverance!

Shiwa Aui then requested, "Now please tell us of the sufferings of animals." Whereupon Milarepa sang:

I bow down to all holy Gurus. Pray protect
All animals from fear with your compassion!

Animals, alas, are ignorant and benighted;
Most stupid men will incarnate among them.
Blind and enslaved by evil Karma,
The ignorant know not Dharma's Truth.
Blind both to evil and to virtue,

They quickly waste their lives away.
Unable to reason and use symbols,
They act like blind automatons;
Unable to distinguish wrong from right,
Like maniacs, they do much wrong.
Some people even say 'tis good
[To be an animal],
Since it does not regret or repent.
Alas, how foolish is this thought!

Then, all stupid life-takers
Will incarnate as beasts;
The fools who know not right from wrong,
And those who harbor vicious thoughts,
Will incarnate as common brutes.
It is hard for me to describe
Their Karmas, but think on my words
And cultivate your minds.

The Repas again asked, "Did you preach the Dharma for sentient beings in only one place, or did you go to different regions in the Six Realms to preach?"

"In accordance with the different capacities, Karmas, and needs of sentient beings," replied the Jetsun, "I manifested myself in different forms at different places to preach the appropriate Dharma for them."

The monks, disciples, patrons, and attendants in the assembly were all deeply impressed with a fear of the great sufferings of Saṃsāra and the lower Realms. With a greater aspiration toward the Dharma, they all exerted themselves in the renunciation of sins and the practice of good deeds.

...   .

At another time, Milarepa flew up into the sky, transforming his body from one to many, and then retracted them back into one. Also he preached various Dharmas in an invisible form, and performed many other miracles.

When Sevan Repa saw Milarepa flying he also held his breath and tried to fly; but all he could do was to walk above the ground. Commenting on this, Milarepa said, "If one has not yet practiced as I have, by venerating my Guru, respecting my brothers, renouncing Saṃsāra, pitying sentient beings, and practicing devotion with great diligence, he should never expect to perform these miracles easily and spontaneously. My son-disciples, if you have not yet completed these virtuous deeds to suffice the cause [of the Supreme Accomplishment], you should never expect to attain it too easily." Whereupon he sang:

> If there be neither Karma nor the required conditions,
> In this life one should not hope to attain Buddhahood.
> He who cannot put all his trust in his Guru
> Should not expect care and blessing in return.
> He who cannot satisfy disciples
> Should not expect to become a Guru.
> He who cannot master his own mind
> Should have no hope of leading others.
> He who cannot hold the Lineage tradition
> Should not aspire towards the Signs and Siddhis.
> He who cannot practice diligently
> Should not have wishful thoughts for Buddhahood.
> He who has not cut the bonds of dualism
> Should not expect an infinite Compassion.
> He who cannot sever the chain of clinging to
> An entity should not expect an all-free View.
> He who has not seen Self-mind in nakedness
> Should not expect to behold the True Essence.
> He who knows not how to cleanse impurities
> Should not expect unceasing Experience.
> He who cannot destroy attachment within
> [Himself], should not expect relaxed Six Senses.
> He who is not expert in Samādhi
> Should not expect the great Omnipresence.
> He who has yet to uproot subtle hopes and fears
> Should never expect the Trikāya to attain.
> He who cannot flawlessly observe moral rules
> Should never expect immediate happiness.
> He who has not completed the Two Provisions
> Should never expect to be a revered Buddha.
> He who cannot obey orders should not hope
> For popularity among his brothers.
> He who has yet to master Self-awareness
> Should not expect freedom from ghosts and Devas.
> He who has yet to master all appearances
> Should not expect to govern the Three Lokas.
> He who has yet to transcend the mundane level
> Should not cherish the thought of "no good and no evil."
> A yogi who heads a monastery

Should not neglect discipline and virtue.
He who does not understand the stages
Of the Experiences should not try
To prove and check those of gifted disciples.
He who has not fully practiced the Pith-Instructions
Should not expect in Bardo to gain Liberation.
He who cannot observe the precepts in perfect order
Should ne'er expect his wishes to be easily fulfilled.
He who cannot observe well the Samaya rules
Should n'er expect Ḍākinīs and Guards to like him.
He who has not obtained the Key Instructions
From logic and the Holy Scriptures
Should not neglect the words and symbols.
He who possesses not the Five Miraculous
Powers, should not make predictions from external signs.
He who has not stablized the Experience,
Should never neglect to cultivate his mind.

· · ·   · · ·   · · ·

On another occasion, the Jetsun's body became invisible to all who
came before him. Some saw light, and some a glowing lamp shining
on his bed; others beheld a rainbow, water, a bar of gold, or a whirl-
wind; and still others could not see anything. Then Repa Shiwa Aui
asked the Jetsun what were the meanings and reasons behind all these
phenomena. Milarepa answered him in this song:

I pray to all Gurus —
Pray enable me to change into many forms.

Listen Shiwa Aui, my dear son,
Who is as good as Rechungpa.
Since I have mastered Earth,
Earth of myself is now a part;
Since I have mastered Water,
Water of myself is now a part;
Since I have mastered Fire,
Fire of myself is now a part;
Since I have mastered Air,
Air of myself is now a part.
Since I have mastered the Void of space,
All manifestations in the Cosmos
Have merged and are identified with me.

Since I have mastered the projection of Prāṇa-Mind,
I can transform my body into any form.
Dear son, if you have faith
In the Accomplished Jetsuns,
You will indeed be blessed
And your wishes fulfilled.

. . .　　. . .　　. . .

Again one day the Jetsun transformed himself into a different body
before each of his disciples and faithful patrons, to preach the Dharma
to them. Also he conjured a child playing with clay beside each
preacher. In short, he performed many miracles in inconceivable varieties. The disciples asked him his reasons for doing so. He replied, "I
am a yogi who sees his own Self-mind, thus I can change and manipulate all manifestations in the outer world to any form and in any
manner I please. Also, I can project and multiply all objects from my
mind and bring them back to it again." Then he sang:

I bow down to all Gurus.

When my body has the Guru's blessing,
It can work many miracles
And many transformations.
When my mouth receives the Guru's
Blessing, it can sing lyric songs
And give Pith-Instructions.
When my mind receives the Guru's blessing
It realizes and is the Buddha.

Fire cannot burn nor water drown me;
Walking like an elephant, I act
And dance with great confidence.

With their different states of mind,
The faithful see my various forms
And hear my different preachings;
By this they will gain Liberation.
But impure men with evil Karmas
Cannot even see my body.
They must suffer for their sins —
Even Buddha cannot help them.

Dear sons, try with diligence to practice
The Dharma. I could talk on without end,
[But what better advice could I give you?]

Alas, pity all sinful men! Seeing them
Deprived of a chance for Liberation,
And bearing all sorrows, my heart is most
Distressed and troubled!
Oh friends, let us try
Firmly to practice our devotion.
Let us forget all worldly things,
For the next life preparing!

Hearing this song, all the son-disciples were inspired with great joy.

[Thus, and in this manner, the Jetsun Milarepa] caused the Buddhist religion to dawn in Tibet, and brought temporal and Ultimate happiness to sentient beings. Having unified forms and Mind, and consolidated the Main and the Ensuing Samādhis, the great Master Yogi, Milarepa, benefited sentient beings through his miraculous powers and melodious songs. These songs were cherished, remembered, and recorded in writing by his heart-son disciples. The major part of Milarepa's songs that are well known in the human world, is now compiled in this volume. It is befitting to state here that to collect all his innumerable songs would be a task quite beyond our reach.

This is the story of Milarepa performing miracles to inspire his disciples, and the end of the last series [of the *Mila Grubum*].
In the foregoing chapters three groups of stories,[6] serving as a good account of the Eight Deeds[7] of [the Jetsun Milarepa] through which he propagated the Practice Transmission in Tibet and bestowed blessing on sentient beings, are related with complete details.

(The End)

NOTES

1 Heavenly Yak: a legendary yak said to dwell in Heaven (T.T.: lHa.gYag.).
2 The Four Formless Heavens, or Realms (T.T.: gZugs.Med.sKye.mChed.

bShi.), are: (1) the Realm of Infinite Space; (2) the Realm of Infinite Consciousness; (3) the Realm of Nothingness; and (4) the Realm of Neither Consciousness nor Non-Consciousness. These Formless Heavens are considered to be the highest Heavens in Saṃsāra; only those who have attained very advanced Samādhis can be born in these Realms. However, according to Buddhism, a birth in these Heavens will not bring one to Liberation, hence it is only a waste of time.

3 Heavens of Form (T.T.: gZugs.Khms.Kyi.lHa.): In this Realm, it is said, there are 17 Heavens. They are:

    (1) Brahmapariṣadya, (2) Brahmapurohita, (3) Mahābrahmā. (These three belong to the Heavens of the First Dhyāna.)

    (4) Parittābha, (5) Apramāṇābha, (6) Ābhāsvara. (These three belong to the Heavens of the Second Dhyāna.)

    (7) Parittaśubha, (8) Apramāṇaśubha, (9) Subhakṛtsna. (These three belong to the Heavens of the Third Dhyāna.)

    (10) Anabhraka, (11) Puṇyaprasava, (12) Bṛhatphala, (13) Avṛha, (14) Atapa, (15) Sudṛsa, (16) Sudarśana, and (17) Mahāmaheśvara. (These eight belong to the Heavens of the Fourth Dhyāna.)

4 Six Elements: the elements of earth, water, fire, air, space, and consciousness. In comparison with sentient beings in the Heavens, human beings are said to possess more elements. For example, in the Heaven of Form, sentient beings do not have the elements of earth, water, and fire; and in the Formless Heavens, sentient beings do not have the elements of earth, water, fire, air, and space, because they possess only the element of consciousness.

5 The-Hell-that-Never-Ceases (T.T.: mNar.Med.dMyal.Wa.): It is said that denizens of this Hell suffer unceasing torment, whereas in other hells, temporary relief of pain is possible.

6 According to the compiler, this book, the *Mila Grubum*, consists of three groups of stories. The first group of stories are those of Milarepa's conquering and conversion of the malignant demons — Stories 1 through 8; the second group are those of Milarepa and his well-endowed disciples — Stories 9 through 44; and the third group are those of various categories — Stories 45 through 61. See the last paragraphs of Story 8 and of Story 44.

7 The Eight Deeds (T.T.: mDsad.Pa.brGyad.): These are the well-known Eight Deeds of Buddha, performed in the eight phases of Buddha's life. They are: (1) descending from the Tuṣita Heaven; (2) entering His mother's womb; (3) birth; (4) renouncing the world; (5) conquering the demons; (6) attaining the Ultimate Enlightenment; (7) setting the Wheel-of-Dharma in motion (preaching); and (8) Nirvāṇa.

On His two mighty wings
Of Wisdom and of Skill,
He flew to the sky of Supreme
Accomplishment, with a mind
Priceless and pure as Heaven's.

He was the Lord Jetsun Mila
Who danced, and sang with joy
In a drama of Totality.
With a mind firm as a diamond
He raised the flag of the Two Siddhis.
To Him, the changeless Vajra,
With a laughing voice that
Rolls the world and heaven,
I pay sincerest homage!

From reading His life story, one will profit;
From hearing His name, one will be freed from pain;
Bestowed will be the power of
Achieving Buddhahood this time.
To those Who remember and venerate Him,
He is the wish-granting jewel, the matchless
        treasure-opener,
The Great Sorcerer, a descendent from a brave Lineage.

Any man of sense who reads his stories
Will be inspired with a wish to follow him.
Those who read, hear, think, and touch
This book will all gain great profit.
With this in mind, to propagate the Dharma
The faithful Chueji Jangtse has arranged the wood-
        blocks
For publication of a late edition of this book.
By this merit may all living
Beings follow Milarepa,
Till they arrive at Buddhahood.
May all men who find this book, ever be born

In a Lineage of the Supreme Vehicle.
May they all meet a perfect Guru, rely
On him, and cherish him like their own eyes —
As Milarepa once did in his lifetime.
[By the merit of publishing this book],
May all Buddhist Schools, Sūtra or Tantra,
Scripture or Devotional, prosper and spread afar.
May all religious leaders everywhere live long.
May all preachers of all Sects agree
With each other in the light of Dharma.
May all Buddhist patrons gain prosperity
And power. May all men complete
Their preparatory work and soon
Enter the one supreme Path of Vajrayāna!
In the Two-in-One Palace of Ḍākinīs,
May they soon become Buddhas of the Ten Perfections!

By the earnest request of the benevolent practicer (sGrub. Pa.Po.),
I, Monk Jhambar Rolbi Lhodroe, have written these auspicious wishes.
May all of our good Vows, both temporal and eternal, soon be fulfilled.

APPENDIX

༄༅།། THE "HUNDRED THOUSAND SONGS OF MILAREPA," ITS ORIGIN, BACKGROUND, FUNCTION, AND TRANSLATION

by GARMA C. C. CHANG

THE *Mila Grubum*,[1] or the "Hundred Thousand Songs of Milarepa," is perhaps the most outstanding masterpiece of Tibetan literature. Its rich contents, fascinating stories, and characteristic style, all revealed through a simple yet graphic expression, have capitvated the hearts and minds of Tibetans from all walks of life for the past eight centuries, providing them with solace and a source of inexhaustible joy and in- spiration. It has been read as the biography of a saint, a guide book for devotions, a manual of Buddhist Yoga, a volume of songs and poems, and even a collection of Tibetan folklore and fairy tales.

In introducing this beloved, holy book of Tibet, I have naturally been concerned lest I do an injustice to it by possible misrepresenta- tion — even profanation. I am inclined to believe that a proper intro- duction to a book of this kind should adhere as closely as possible to an "indigenous style," for none could know better or feel more in- timate with the subject matter of the *Mila Grubum* than the owners of the book themselves — the Tibetan people who have inherited it and have lived with it for centuries. With this in mind I present this book to readers under three topics: (1) the life and contribution of Milarepa; (2) the central teaching of Tibetan Tantrism; and (3) the translation.

THE LIFE AND CONTRIBUTION OF MILAREPA

Milarepa, the great Buddhist saint and poet of Tibet, was born A.D. 1052[2] and died in 1135. His youth was full of misfortunes and sorrows. Following the early death of his father, his relatives treacher- ously and shamelessly seized his vast patrimony. After many years of hard labor, poverty, and humiliation, he was finally persuaded by his

679

mother to take revenge upon the wrongdoers through magic, for they were much too powerful to be vanquished by ordinary means. He succeeded in obtaining, through his sincere devotion and service to a teacher of sorcery, a powerful spell, by means of which he assassinated many of his relatives and wrought great havoc on his native valley by destroying the harvest with hailstorms.

Not long after, he repented of his sinful deeds, and determined to seek salvation by devoting the rest of his life to the practice of the Dharma. Despite the fact that meanwhile he was initiated into the profound teachings of the "Great Perfection" (T.T.: rDsogs.Pa.Chen.Po.) by an enlightened lama, the shadows of sin and pride still made it impossible for him to make any spiritual progress. The lama then sent him to the famous Guru — Marpa the Translator — who had just returned from India after many years of study and practice there.

The day before Milarepa arrived, both Marpa and his wife dreamed of goddesses who prophesied the coming of a disciple who would one day become the greatest teacher of Tibet, bringing salvation to innumerable sentient beings, bestowing Enlightenment upon countless Dharma devotees, and glorifying the immaculate doctrine of Buddhism.

Perceiving Milarepa's past sins and his great potential capacities, and wishing to clear away all hindrances that might otherwise block his spiritual growth, Marpa relentlessly put him on trial by imposing upon him severe mental and physical penances. Milarepa was ordered to build, single-handed, one house after another on a desolate mountain, then to tear them down again for no apparent reason. In return for long years of service, devotion, and obedience to Marpa, Milarepa received only humiliation and unjustified harsh treatment. At last he was accepted as a disciple, and rewarded with the longed-for instructions. Then, for eleven continuous months, he meditated alone in a cave, where he finally attained direct Realization and an initial achievement on the Path to Bodhi.

By this time, Milarepa had been separated from his family for many years. One day, while meditating in the cave, he fell asleep and dreamed that he returned home and saw the bones of his mother lying in the ruins of his house. He then thought that she must have died during his long absence. He saw his only sister as a vagabond beggar, his house and fields deserted and overgrown with a tangle of rank weeds. He awoke weeping bitterly, calling the names of his mother and sister, his pillow wet with tears.

Stricken with grief and longing to see his mother, he left Marpa and went back to his home village, where all the premonitions of his dream were confirmed. Witnessing this painful human existence helplessly and futilely consumed in fleeting evanescence, an anguish of desire to renounce the world wrung his heart. He made a solemn vow that he would meditate on a remote mountain uninterruptedly until he reached the Ultimate Enlightenment.

This vow he kept. For twelve consecutive years he meditated alone in a cave, living on nothing but nettles, until his whole body became greenish in hue. As a consequence of this consistent effort, he finally earned his reward — the realization of Ultimate Enlightenment. After this, his fame gradually spread over the whole of Tibet and Nepal. In his later years he was called by all Tibetans, "Jetsun Milarepa" ("Holy Milarepa"), and is regarded to this day as indisputably the greatest poet, yogi, and saint in Tibetan history.

Milarepa had a fine voice, and loved to sing. Even when he was a boy, he was regarded by his countrymen as an excellent singer of folksongs. Sainthood and Enlightenment only made him sing more frequently and joyfully than before. When his patrons and disciples made a request, or put a question to him, or a dispute arose, he answered them not in dull prose but in freely flowing poems or lyric songs composed spontaneously. No one knows how many songs or "poems" he "composed" in his lifetime. Tibetans believe there were close to one hundred thousand. This claim may not be an exaggeration, if we consider that throughout almost half of his life Milarepa used songs to communicate his ideas in his teaching and conversation. Even if we discount this seemingly exaggerated claim, we must nevertheless admit that he was an extraordinarily prolific "composer" of songs. For him there was no difficulty in creating a new song at any moment, for, in the genius of his enlightened mind, the fountain of inspiration was inexhaustible.

In his songs, Milarepa has left us a treasury of valuable information on his personal yogic experience, and advice and instruction concerning the practical problems of meditation. To serious yogis and Dharma practitioners, they are indeed a most precious guide. Speculative and scholarly writings are abundant in Buddhist literature, but rarely can one find a volume having such life and vitality, and generating a magnetic force bright and powerful enough to dispel the darkness of grief and bring hope and joy to all.

Unlike many religious leaders, who exerted themselves in various tasks for the creation of their new Orders, Milarepa never tried to build a temple, form a group, or set up an organization of any sort, but faithfully followed his Guru's injunctions by leading the life of a true mendicant yogi in the remote mountains, the life of a saint-troubadour, wandering from place to place to preach the holy Dharma through his songs. Also, differing from those pedantic scholars and dogmatic Tantric yogis who either adhered to ideas and words or to rites and forms, Milarepa cast away all erudite Buddhist studies and cumbersome Tantric rituals, and marched directly toward Buddhahood by way of simple understanding and persistent practice. As a result, his teachings were also more precise, direct, and simple than those of conventional Tantrism, and well deserve being called the *quintessential teachings of practical Buddhism*. Though Milarepa was ridiculed by a number of jealous scholars of his time as being an ignorant hermit who knew nothing about Buddhism, history has proved that his teachings were far superior and more influential than those of any learned Budhist scholar of his day.

Through the illustration of his own life, Milarepa set for all Budhists an example of the perfect Bodhisattva, and a model of the incorruptible life of a genuine practitioner of Buddhist Tantrism. His life is an unmistakable testimony to the unity and interdependency of all Buddhist teachings — Theravāda, Mahāyāna, and Vajrayāna — for Buddahood is not attainable if any of the three are lacking. He made it clear to all that poverty is not a kind of deprivation, but rather a necessary way of emanicpating oneself from the tyranny of material possessions; that Tantric practice by no means implies indulgence and laxity, but hard labor, strict discipline, and steadfast perseverance; that without resolute renunciation and uncompromising discipline, as Guatama Buddha Himself stressed, all the sublime ideas and dazzling images depicted in Mahāyāna and Tantric Buddhism are no better than magnificent illusions.

Milarepa was one of the very few Buddhist saints whose transmitted teachings have given birth to more enlightened beings than have any of the Mahāyāna Buddhist Schools, except Ch'an Buddhism in China. Hui Neng, the founder of Ch'an, was perhaps the only figure in Buddhist history whose influence and contribution can, in various aspects, rival those of Milarepa.

These two great sages also had many other things in common. They both laid stress on actual practice and direct Realization, and in both instances their teachings were characterized by extreme simplicity and straightforwardness. But the teaching of Milarepa seems to be more thorough, complete, and "advanced" than that of Hui Neng because, unlike Hui Neng, who put all his emphasis on the Prajñāpāramitā, Milarepa accentuated *all* the essential teachings of Buddhism. In stressing the importance of the Dharmakāya, both are alike; but as to the teaching of the other two Kāyas — the manifestation, and the dynamic force of Buddhahood — Milarepa's seems to be the more thorough. Thus, through his life-example, Milarepa preached and demonstrated the unity and interdependency of all the essential teachings of Buddhism. Among his many important contributions, this is perhaps the greatest and the most unique one of all.

Those who have a serious interest in Milarepa's life and work should also read another important Tibetan work, "The Jetsun Milarepa *Khabum*," or "*Namthar*" — "The Biography of Milarepa," translated by the late Lama Kazi Dawa-Samdup and edited with an Introduction and annotations by Dr. W. Y. Evans-Wentz, under the title, "Tibet's Great Yogi, Milarepa," (Oxford University Press, 1951). A careful study of this celebrated book will not only broaden the reader's understanding of Milarepa's life and work, but will bring to him a broader comprehension of the spirit and teaching of Tibetan Buddhism.

THE CENTRAL TEACHING OF TIBETAN TANTRISM

A better understanding and deeper appreciation of the songs of Milarepa will be reached if a good knowledge of Buddhism in general, and a fair grasp of Tibetan Tantrism in particular, is acquired. In order to help those who may not have had such a background, a brief summary of the essential teachings of Tibetan Tantrism is given in the following pages. Information on general Buddhism is not included, since this may be obtained from sources easily available to all. It goes without saying that this brief summary is less than adequate to represent the vast and comprehensive contents of the Tibetan Tantra. One cannot expect, therefore, to glean from these brief lines more than a hint of the essential, underlying principles.

Tibetan Tantrism is a form of practical Buddhism abounding in methods and techniques for carrying out the practice of all the Mahāyāna teachings. In contrast to the "theoretical" forms of Buddhism, such as Sautrāntika, Vaibhāṣika, Mādhayamika, Yogācāra, Hua Yen, Tien Tai, etc., Buddhist Tantrism lays most of its stress on *practice* and *Realization*, rather than on philosophical speculations. Its central principles and practices may be summarized as follows:

1. That all existence and manifestation can be found in one's experience, that this experience is within one's own mind, and that Mind is the source and creator of all things.

2. That Mind is an infinitely vast, unfathomably deep complex of marvels, its immensity and depth being inaccessible to the uninitiated.

3. That he who has come to a thorough realization and perfect mastership of his own mind is a Buddha, and that those who have not done so are unenlightened sentient beings.

4. That sentient beings and Buddhas are, in essence, identical. Buddhas are enlightened sentient beings, and sentient beings unenlightened Buddhas.

5. That this infinite, all-embracing Buddha-Mind is beyond comprehension and attributes. The best and closest definition might be:

"Buddha-Mind is a GREAT ILLUMINATING-VOID
AWARENESS."

6. That the consciousness of sentient beings is of limited awareness; the consciousness of an advanced yogi, of illuminating awareness; the consciousness of an enlightened Bodhisattva, of illuminating-void awareness; and the "consciousness" of Buddha, the GREAT ILLUMINATING-VOID AWARENESS.

7. That all Buddhist teachings are merely "exaltations," preparations, and directions leading one toward the unfoldment of this GREAT ILLUMINATING-VOID AWARENESS.

8. That infinite compassion, merit, and marvels will spontaneously come forth when this Buddha-Mind is fully unfolded.

9. That to unfold this Buddha-Mind, two major approaches or Paths are provided for differently disposed individuals: the Path of Means, and the Path of Liberation. The former stresses an approach to Buddhahood through the practice of taming the Prāṇa, and the latter an approach through the practice of taming the mind. Both approaches, however, are based on the truism of the IDENTICALITY OF MIND AND PRĀṆA.[3] (T.T.: Rluñ.Sems.dWyer.Med.), which is the fundamental theorem of Tantrism.

The principle of the Identicality of Mind and Prāṇa may be briefly stated thus: The world encompasses and is made up of various contrasting forces in an "antithetical" form of relationship — positive and negative, noumenon and phenomenon, potentiality and manifestation, vitality and voidness, Mind and Prāṇa, and the like. Each of these dualities, though apparently antithetical, is an inseparable unity. The dual forces that we see about us are, in fact, one "entity" manifesting in two different forms or stages. Hence, if one's consciousness or mind is disciplined, tamed, transformed, extended, sharpened, illuminated, and sublimated, so will be his Prāṇas, and vice versa. The practice that stresses taming the Prāṇa is called the "Yoga with Form," or the "Path of Means." The practice that stresses taming the mind is called the "Yoga without Form," or the "Path of Liberation." The former is an exertive type of Yoga practice, and the latter a natural and effortless one, known as Mahāmudrā.[4]

(1) *The Path of Means:* The main practices of the Path of Means contain the following eight steps:

(A) The cultivation of altruistic thoughts, and basic training in the discipline of the Bodhisattva.

(B) The four fundamental preparatory practices, which contain:
(a) One hundred thousand obeisances to the Buddhas. This practice is for the purpose of cleansing all bodily sins and hindrances, thus enabling one to meditate without being handicapped by physical impediments.
(b) One hundred thousand recitations of repentance prayers. When properly performed, this cleanses mental obstructions and sins, clearing out all mental hindrances that may block spiritual growth.
(c) One hundred thousand repetitions of the prayer to one's Guru of the Guru Yoga Practice. This brings protection and blessings from one's Guru.
(d) Making one hundred thousand Special Offerings. This will create favorable conditions for one's devotions.

(C) The Patron Buddha Yoga, a training for identifying and unifying oneself with a divine Buddha as assigned to one by his Guru. This Yoga consists of mantra recitations, visualization, concentration, and breathing exercises.

(D) The advanced form of breathing exercises and their concomitant and subsidiary practices, including the Yogas of Dream, of Transformation, of Union, and of Light — generally known as the Perfecting Yogas.

(E) Guiding the subtle Prāṇa-Mind (T.T.: Rluñ.Sems.) into the Central Channel, thus successively opening the four main Cakras ("psychic" centers) and transforming the mundane consciousness into transcendal Wisdom.

(F) Applying the power of Prāṇa-Mind to bring about or to vanquish at will, one's death, Bardo, and reborn state, thus achieving emancipation from Saṃsāra.

(G) Applying the power of Prāṇa-Mind to master the mind-projection performances.

(H) Sublimating and perfecting the Prāṇa-Mind into the Three Bodies of Buddhahood.

(2) *The Path of Liberation,* or the Yoga without Form, is the simplest and most direct approach toward the Buddha-Mind. It is a natural and spontaneous practice, bypassing many preparations, strenuous exercises, and even successive stages as laid down in other types of Yoga. Its essence consists in the Guru's capability of bringing to his disciple a glimpse of the Innate Buddha-Mind in its primordial and natural state. With this initial and direct "glimpsing experience," the disciple gradually learns to sustain, expand, and deepen his realization of this Innate Mind. Eventually he will consummate this realization to its full blossoming in Perfect Enlightenment. This practice is called Mahāmudrā.

(A) The first glimps of the Innate Mind can be acquired either through practicing Mahāmudrā Yoga by oneself, or through receiving a "Pointing-out" demonstration from one's Guru. The former way is to follow the Guru's instructions and meditate alone; the latter consists of an effort by the Guru to open the disciple's mind instantaneously. Both approaches, however, require the continuous practice of Mahāmudrā Yoga to deepen and perfect one's experience.

(B) The central teaching of Mahāmudrā consists of two major points: relaxation, and effortlessness. All pains and desires are of a tense nature. But Liberation, in contrast, is another name for "perfect relaxation." Dominated by long-established habits, however, average men find it most difficult, if not entirely impossible, to reach a state of deep relaxation; so instructions and practices are needed to enable them to attain such a state. The primary concern of Mahāmudrā, therefore, is to instruct the yogi on how to relax the mind and thus induce in him the unfolding of his Primordial Mind. Paradoxically, effortlessness is even more difficult to achieve than relaxation. It requires long practice to become "effortless" at all times and under all circumstances. If one can keep his mind always relaxed, spontaneous, and free of clinging, the Innate Buddha-Mind will soon dawn upon him.

(3) *The Path of Means and The Path of Liberation,* exist only in the beginning stages. In the advanced stages these two Paths converge and become one. It is to the advantage of a yogi, in order to hasten

his spiritual progress, if he can either practice both teachings at the same time or use one to supplement the other. Most of the great yogis of Tibet practiced both Paths, as did Milarepa.

THE TRANSLATION OF THE BOOK

To the best knowledge of the translator, the *Mila Grubum*, or the "Hundred Thousand Songs of Milarepa," has never before been completely translated from Tibetan into any major foreign language. Translations of several sections, however, have been available for some time. Many thoughtful and interested readers may be curious as to why an important work such as this has never been fully translated. There are many reasons for this. In addition to the depth of the work itself, a number of technical difficulties are involved. Scholars of Tibetan Buddhism do not find it very difficult to translate the conventional type of Buddhist Sūtras and Śāstras, for they are all written with established terminologies, phraseologies, and styles. The enigmatic passages of a Tibetan text frequently can be deciphered by means of a comparative study of the equivalent text in the Chinese or Sanskrit language. But nothing of this kind is available in the case of the *Mila Grubum*; its language, style, and subject matter are in many ways different from those of conventional Buddhist texts. It was written not only in colloquial Tibetan, but in a form of ancient colloquialism strongly tinged with a flavor of the local dialect of Southwestern Tibet. The particular phrases with which Milarepa expressed his Tantric ideas and mystical experiences, present another formidable problem of translation. Moreover, the major part of the book is largely composed of verses and songs of an "uncommon" type, which further increases the difficulties.

Being fully aware of these difficulties, I have undertaken this formidable task not without apprehension and concern. I have always been of the opinion that a better translation of the Buddhist classics can be achieved only by pooling together the talents of many Buddhist scholars (in different fields) to make a joint effort in the task, as did King James of England with the translation of the Bible, and Emperors Tai Tsung and Khri.Sroñ.lDe.bTsan. of China and Tibet with the translations of Buddhist Sūtras in the Tang period. Individual efforts in this type of undertaking are always difficult. It is my hope, therefore, not to make a perfect translation, but rather to see that this important work of Tibetan Buddhism is soon made available to the world. As a Chinese proverb has said, "The purpose of my throwing a brick is to induce people to cast their jade." My greatest desire is to see that this pioneer translation, imperfect as it may be, rouses a wider interest in the work itself, and thus serves as a prelude to more and better translations of the *Mila Grubum* to follow.

Because no clear statement appears in the book, the author or compiler of the *Mila Grubum* is not clearly known. Except in Stories 29, 30, and 31, where the compilers' names — Shiwa.Hod. and Ñan. rDson.sTon.Pa. — are given, the name of the compiler of the vast majority of the stories — a total of 58 — is not clearly mentioned. It is interesting to note, however, that these stories seem to have a uniform style, and, when compared with Stories 29, 30, and 31, they reveal an outstanding difference, flavor, and superior quality. Beyond any doubt they were written by another author. I therefore assume that this compiler or author is the same person as the author of the *Mila Khabum*, or *Namthar* (Mi.La.bKah.hBum., or .rNam.Thar. — the "Biography of Milarepa"), namely, the fabulous and mysterious yogi, gTsañ.sMyoñ.Heruka. — "The Mad Yogi from gTsañ"[5] — who was a disciple of Phag.Mo.Gru.Pa. (1110-1170), the celebrated pupil of Gambopa (1079-1161), Milarepa's chief disciple. Another strong piece of evidence seems also to support this opinion: in the *Mila Khabum*, or *Namthar*, from Folio 109 to Folio 113, there is a detailed account of Milarepa's life story which is identical with that of the *Grubum*; even the sequence of the stories in the two books is in perfect correspondence. There seems to be no other explanation than the fact that both books were compiled by the same person, either in the latter part of the 12th or in the beginning of the 13th century.

Professor Herbert V. Guenther, of the Sanskrit University, Varanasi, India, was so kind as to do some research for me on this problem. His findings are stated in a letter to me, as follows: " . . . just to let you know that your surmise that the biography of Mi.La.Ras.Pa. [the *Mila Khabum*] is not by Ras.Chuñ.Pa. [Rechungpa] but by the "Insane Yogi" is correct. While I was studying my sÑan.r.Gyud., I came across the following line: 'Dur.Khrod.Myul.Bahi.rNal.hByor.Pa.Sañs. rGyas.rGyal.mTshan.gTsañ.Pa.He.Ru.Ka.Rus.Pahi.rGyan.Can.Sogs. Du. Mahi.Miñ.Can.Gis.bKod.Pa.' The same names occur at the end of Mi.La.Ras.Pa's rNam.Thar. It seems that the confusion with Ras.Chuñ. Pa. is due to the fact that gTsan.Pa.Heruka is considered as an incarnation of Ras.Chuñ.Pa. and as one of the disciples of Phag.Mo.Gru. Pa . . . . By this strong evidence the authorship of both the *Mila Khabum* and the *Mila Grubum* is thus established to be by Sañs.rGyas. rGyal.mTshan, the 'Insane Yogi from gTsañ,' who bears many different names."

The sequence of stories appearing in the *Mila Grubum* seems to have been arranged, not in the strict chronological order of Milarepa's life, but rather into three groups according to the contents of the stories. Stories of Milarepa's encounters with malignant spirits are found in the first part of the book; stories of Milarepa and his human disciples, in the middle part; and stories of a more varied and general nature, at the end. This classification, of course, should not be treated too rigidily, for most of the stories contain, in some measure, all three elements.

The Tibetan text of the *Mila Grubum* has four major versions — those of Peking, of Narthang, of Dege, and of Lhasa. The Lhasa edition, containing 319 wood-printed folios and 61 stories, has been used in this translation. I believe this edition to be the latest publication among the four, being more or less a reproduction of the Dege version.

Because of the complexity and particularity of Tibetan Buddhist terminology, explanatory notes for these terms are necessary. Nevertheless, I have tried to make these notes as simple as possible to avoid over-elaboration, lest they become a burden rather than a help to the general reader and thus impede the reading of the text itself.

The Tibetan names, both of places and persons, *are all rendered phonetically*[6] in order to avoid the cumbersome, confusing, and impractical transliteration of Tibetan words, e.g., instead of sNan.gYon., "Nyan Yuan"; Mi.La.Ras.Pa., "Milarepa"; gTsug.Tor.rNam.rGyal., "Tsudor Namjal"; Zla.Wa.bZañ.Po., "Dawazungpo," etc. This simplification is not only desirable and necessary from a practical viewpoint, but is also founded on the very fact that the Tibetans themselves have for several centuries abandoned pronouncing these cumbersome prefixes and suffixes in their everyday speech as well as in their reading. Nevertheless, to help scholars of Tibetanology in identifying these names, a list of important Tibetan names and terms is attached at the end of this book, wherein both the pronunciation and transliteration are given. The Romanization of Tibetan words in the book is based on the Sarat Chandra Das system.[7]

For the same reason Tibetan diacritical marks are omitted in the text, but included in the notes.

In the year 1950, when I was in retreat at Kalimpong, India, Lady Yutog, a devout Tibetan noblewoman, came to visit me. She was interested to hear that I, a young Chinese, who had spent a number of years studying Tibetan Buddhism in Eastern Tibet, was now practicing meditation at Kalimpong. After an exchange of information and ideas, she appeared to be delighted. The second morning she came to see me again, bringing with her a huge Tibetan book wrapped in an elegant yellow silk scarf, and said to me, "This is the *Mila Grubum.* I now offer it to you, for I understand how much this book would mean to a person in retreat. My greatest hope is, however, to see the message of Milarepa reach every corner of the globe. I hope you will translate this book into English some day, so that many people can read it and profit from it." Jubilantly I accepted this wonderful gift, for this was just the book I had been painstakingly seeking ever since I had lost all my Tibetan books during my escape into India from China.

In retrospect, now that the translation is completed, I feel more grateful than ever to Lady Yutog for this inspiring and deeply significant visit. Under divine wisdom and guidance she brought to me a precious gift, together with insight into an important mission and challenge — one which I accepted with joy and inspiration during a critical period in my life.

NOTES

1 *Mila Grubum* represents the Tibetan pronunciation of the title. The transliteration would be: Mi.La.Ras.Pahi.mGur.hBum.

2 According to "The Blue Annals," p. 427, Milarepa was born A.D. 1040 and died A.D. 1123. But according to the *Mila Khabum*, or *Namthar*, the dates should be 1052 and 1135.

3 Prāṇa: a Sanskrit term, equivalent to the Tibetan term Rluṅ. and to the Chinese term Ch'i, conveying various meanings: air, energy, vital force, breathing, propensity, and so forth. An exact translation of this term into English is extremely difficult.

4 A renowned version of the Mahāmudrā system is set forth in English translation, along with Chang's "Yogic Commentary" thereon, in "Tibetan Yoga and Secret Doctrines," 2nd ed., edited by Dr. W. Y. Evans-Wentz (Oxford University Press, 1958).

5 Although the text of the *Mila Khabum* opens with Rechungpa's request to Milarepa to relate his life story in the very beginning of the book as well as in each of its successive chapters, this by no means suggests that Rechungpa was the author of the *Mila Khabum*, as some scholars are inclined to believe. On the contrary, this fact provides strong evidence that Rechungpa was an actor in the "drama of the *Mila Khabum*" as portrayed by the author, rather than the author himself. The fact that gTsaṅ.sMyon.Heruka was the author of the *Mila Khabum* is well known in Tibet.

6 In the case of personal names ending in **ཟ** *Pa* instead of *Ba* is used, e.g., Milare*pa*, not Milare*ba*, and Rechung*pa*, not Rechung*ba*, though phonetically "Pa" should be pronounced "Ba" in modern Tibetan. This compromise seems to be necessary since these names are now more or less established in the West.

7 In order to keep the transliteration as close to the "Tibetan way" as possible, the letter **བ** (Ba) is also transliterated as "Wa" after the prefix **ད** (Da), e.g., dWañ-bShi., not dBañ.bShi. This is because all Tibetans invariably pronounce it as "Wa." This, of course, should not be mistakenly identified with the other Wa (**ཝ**), the 20th consonant. This rule is also true in the case where the letter is used to form a noun, e.g., dGe.Wa., not dGe.Ba. The root of each Tibetan word is always capitalized to facilitate identification. In the case of **ཕ**, **ཙ** , **ཚ** , **ཛ** , and **ཤ** — Pha, Tsa, Tsha, Dsa, and Sha — only the first letter of the root is capitalized. Also note: "T.T." stands for Tibetan Transliteration.

GLOSSARY

Ālaya Consciousness — the "Store" Consciousness. The function of this consciousness is to preserve the "seeds" of mental impressions. Memory and learning are made possible because of this consciousness. In a loose sense, it can also be regarded as the "Primordial Consciousness" or "Universal Consciousness."

Bardo — the intermediate stage between death and rebirth.

Bodhi — Buddhahood, or that which concerns Buddhahood.

Bodhi-Mind (Skt.: Bodhicitta) — the aspiration to Buddhahood; the determination to practice all the virtuous deeds that lead toward Buddhahood; the enlightened insight into immanent Reality; the great compassionate Vow to serve, benefit, and deliver all sentient beings.

Bodhisattva — a man who has taken a vow to strive for Enlightenment and save all sentient beings; a man who aspires to Buddhahood and altruistic deeds; an enlightened being; a follower of Mahāyāna Buddhism.

Bon Religion — the aboriginal religion of Tibet.

Dākinīs — goddesses, or female deities.

Deva — a general term for gods, angels, or heavenly beings.

Dharma — a term having two main usages: (1) to signify object, matter, or thing; (2) to mean the teaching and doctrine of Buddhism, hence, the religious truth and Law.

Dharmadhātu — Totality, or the realm of Ultimate Reality.

Dharmakāya — the "Body of Truth," or the real "Body" of Buddha, which is formless, omnipresent, ultimate, and yet void.

Dhyāna — an equivalent of Samādhi which, according to the Buddhist version, denotes a group of pure concentrative states.

Dumo's Fire — The "mystic" heat that is produced in the Navel Center through the practice of Heat Yoga.

Eight Worldly Winds, or Eight Worldly Dharmas — a metaphoric term denoting the "winds," or influences, which fan the desires and passions, i.e.: gain, loss; defamation, eulogy; praise, ridicule; sorrow, joy.

Experience and Realization (T.T.: Ñams.Dañ.rTog.Pa.) — The former term denotes the Yogi's experiences, understandings, and insights prior to Enlightenment; the latter denotes the real Enlightenment. The resemblance of the two often confuses a yogi into mistaking the former for the latter.

Foundation, Path, and Fruit — Foundation is the immanent Buddha-nature; Path is the action or practice that leads toward the unfoldment of the Buddha-nature; Fruit is its realization.

Jetsun — The Revered One (a title).

Kleśas — the worldly desires and impulses that cause one to wander in Saṃsāra.

Among them, three are most prominent: lust, hatred, and ignorance.

Mahāmudrā — the most important teaching of Tibetan Tantrism, by which one is led to the realization of the Dharmakāya; the practical verbal instruction on how to meditate on the Void.

Maṇḍala — meaning "circle" or "center." A maṇḍala is an extremely complex pictorial design that symbolizes the phenomenal world of Tantric Buddhas.

Nhamdog — the disturbing and wavering thoughts which one encounters in meditation; wrong or uncontrollable thoughts; misconception or misjudgment.

Nirmāṇakāya — the transformation or incarnation Body of a Buddha.

Pāramitās — the spiritual deeds of a Bodhisattva that bring him to Buddhahood.

Prajñā — Transcendental Wisdom, or the supramundane insight into Reality.

Prāṇa — Prāṇa conveys various meaning's such as air, breath, energy, wind, vitality, and so forth. Yogically speaking, Prāṇa is the vital force in the physical body to be tamed and mastered in order to achieve the total transformation of mind and energy.

Prāṇa-Mind (T.T.: Rluñ.Sems.) — According to Tibetan Tantrism, mind and Prāṇa are but two facets of one entity. They should never be treated as two separate things. If one's mind is disciplined, transformed, extended, sharpened, illuminated . . . so also is one's Prāṇa — the vital force that gives birth to all manifestations.

Samādhi — a pure concentrative state.

Saṃsāra — the wheel of life and death; the migration through many rebirths; the doctrine of reincarnation.

Sūnyatā — voidness or emptiness; that which denies the viewpoints based on existence or non-existence, being or non-being; the doctrine that holds that all becomings in the phenomenal world are devoid of self-nature, entity, or substance, that they are illusorily existent but not truly so; the all-inclusive Totality seen by an enlightened mind.

The Tantra — the holy scriptures of Tantrism.

Tantrism — the doctrine and teaching of Tantrayāna, or Vijrayāna; one School of Mahāyāna Buddhism; "esoteric" Mahāyāna Buddhism.

Three Main Channels, or Nāḍis — the three "mystical nerve channels" through which all supramundane knowledge and power are gained; through the Central Channel the Dharmakāya is realized, and through the right and left Channels, the Sambhogakāya and Nirmāṇakāya are realized.

Three Precious Ones, or the Three Gems (Skt.: Triratna) — the Buddha — the Enlightened One; the Dharma — His teachings; and the Saṅgha — the advanced or enlightened Sages.

Two Truths — the expedient truth and the final truth.

Whispered Transmission — the Ghagyuba School of Tibetan Buddhism, founded by Marpa and Milarepa.

TABLE OF TIBETAN WORDS

694

Dagbo	Dags.Po.
Dagbo Lhaje	Dags.Po.lHa.rJe.
Dagmema	bDag.Med.Ma.
Dagmo Ridra	sTag.Mo.Ri.bKra.
Damala Richroma	Ta.Ma.La.Ri.Khrod.Ma.
Darsen Gharmo	Dar.Señ.dKar.Mo.
Daugom Repa Dorje Wonshu	sTag.sGom.Ras.Pa.rDor.rJe.dWañ. Phyug.
Dawazungpo	Zla.Wa.bZañ.Po.
Degar Drozonma	gTad.dKar.hGro.bZañ.Ma.
Dembu [Lady]	lHa.lCam.lDem.Bu.
Dem Chog	bDe.mChog.
Den Yi	gDan.bShi.
Deut Jal	sTod.rGyal.
Dewashun	bDe.Wa.sKyoñ.
Dhamba Jhaupu	Dam.Ba.rGyags.Phu.
Dhamo	sTa.Mo.
Dhampa Sangje [of] Dinrin	Dam.Pa.Sañs.rGyas., Tiñ.Riñ.
Dhar Lho	Dar.Blo.
Dharma Aui	Dar.Ma.Hod.
Dharma Bodhi [of India]	Dharma.Bodhi., rGya.Gar.
Dharma Wonshu	Dar.Ma.dWañ.Phyug.
Dhawa Norbu	Zla.Wa.Nor.Bu.
Dinma	Diñ.Ma.
Dinma Drin	Diñ.Ma.Brin.
Din Ri	Diñ.Ri.
Din Ri Namar	Diñ.Ri.sNa.dMar.
Di Se	Ti.Se.
Dodejan	mDo.sDe.rGyan.
Dodra	mDo.bKra.
Dogar Nya	lTo.dKar.Na.
Doh	rDo.
Dor Draug Rechung	rDo.Grags.Ras.Chuñ.
Dorje-Chang	rDo.rJe.hChañ.
Dorje Danyi	rDo.rJe.gDan.bShi.
Dorje Paumo	rDo.rJe.Phag.Mo.
Dorje Semba	rDo.rJe.Sems.Pa.
Dorje Tson	rDo.rJe.rDsoñ.
Dormo	rDor.Mo.
Dochin	hDo.Chen.
Drajadorje	Brag.sKya.rDo.rJe
Drang Sung	Drañ.Sroñ.
Drashi Oma Chuwu	bKra.Çis.Ho.Mahi.Chu.Wo.
Drashi Tse	bKra.Çis.brTsegs.
Drashi Tserinma	bKra.Çis.Tshe.Riñ.Ma.
Draugmar Bouto	Brag.dMar.sPo.mTho.
Draug Srin Mo	Brag.Srin.Mo.
Dre	hBre.
Dre Dun	hBre.sTon.
Dre Dun Drashi Bar	hBre.sTon.bKra.Çis.hBar.
Dreloon Joomoo	hDre.Luñ.sKyog.Mo.
Dre Tze	hBre.rTse.

Drigom Linkawa	hBri.sGom.Gliñ.Kha.Wa.
Drigom Repa	hBri.sGom.Ras.Pa.
Drin	Brin.
Dritsam	hBrig.mTshams.
Drogmanzulema	hBrog.sMan.Zul.Le.Ma.
Drol Ma [Tārā]	sGrol.Ma.
Dronso Charwa	Grañ.So.Khra.Wa.
Dro Tang**	Gro.Thañ.
Drowazunmo	hGro.Wa.bZañ.Mo.
Dro Wo [Valley]	Gro.Wo.
Duinjo's [Wondrous Cow]	hDod.hJohi.Ba.Mo.
Dumo	gTum.Mo.
Dumo Ngosangma	gTum.Mo.sÑo.Sañs.Ma.
Dunba Dharmadraug	sTon.Pa.Dar.Ma.Grags.
Dungom Repa	sTon.sGom.Ras.Pa.
Gadaya [Cave]	Ka.Daya.
Galugha	dGah.Klu.dGah.
Gambo Dar	sGam.Po.gDar.
Gambopa	sGam.Po.Pa.
Garakhache [Guest House]	Ga.Ra.Kha.Che.
Gawojobo	dGah.Wo.hJog.Po.
Gebha Lesum	Gad.Pa.Gle.gSum.
Gelugpa	dGe.Lugs.Pa.
Ghadampa	bKah.sDom.Pa. [or] bKah.gDams.Pa.
Ghadaya	Ka.Ta.Ya.
Ghagyu	bKah.rGyud.
Ghagyuba	bKah.rGyud.Pa.
Gog Tang	lKog.Thañ.
Goh [Valley]	Go.Luñ.
Gung Tang	Guñ.Thañ.
Gungtuzunpo	Kuñ.Du.bZañ.Po.
Guru Tsems Chin [of] La Dud	Guru.Tsems.Chen., La.sTod.
Gu Tang	Ku.Thañ.
Halo [flower]	Ha.Lo.
Heruka Galbo	He.Ru.Ka.Gal.Po.
Jal	rGyal.
Jarbo Ton Drem [or] Jarbo Tang Drem	Gyal.Po.Thañ.hGrem.
Jaung Chub Tsong	Byañ.Chub.rDsoñ.
Jeba Dorje	dGyes.Pa.rDo.rJe.
Jen [Valley]	gCen.Luñ.
Jenlun Ngan Tson	gCen.Luñ.Ñan.rDsoñ.
Jetsun	rJe.bTsun.
Jhachil Lama	rGya.mChil.
Jhajogri [Monastery]	rGya.lCags.Ri.
Jhal Khrum	rGyal.Khrom.
Jhambar Rolbi Lhadroe	hJam.dPal.Rol.Pahi.bLo.Gros.
Jham Mei	lCam.Me.
Jhunma [and] Roma	rKyañ.Ma., Ro.Ma.
Ji Dron (Mang Yul Ji Dron)	sKyid.Groñ.

Jidun	Kyi.sTon.
Jipu Nimadson	sKyid.Phug.Ñi.Ma.rDsoñ.
Jolmo [Singing bird]	hJol.Mo.
Jomo	Jo.Mo.
Jomo Chod Dan	Jo.Mo.mChod.rTen.
Joro Dritsam	lCo.Ro.hBrig.mTshams.
Jo Shag	Jo.Çag.
Joupuva	rGyags.Phu.Wa.
Jowo Shakja	Jo.Wo.Shagja.
Jun Chub Tsong	Byañ.Chub.rDsoñ.
Jundhagho	Byañ.rTa.sGo.
Jung	gCuñ.
Jung Bo	hByuñ.Po.
Jungron	Coñ.Roñ.
Junpan Nanka Tsang	rKyañ.Phan.Nam.mKhah.rDsoñ.
Jupan Drinzonma	Cod.Pan.mGrin.bZañ.Ma.
Jurmo [fish]	Gyur.Mo.Ña.
Kar Chon Repa	mKhar.Chuñ.Ras.Pa.
Khum Bu	Khum.Bu.
Ko Kom	Ko.Kom.
Kollo Dompa	hKhor.Lo.sTom.Pa.
Ku Ju	Khu.Byug.
Labar Shawa	Lha.hBar.Bya.Wa.
Ladgu Lungu	La.dGu.Luñ.dGu.
Lan [tribe]	Rus.Glan.
Lan Gom Repa	Glan.sGom.Ras.Pa.
Langgo Ludu Tson	Glañ.sGo.Klu.bDud.rDsoñ.
Lapu	La.Phug.
Lapu Paima Tson	La.Phug.Padma.rDsoñ.
Lashi [Snow Mountain]	La.Phyi.
La Shin	La.Shiñ.
Lese	Legs.Se.
Lesebum	Legs.Se.hBum.
Lha Dro [of] Drin	Brin.lHa.Bro.
Lhaje Nu Chon	lHa.rJe.gNubs.Chuñ.
Lhaman Jalmo	lHa.sMan.rGyal.Mo.
Lhasa Chrunon	Lha.Sa.hPhrul.sNañ.
Lhaze [Temple]	La.Ze.
Lho Draug Wa	lHo.Brag.Wa.
Ligor Sharu	Li.sKor.Phya.Ru.
Linba	Liñ.Ba.
Linba Draug	Liñ.Ba.Brag.
Lodahan [River — see Lohida]	Lo.Ta.Han.
Lodan Sherab	bLo.lDan.Çes.Rab.
Lodun	Lo.sTon.
Londun Gedun	Lo.sTon.dGe.hDun.
Lodun Gedunbum	Lo.sTon.dGe.hDun.hBum.
Lohida [River — see Lodahan]	Lo.Hi.Ta.
Loro	Lo.Ro.
Lowo [Lake]	gLo.Wo.mTsho.

Ma Goun	Ma.mGon.
Mamo	Ma.Mo.
Mamo Tson	Ma.Mo.rDsoñ.
Man Chu [Manlun Chubar]	sMan.Chu.
Mang	Mañ.
Mang Yul	Mañ.Yul.
Mang Yul Ji Dron	Mañ.Yul.sKyid.Groñ.
Manlun Chubar	sMan.Luñ.Chu.Bar.
Mannmo	sMan.Mo.
Ma Päm	Ma.Pham.
Marngo	Mar.rÑog.
Marpa	Mar.Pa.
Medripa [Skt.: Maitṛpa]	Me.Dris.Pa.
Megom Repa	Mes.sGom.Ras.Pa.
Menlha [Mount]	sMan.lHa.Ri.
Mijurpa [Buddha]	Mi.hGyur.Pa.
Mila Shirab Jhantsan	Mi.La.Çes.Rab.rGyal.mTshan.
Miyo Lonzonma	Mi.gYo.Kloñ.bZañ.Ma.
Mon [Yul]	Mon.Yul.
Nagchar	sNag.Phrar.
Nam Lo	gNam.Lo.
Nam Men [Karma]	rNam.sMin.
Namtsoshumo	gNam.mTsho.Phyug.Mo.
Naro Bhun Chun	Na.Ro.Bon.Chuñ.
Naro Chu Dru	Naro.Chos.Drug.
Ngan Tson	Ñan.rDsoñ.
Ngan Tson Dewa Shun	Ñan.rDsoñ.bDe.Wa.sKyoñ.
Ngan Tson Dunba Shun Chub Jhalbo	Ñan.rDsoñ.sTon.Pa.Byañ.Chub.rGyal. Po.
Ngan Tson Dunba Bodhiradza	Ñan.rDsoñ.sTon.Pa.Bhodhi.Ra.Dsa.
Ngogang	sÑo.sKañ.
Ngogom Repa Dharma Wonshu Shawa	sÑo.sGom.Ras.Pa.Dar.Ma.dWañ. Phyug.Bya.Wa.
Ngomi	rÑog.Mis.
Ngunbatso	mÑon.Pa.mDsod.
Ngundojan	mÑon.rTog.rGyan.
Nhamdog	rNam.rTog.
Ningmaba	rÑiñ.Ma.Pa.
Nin Lung	rÑiñ.rLuñ.
Nonyul [Mountain]	sNañ.Yul.
Nu Yin	gNod.sByin.
Nya	gÑah.
Nya Chen Yor Mo	Ña.Chen.Yor.Mo.
Nyal	gÑal.
Nyan Chung Repa	gÑan.Chuñ.Ras.Pa.
Nyang [Upper]	Myañ.sTod.
Nyan Jue	sNan.brGyud.
Nya Non	gÑah.Nañ.
Nya Non Tsar Ma	gÑah.Nañ.rTsar.Mar.
Nyantsa Karjan	Myañ.Tsha.dKar.rGyan.
Nyan Yuan [Cave]	sÑan.gYon.

Nyi Shang	sÑi.Çañs.
Nyi Shang Gur Da	sÑi.Çañs.Gur.rTa.
Nyi Shang Ka Daya	sÑi.Çabs.Ka.Taya.
Nyi Tong	Ñi.mThoñs.
Nyi Wa	sÑi.Wa.
Nyurumpa	sÑug.Rum.Pa.
Og Men	Hog.Min.
Oujen [Pure Land of]	Ao.rGyan.
Padru	Pha.Drug.
Pagmo	Phag.Mo.
Pakshu	Pakçu.
Pan [region]	hPhan.Yul.
Pat Ma Tod Tchin [Padma Sambhava]	Pat.Ma.Thod.Phreñ.
Paugba Wadi	hPhags.Pa.Wa.Ti.
Phuyagzha	Phu.Yag.Za.
[Queen of the Azure Height]	mThon.mThiñ.rGyal.Mo.
Radun Dharma Lhodre	Ra.sTon.Dar.Ma.Blo.Gros.
Ragma	Rag.Ma.
Ra La [Goat Hill]	Ra.La.
Ramdin Nampu	Ram.sDiñs.gNam.Phug.
Rechin [Meditation Cave]	sGrub.Phug.Ras.Chen.
Rechung Dor Draug Shawa	Ras.Chuñ.rDo.Grags.Bya.Ba.
Rechung Dorje Draugpa	Ras.Chuñ.rDo.rJe.Grags.Pa.
Regba Dhujen	Reg.Pa.Dug.Can.
Riga Daya [Cave]	Ri.Ka.Taya.Phug.
Rig Ma	Rig.Ma.
Rin Chin Drag	Rin.Chen.Grags.
Riwo Balnbar	Ri.Wo.dPal.hBar.
Roma	Ro.Ma.
Ron Chon Repa	Roñ.Chuñ.Ras.Pa.
Rondunlaga	Roñ.sTon.lHa.dGah.
Runpu	Ron.Phug.
Sahle Aui	Sa.Le.Hod.
Sajya [Monstery]	Sa.sKyar.
Samye [Temple]	bSam.Yas.
San Chia Yogi	San.Ca.Dso.Ki.
Sangdan Dranma	bSam.gDan.sGron.Ma.
Sangje Jhap	Sañs.rGyas.sKyabs.
Seba [Valley]	Se.Pa.Luñ.
Semodo	Se.Mo.Do.
Sendentsema	Señ.lDeñ.Tsher.Ma.
Sen Ding	Señ.lDeñ.
Sevan Dunchon Shawa	Se.Wan.sTon.Chuñ.Bya.Wa.
Sevan Jashi	Se.Wan.bKra.Çis.
Sevan Jashi Bar	Se.Wan.bKra.Çis.hBar.
Sevan Repa	Se.Wan.Ras.Pa.
Seyi Lhamo	bSehi.Lha.Mo.
Shadulwa Tsinpa	Bya.hDul.Wa.hDsin.Pa.

Shajaguna	Çakya.Gu.Na.
Shambo	Çam.Po.
Shamboche	Phyam.Po.Che.
Shangchub Bar	Byañ.Chub.hBar.
Shangon Repa	gÇen.bsGom.Ras.Pa.
Shapa Linpa	Ça.Pa.gLiñ.Pa.
Shar Bo	Byar.Po.
Shar Mo	Byar.Mo.
Sha Yul [region]	Bya.Yul.
Shin Dre	gÇin.hDre.
Shen Gom Repa	gÇen.bsGom.Ras.Pa.
Sherpug Chushin Dson	Çer.Phug.Chu.Çiñ.rDsoñ.
Shilabharo [of Nepal]	Çi.La.Bha.Ro., Bal.Po.
Shindormo	gÇen.rDor.Mo.
Shiwa Aui	Shi.Wa.Ḥod.
Shri Ri	Çri.Ri.
Shumo Semodo	Phyug.Mo.Se.Mo.Do.
Shun Chub Jarbo	Byañ.Chub.rGyal.Po.
Sidpa Bardo	Srid.Pa.Bar.Do.
Singalin	Siñ.Ga.Gliñ.
Sinhala	Señ.Ha.La.
Srinmo	Srin.Mo.
Sudnam Rinchin	bSod.Nams.Rin.Chen.
Sungdue	gSañ.hDus.
Sungwa Nyinbo	gSañ.Wa.sÑiñ.Po.
Sungwong Dueba	gSañ.Wa.hDus.Pa.
Tantra [of the Wrathful and Peaceful Buddhas]	Shi.Khrohi.rGyud.
Tārā [Drol Ma]	sGrol.Ma.
Ta Zig	rTa.Zig.
Tig Le	Thig.Le.
Tingeyalzunma	mThiñ.Gi.Shal.bZañ.Ma.
Tong Lha	Thoñ.La.
Tsamlin	hDsam.gLiñ.
Tsang	gTsañ.
Tsanbudrisha	hDsam.Bu.Tri.Ça.
Tsan Rigs	bTsan.Rigs.
Tsapu Repa	rTsa.Phu.Ras.Pa.
Tsar Ma	rTsar.Ma.
Tsem Chin Guru [of] La Dud	Tshems.Chen.Gu.Ru., La.sTod.
Tserinma	Tse.Riñ.Ma.
Tsese	mDses.Se.
Tsiba Gonti Tson	rTsig.Pa.rKoñ.mThil.rDsoñ
Tsiwo Repa	rDsi.Wo.Ras.Pa.
Tsomanma	mTso.sMan.Ma.
Tsonlung [Cave]	mTshoñ.Luñ.Brag.
Tsudor Namjhal	gTsug.Tor.rNam.rGyal.
Tubhaga	Thos.Pa.dGah.
Tuntin	mThon.mThiñ.
Wadi	Wa.Ti.

Wa Jal	Wa.rGyal.
Wala Tsandra	Wa.La.Tsandra.
Weu	dWus.
Weu [and] Tsang	dWus., gTsañ
Wurmo	Hur.Mo.
Wutso Gabar Jalbo	dWu.gTso.dGah.hBar.rGyal.Po.
Yagder	gYag.sDer.
Yagru	gYag.Ru.
Yang Nge	gYeñ.Ñe.
Yaugru Tangbha	gYag.Ru.Thañ.Pa.
Yei Ru Jang	gYas.Ru.Byañ.
Ye Rang [and] Ko Kom [King of]	Ye.Rañ., Kho.Khom.
Ye Shin Dsu Pud	Ye.gÇen.gTsug.Phud.
Yidagmo	gShi.bDag.Mo.
Yidham	Yi.Dam.
Yolmo	Yol.Mo.
Yaugra Tangbha	gYag.Ru.Thañ.Pa.
Yundun	gYuñ.sTon.
Yunlaza	Yañ.La.Za.
Yuru Kradrag	gYu.Ru.Khra.hBrug.
Zhaoo	Za.Hog.
Zung Ghar [Tradition]	Zañs.dKar.Lugs.

*The word-ending "ang" should be pronounced as "äng" throughout.
**"Tang" should be pronounced as "Ton," or "Täng."

INDEX

INDEX

Abhāsvara, 673n3

Abhidharma Kośa (Ngunbatso Sastra), 466

Abhismayālaṅkāra (Ngundojan Sastra), 446

Absolute Reality, 55n12

Absolute Truth, 324, 325, 331n15

Absolute Universality, see Dharmadhātu

Accomplishment (Fruit), 126, 130nn 5,6,7; see also Wisdom of Accomplishment

Accomplishment-of-Freedom-from-Obstacles, 187, 189n49

Accomplishments: concealment of, 525-26; of Milarepa, 369, 393-95; worldly (miraculous powers), offer of, by Dākinīs, to Milarepa, 322-23

Accumulation of merits, 45, 55n22, 77, 86n11

Act-of-Insanity, 331n2

Action, 69-70, 72n3, 79-80, 212

Action of Equality, 342, 355n13, 456, 462n2

Activity, 250

Activity, daily, 93, 94n5

Actual-Meditation-State (Main Samādhi), 105n11

Address to worldly Dākinīs, by Milarepa, 319-22

Ādi Buddha, 214n1

Ādiyoga Vehicle, 258n5

Advice: of female demons, to Milarepa, 304-7; of Milarepa, to Gambopa, 491-95, to Rechungpa, 400-1, 586-89, 643-45

Affirmation and negation, 56n40

After-Meditation-State (Ensuing Samādhi), 105n11

Ah, 455n1, 617

Ah Shea Vital Heat, 166; see also Vital Heat Yoga

Ah Tsa Ma demons, 13, 21n5, 59

Ah Tung, 109, 113n12

Ahdsidharata, 318

Ahkaru staff, gift of Dipupa, to Milarepa, 421, 426

Ahru of Bhamen, 589

Ahrura (drug), 288-94 passim; gift of, to Gambopa, by Milarepa, 492, 497n28

Ahtsarya Bodhi Radsa, see Bodhi Radsa

Ālaya Consciousness, 52, 55n11, 56n-38, 107, 112n1, 123, 132, 135n1, 199n10, 269-70

Ālaya-vijñāna, see Ālaya Consciousness

All-knowing Wisdom, 372-73n2

All-Merciful Mother Tārā, 288, 294

All-sources Consciousness, 56n38

Alms, non-discrimination in begging, 152, 156n3

Aloewood staff, gift of Dipupa, to Milarepa, 401

Anabhraka, 673n3

Angels: appearance in pigeon form, 88-93; see also Devas

Animals, 9n16; sufferings of, 667-68

Anuttara Tantra, 22n27, 67n18, 258-n5, 614n4

Anuttara Tantra Initiations, 551n2

Anuyoga Vehicle, 258n5

Apparition of dead man, Bonist trick, 616

Apramāṇābha, 673n3

Apramāṇaśubha, 673n3

Arhats, 262, 274n1

Arising of Self-Buddha Pride (Identification-with-Buddha), 332n17

Arising Yoga, 19, 22n27, 63, 67n18, 70, 76, 86n7, 187n5, 199n1, 348, 352, 376-77, 405, 515, 519n1, 551-n2

Asaṅga, 195

Ashes, dispersal of, by Gambopa, 491

Assurances, 142

Asuras (Non-men), 9n16, 21-22n17, 501, 570; sufferings of, 664

Atapa, 673n3

705

Fourth Body of Buddha (Svābhāvika-kāya), 506n9
Friendliness, Unlimited, 188n25
Fruit (Accomplishment), 126, 130n-n5,6,7, 212
Fruit-bearing Consciousness (Ālaya Consciousness), 112n1
Full-ripening Karma, see Karma, ripened

Gambopa, 456, 462, 463-96, 545
Gaṇêsa, 10n33
Garakhache Guest House, 150-56 passim
Gāruḍa, 10n33
Gāruda bird (Golden Eagle or King-bird Eagle), 6, 10n29
Gautama Buddha, 140, 342, 682; see also Buddha; Sākyamuni
gCod Yoga, 66n4
gGod. School, 402n5
Gebha Lesum, 136
Gelugba School, see Yellow School
General Buddhist Rules, 414, 420n6
Geninma, 414, 420n5
Gesar, King, 306, 311n8
Ghadamba Lama, 472-76 passim
Ghadamba School, 466, 496n8
Ghadaya, 275
Ghagyuba School, 36n12, 258n5, 496-n1; see also Whispered Transmission School
Ghagyuba traditions, 476-77
"Gift from Man and Deity," 294
Gifts: from King of Ye Rang and Ko Kom, to Milarepa, 288-94; of people, to Lamas and story-tellers, 108, 113n7
Girl: dream-messenger to Milarepa, 200; green, appearance and prophecy to Milarepa, in a dream, 159; in prophetic vision of Gambopa, 470
Girl follower of Milarepa, 533-35
Glory, of the yogi, 576-77
Goat Hill (Ra La), 108
Goats, 442-43, 449
God and father image, 244
Goddess, semihuman, 544, 548n1
Goddess and mother image, 244
Goddesses, 78
Goh Valley, 187

Gold: farewell offering by Rechungpa, to Milarepa, 399; gift of, by Milarepa, to Rechungpa, 398, 646, by Rechungpa, to Lady Dembu, 647-48; indifference of Dharma Bodhi to, 368; offer of, to Milarepa, 183, by Sahle Aui, to Milarepa, 409, 414; offering of, by Gambopa, to Milarepa, 473; offering of, by Milarepa, to Marpa, 473, refused, accepted from, and returned to Sahle Aui, by Milarepa, 410, 414
Golden Eagle (King-bird Eagle) 6, 10n29
Golden Light Sūtra, 467
"Golden Rosary," 353
Good, 86n3
Good-offering, 59, 66n4
Good River, 13
Gordag, 534, 540n8
Grace-waves, see Waves of grace
Gray Cave of Dorje Tson, 225
Gray Rock Vajra Enclosure, 97-103 passim
Gray School (Sajyaba School), 36n12, 189n43, 258n5
Great Affair (Enlightenment), 144, 149n7
Great Bliss, 54, 57n43, 246, 248
Great Bliss of Precious Words, 399
Great Compassion Lotus Sūtra, 463, 496n2
Great Compassionate Mind, see also Bodhi-Mind
Great Conquering Demon Cave, 570
Great Demons, attack on Milarepa, 297-310
Great Illuminating-Void Awareness, 684
Great Light, 165; see also Clear Light
Great Perfection, 249, 258n11, 580, 583n2
Great Sorceror (nickname of Milarepa), 3, 9n11
Great Symbol meditation, see Mahā-mudrā meditation
Great Tree of Sumeru, 15, 21-22n17
Great Vehicle, see Mahāyāna Buddhism
Great Wisdom, 170
Green yogi, Gambopa's vision of, 467

716 INDEX

Jhunma, *see* Left Channel
Jidun, 401
Jipu Nimadson, 442
Jo Shag (Jowo Shagja), 585, 595, 604n1
Jomo, 174, 188n32
Jomo Chod Dan (Stūpa of the Hostess), 465
Joro Dritsam, 259
Joupuva, 23
Jowo Shagja (Jo Shag), 585, 595, 604n1
Joyous Heaven, 410
Jundhagho (North Horse Gate), 150
Jung, C. G., 112n1
Junpan Nanka Tsan (Sky Castle of Junpan), 68, 72n1
Jupan Drinzonma, 313-30 *passim*
Jupiter, 36n7

Ka Be ornaments, 172, 188n29
Ka Shi Ka cloth, 288-94 *passim*
Kalirāja, 506n6
Kapāla (skull-cup), 380, 392, 396n-13
Kar Chon Repa, 205-6
Karma, 136, 148n1, 634-35, 663-64; ripened, 13, 21n6, 14, *see also* Law of Karma
Karma Mudrā, 135 and 135n6, 352, 357-61, 361n5, 640-41
Karma of Wishes, 189n31
Key-Instructions (Pith-Instructions), 183, 189n42; Dharma Bodhi on, 370-71
Key-words of the Five Elements, 377, 396n3
Khandroma (Ḍākinīs), 331n8
Khri.Sroñ.lDe.bTsan., Emperor, 687
Khum Bu, 334
Kin, spiritual, of Milarepa, 533-34
King of Ko Kom, 401
King of the Mighty Wheel (Cakravarti), 399, 401n2
King of the Nāgas, 296, 357
King of Ye Rang and Ko Kom, 288-90
Kleśas, 13, 21n7, 47-48, 56n26, 56n-27, 76, 86n3, 86n6, 92-93, 152, 244, 351; *see also* Five Poisonous Cravings; Passion-Bodhis

Knowledge (View), 142, 149n6
Kriya Tantra, 614n4
Kriyātantra Vehicle, 258n5
Krunkol Exercises, 364, 365n2
Kṣāntyṛṣi, 506n6
Ku Ju, 467, 523, 578, 653-55
Kurukullā, Goddess, 183
Kyi, 360, 361n5

La Shin, 408, 615
Labar Shawa, 62-64
Làdgu Lungu, 20
Lamp of Illuminating Wisdom, 399
Lan Gom Repa, 456-62
Langgo Ludu Tson, 257
Lapu, 242
Lark, 85
Las, 360, 361n5
Lashi Snow Mountain, 11, 26, 200, 294, 567-69, 570
"Laughing Vajra" (name given Milarepa), 333
Law (Dharma), 8n3
Law-of-Causation, 336, 348
Law of Karma, 17-18, 302
Le, 360
Leading Awareness into the Path, 141
Leakless Samādhi, 497n22
Learning, 397-98
Left Channel, 10n28, 478; *see also* Three Channels
Leprosy, 109-10, 113n10
Lese, 552
Lesebum, 11, 28-29, 398, 557-62
Lha, 54n8
Lha Dro of Drin, 649
Lhaju Nu Chon, 160
Lhaman Jalmo, 357
Lhasa, 585
Lhasa Chrunon Temple, 265, 274n4
Lho Draug Wa, 161, 187n3; *see also* Marpa
Liberation, 128-29, 130n15, 672-73n-2; by Milarepa, of dead man reborn as insect, 616-17
Life-Essence, 37n19
Life Prāṇa, 163, 188n10, 479
Life-Tree, 71, 73n7
Light Cave of Runpu, 114
Light-of-Death (Dharmakāya), 343, 352